THE

UNITED STATES
PONY CLUB
MANUAL OF
HORSEMANSHIP

Also by Susan E. Harris

Horsemanship in Pictures
Grooming to Win, Third Edition
Horse Gaits, Balance, and Movement

THE
UNITED STATES PONY CLUB
MANUAL OF
HORSEMANSHIP

BASICS FOR BEGINNERS/D LEVEL
SECOND EDITION

Written and illustrated by
Susan E. Harris

The United States Pony Clubs, Inc.

WILEY

John Wiley & Sons, Inc.

Howell Book House
Published by John Wiley & Sons, Inc., Hoboken, New Jersey

For general information on our other products and services or to obtain technical support please contact our Customer Care Department within the U.S. at (877) 762-2974, outside the U.S. at (317) 572-3993 or fax (317) 572-4002.

John Wiley & Sons, Inc., also publishes its books in a variety of electronic formats and by print-on-demand. Not all content that is available in standard print versions of this book may appear or be packaged in all book formats. If you have purchased a version of this book that did not include media that is referenced by or accompanies a standard print version, you may request this media by visiting http://booksupport.wiley.com. For more information about Wiley products, visit us at www.wiley.com.

ISBN: 978-1-118-12378-2 (paper)
ISBN: 978-1-118-22476-2 (ebk)
ISBN: 978-1-118-23006-0 (ebk)
ISBN: 978-1-118-23014-5 (ebk)

Printed in the United States of America

10 9 8 7 6 5 4 3 2 1

Second Edition

Photographs by Shelley Mann, USPC
Illustrations by Susan E. Harris
Book design by Lissa Auciello-Brogan
Cover design by Wendy Mount
Book production by John Wiley & Sons, Inc. Composition Services

Contents

A Note from the United States Pony Clubs, Inc.

We suspect that the first requests from USPC members for a manual of their own were received in 1954, when the first U.S. clubs were founded. By 1979, when the Instruction Council rewrote the USPC Standards, it was determined that there was a need for one source of information members could consult as they progress through the rating levels. The first United States Pony Club manual that matched our standards and used terms specific to North America was created in 1994. The USPC Standards were revised again in 2009, creating a need for this newly revised D Level Manual.

Author and illustrator Susan E. Harris, an experienced and successful riding instructor, has received guidance from an advisory panel that represents years of teaching, coaching, and examining riding and horse management skills within the USPC. We wish to express our thanks to the Standards and Curriculum Chair, Kim Lowman Vollmer, and her D Manual Committee for their hours of dedication in revising and updating this book.

The USPC's Mission

The United States Pony Clubs, Inc. develops character, leadership, confidence, and a sense of community in youth through a program that teaches the care of horses and ponies, riding, and mounted sports.

Core Values of the USPC

- *Horsemanship* with respect to health care, nutrition, stable management, handling, and riding a mount safely, correctly, and with confidence.

- *Organized teamwork* including cooperation, communication, responsibility, leadership, mentoring, teaching, and fostering a supportive yet competitive environment.
- *Respect* for the horse and self through horsemanship, for land through land conservation, and for others through service and teamwork.
- *Service* by providing an opportunity for members, parents, and others to support the Pony Club program locally, regionally, and nationally through volunteerism.
- *Education* at an individual pace to achieve personal goals and expand knowledge through teaching others.

Sportsmanship, Stewardship, and Leadership through Horsemanship

A Note to Parents

Pony Club started in Great Britain in 1928 with 700 members. By 1992 there were more than 125,000 members in 27 countries, making it the largest junior equestrian group in the world. Each club is run by a volunteer District Commissioner and other elected officers and each USPC Riding Center is run by a Central Administrator. At this writing, the United States Pony Clubs have over 10,000 members in more than 600 clubs or riding centers.

This *USPC Manual of Horsemanship* is written especially for Pony Club members and for the volunteers who teach and lead them, but it will also be helpful to anyone who wants to learn or teach good horsemanship. In this manual, and in the two to follow, the emphasis is on how children learn, rather than on subject matter for its own sake. Progress along a continuum of learning is stressed, not the mere acquisition of facts.

This manual provides an introduction to the curriculum of the USPC and will help children meet the current USPC Standards of Proficiency. However, the levels of proficiency required by the standards cannot be achieved by book work alone. Much practical hands-on learning is essential, as is good mounted instruction at all levels. As in any course of study, effective teaching and learning require outside reading and supplemental material. Material from the USPC's most recently published standards and reading lists, as well as individual teachers' resources, will be necessary to augment this material. Pony Club's philosophy is to teach a basic and safe method to accomplish horsemanship tasks. There is no one "Pony Club" way, but there is a safe and careful way to get the job done so that you and your horse or pony are as happy as possible in this sport.

Pony Club supports the ideal of a thoroughly happy, comfortable horse person, riding across a natural countryside with complete confidence and perfect balance on a horse or pony equally happy and confident and free from pain or bewilderment.

The USPC's Program

The United States Pony Clubs, Inc., an educational organization for youth, provides a program that teaches riding, mounted sports, and the care of horses and ponies, thereby developing responsibility, sportsmanship, moral judgment, leadership, and self-confidence.

Guiding Beliefs of the USPC

- The USPC is an educational organization that progressively develops the well-rounded horse person.
- The well-rounded horse person is capable of riding safely and tactfully on the flat, over fences, and in the open.
- Knowledgeable care of horses and ponies (horse management) is basic to the well-rounded horse person.
- The USPC is committed to the well-being of the horse.
- Fair and friendly competitions develop teamwork and sportsmanship.
- Fun and friendship are part of Pony Club.
- Pony Club requires parental and volunteer involvement and support.
- The USPC is committed to safety.
- The local club is the core of the USPC.

This book is not intended as a substitute for professional advice and guidance in the field of horseback riding. A young person should take part in the activities discussed in this book only under the supervision of a knowledgeable adult.

PART I

For Children and Parents: Getting Started Right

The ideal of Pony Club is a happy, comfortable young rider with confidence and balance on a pony equally happy and confident and free from pain or bewilderment.

1

About Pony Club, Learning to Ride, and Selecting a Pony

Pony Club is for anyone up to 25 years old who is interested in horses and riding. It was started in England in 1928 to teach horsemanship, horse and pony care, safety, and good sportsmanship to young people who could not otherwise afford expensive lessons. The United States joined the program in 1954. Today there are more than 600 U.S. Pony Clubs and USPC Riding Centers with more than 10,000 members.

Pony Club mounts may be horses or ponies. In Pony Club, the word *pony* is used for all mounts used by young people, regardless of size or breed.

Pony Club teaches English riding, emphasizing the Balanced Seat. There are ten levels, called *ratings*, with clear standards for each level. Pony Club members start out as unrated. They learn at their own pace and take the test for each rating when they are ready. Each rating includes riding tests, stable management, and oral testing. Testing for the first five ratings (D-1 through C-2) is done by local examiners. The C-3 rating is tested by national examiners, and so national ratings can begin at the C-3 or H-B level and go up to the A level. Specialty ratings are available at these upper levels in the dressage and show jumping tracks. These upper levels require a high degree of skill, knowledge, and horsemanship experience.

This book covers the Pony Club D Level, which includes the D-1, D-2, and D-3 ratings. This level introduces the fun and challenge of riding, while building a foundation of safety habits and knowledge of the daily care of a pony and his tack. In the D-1 through D-3 levels, Pony Club members learn to ride independently, with control and a secure position at the walk, trot, and canter, and over low fences, if desired, in the ring and in the open. (The next manuals will cover the C, B, and A levels.)

The core of the Pony Club program is Pony Club meetings and lessons, where both riding and horse management are taught. Club members come to these meetings with their ponies for riding lessons, horse management instruction, mounted games, and other activities. Horse care and safety are always stressed, and members are expected to take care of themselves and their ponies as much as possible (with adult supervision). There are also unmounted meetings for various projects, learning, and fun!

Local Pony Clubs and USPC Riding Centers send teams of members to local, regional, and national competitive rallies in eventing, show jumping, dressage, mounted games, tetrathlon (a competition that includes riding, running, swimming, and marksmanship), and polocrosse (a combination of lacrosse and polo). In Pony Club competitions, teamwork, horse management, good horsemanship, and good sportsmanship are just as important as performance. Parents are not allowed to help or coach their children during a competitive rally; instead, Pony Club members work together as a team and help each other (with supervision by the Horse Management judges).

Unmounted instruction. Pony Club members learn horsemanship, horse care and management, and gain horse knowledge.

Teamwork. Pony Club members help each other at a competitive rally. Parents may not help or coach their children at competitive rallies. Instead, children must work as a team, helped by Horse Management judges.

Many Pony Clubs and USPC Riding Centers sponsor clinics with well-known instructors, or take part in such activities as foxhunting, polo, distance riding, vaulting, and driving. Pony Club camps are also popular, and often include special clinics or activities. Quiz, which is like a horse knowledge contest, is an unmounted activity that Pony Club members enjoy, especially during the winter. They can compete up to the national level at Pony Club Championships.

A week-long Pony Club Festival is held every three years at the Horse Park in Lexington, Kentucky. It includes the Pony Club Championships, along with several days of clinics, workshops, and special activities for Pony Club members and their parents. Many families like to attend the Festival as a family vacation.

Pony Clubs are active in more than twenty countries around the world, and there is an exchange program for members of Pony Clubs in the United States and other countries.

If you want more information about Pony Club or a USPC Riding Center near you, or if you would like to start a Pony Club in your area, contact:

The United States Pony Clubs, Inc.
The Kentucky Horse Park
4041 Iron Works Parkway
Lexington, KY 40511
www.ponyclub.org
(859) 254-PONY (7669)

What You Need to Learn to Ride

This book and this level of horsemanship are about good basics for getting started right. You will need lessons before you can think about having a pony of your own. It is much easier to learn and have fun with good instruction, and it is kinder to your pony. The right pony, instructor, equipment, and place to ride can make a big difference in how easy it is, how safe you are, and how much you and your pony enjoy the whole experience.

A Good Instructor

Look for a good instructor first—preferably an experienced USPC instructor who is familiar with Pony Club's programs, requirements, and methods of teaching. Good instructors will be safety minded, know their subject and make it easy to understand, and care about ponies and young people. A good riding program or USPC Riding Center will be safe and well organized, with horses

Mounted games are popular Pony Club activities that are fun for children and ponies, too.

and ponies that are well cared for, and a clean, safe, and orderly stable and riding area. Above all, the program should teach good horsemanship—which means understanding, handling, and caring for ponies—not just riding.

The Right Pony and Equipment

You should start out on a reliable beginner's pony. Such a pony is quiet, well trained, and will respond correctly when you ask him in the proper way. Being *over-mounted* means riding a horse or pony who is too much for you. This is frightening, dangerous, and no fun at all! As you become a better rider, you will be ready to ride a more advanced pony.

When you get a pony of your own, you will need the right tack and equipment for the kind of riding you are doing. Pony Club recommends an all-purpose balanced seat saddle, which must fit both the rider and the pony. (For more information about choosing tack and equipment, see chapter 12, "Tack.") Tack does not have to be new or expensive, but it must be in good repair and condition and fit your pony.

Dress for Safety

To learn to ride, you need clothes that are safe and comfortable for riding and working around ponies. The most important item is a properly fitted safety helmet, which must be made to Standard F1163 of the American Society for Testing Materials (ASTM) and tested by the Safety Equipment Institute (SEI). (Look for the ASTM/SEI label inside the helmet.) This helmet *must* be worn with the chin-strap fastened and properly fitted *whenever you are on a horse or pony*. In case of a fall, a helmet could prevent a serious head injury or even save your life!

You will also need safe shoes or boots, long pants, and comfortable, washable clothes. (See chapter 13, "Dress and Turnout," for details.) These don't have to be expensive show clothes. Many Pony Clubs have used tack and clothing exchanges where you may be able to find outgrown items at bargain prices.

Where Will You Ride?

Where you ride depends on where you live and what kind of space you have at home or nearby. You will need a fairly level area about 60 by 120 feet or larger for basic ring work, and you will also want to ride in an open area like a large field or pasture and on trails. The area should be free of holes, machinery, wire, and other dangerous things. Streets and roads are a poor place to ride a pony, and they can be quite dangerous. If you don't have a good place to ride at home, you may find that it is better to keep your pony at a stable that has safer places to ride.

Safety

Whenever people and horses are together, safety must always come first. No one wants to get hurt, injure someone else, or see an animal get hurt. The best way to be safe around horses and ponies is to become an educated horse person and follow good safety practices *all the time*. In Pony Club, safety is taught from the very beginning and checked in everything you do at every level. Far from stopping the fun, this lets everyone enjoy riding and being around horses and ponies without unnecessary risk.

A child's pony should be gentle, friendly, and easy for a child to handle.

A horse or pony is a big, powerful animal with feelings and a mind of his own. Even the gentlest pony thinks and acts like an animal, not like a machine or a person, and any animal can surprise you. Most accidents happen when someone doesn't know enough about horses and safety, doesn't think, or gets careless about safety practices. A knowledgeable adult should always be in charge of any activity that involves children and horses.

Like any other sport, riding is about as safe as you make it. Every rider should start with a good foundation of basic skills and knowledge and have plenty of experience and confidence at one level before trying to move up to the next level. However, some people get into trouble because they want to try more advanced activities before their basics are solid, or because they are in a hurry to compete or to get the highest possible rating as quickly as they can. This can lead to being over-mounted or trying to do difficult and demanding kinds of riding before you or your pony are ready. This is dangerous, unfair to your pony, and no fun at all! If you take time to learn everything in each level thoroughly before thinking about a higher rating, and don't get carried away by competition, you and your pony will be safer and will enjoy your riding much more.

The Balanced Seat

There are different seats or styles of riding for different purposes. The USPC teaches the Balanced Seat, which is an all-purpose seat. It is riding by balance, not by strength or force. This kind of riding is based on a modified dressage seat and includes riding on the flat (ring riding), jumping, and riding in the open (trail riding and cross-country jumping). With a good basis in the Balanced Seat, a rider can adapt to any style of riding.

A Pony of Your Own?

Most horse lovers dream of having their own horse or pony, but it is not necessary to own a pony to join a Pony Club or USPC Riding Center or to take part in Pony Club mounted activities. You may be able to use a lesson pony or a leased or borrowed pony if you do not have your own. However, you are expected to take as much care as possible of any pony you use.

Are You Ready for a Pony?

If you want to have your own pony, you have a lot of planning to do. Can your family afford to keep a pony? The cost of feed, health care, foot trimming or shoeing, maintaining the stable and equipment, and other expenses will add up to more than the cost of buying a pony. Do you have a good place to keep a pony at home, or will you board him someplace else? Do you know an experienced horse person who will help you learn all you need to know about keeping your pony safe, healthy, and well cared for? Above all, do you have the time and interest to work with your pony and take care of him *every day*, even on days when you can't ride him?

No matter how much you want a pony, take your time and make sure you are ready for all that owning involves. It is better to take riding lessons and learn good basic pony care first. This can be fun, and it may help you convince your parents that you really are ready for a pony of your own.

Leasing a Pony

Leasing a pony is one way to have a pony without buying one. The owners may be too busy to ride as much as they would like, and might lease their pony so that he gets more attention and exercise. Older kids who go off to college might lease their pony while they are away. Advanced riders sometimes lease a horse for the summer to pass an upper level rating. Sometimes owners will lease a pony to a good home, even if they do not want to sell him. There are risks and benefits to both parties.

If you are not able to ride every day, a partial lease might work for you. A partial lease is an arrangement where you share riding, cost, and horse care responsibilities with the owner.

Leasing a pony should involve a written agreement (sample lease contracts can be found online). A lease is for an agreed-on period, usually a year. The lease contract should cover who is responsible for paying for the following: board, feed, supplements, regular vet care, special vet care, trimming or shoeing, deworming, dental care, any damage the pony may cause, and any other expenses. The lessor (the owner) should provide you with past vet records and a deworming schedule. You should also discuss whether you will be using the pony's tack or your own. You need to know what kind of care you will be expected to provide for the pony, and whether you can take him to lessons, competitions, and ratings. Some owners will lease a pony only if he stays at their stable so they can supervise his care. Some owners ask to be paid for the use of the pony, others don't. Before your parents lease a pony, you should try out the pony several times to be sure that you can ride, handle, and care for him. You may even wish to have a trial period built into your lease agreement.

Note to Parents

About Riding and Your Child

Parents who are experienced horse persons will already know what owning a pony entails, particularly if they are familiar with Pony Club. The following information will help parents who are new to horses and riding.

What Are the Benefits of Riding?

Riding, and especially owning a horse or pony, is not a cheap sport, but it can have great benefits for children and families. Riding is a healthy outdoor sport; it can be enjoyed alone, in a group, as part of a team or as a family activity, and this enjoyment can be lifelong. Children are naturally attracted to animals and to the challenge of riding. Riding and caring for a pony can teach them kindness, patience, responsibility, and perseverance, while taking instruction and working with other young riders can help instill self-discipline, good sportsmanship, and self-esteem. Of course, these virtues don't come automatically from taking riding lessons or buying a pony; they require guidance, leadership, and, ideally, family participation. Sharing the joys, work, growth, and challenges of riding is a good way to bring children and families together, and it gives children a healthy and positive outlet for their interest, time, and energy.

For some children, riding may be an avenue for high achievement or even a career. While the challenge of competition is important to some, riding can also be enjoyed simply as a wholesome recreation that puts us in touch with nature and with a wonderful and responsive animal.

At What Age Should a Child Begin Riding?
According to Dr. Doris Bixby Hammett of the American Medical Equestrian Association, to be ready to ride a child should have the following:

- An interest in ponies and the desire to ride and learn.
- Enough muscle strength to maintain a safe and balanced position, and neck muscles strong enough to support properly fitted protective headgear.
- The balance to stay on the pony in motion.
- The ability to understand instructions and follow directions.
- A long enough attention span for instruction.

While some very young children enjoy petting, brushing, and being around ponies (with careful adult supervision), and being led around on a pony for short periods, most are not ready to begin regular riding lessons in a group until they are 7 or older. Your child will enjoy riding and Pony Club more if you wait until she is ready and eager for the experience.

How You Can Help Your Child
Your child's start in riding and her first pony will involve some new responsibilities. You don't have to be an expert horse person to see

that your child has the necessary adult help, guidance, and supervision, or to be in touch with how she is getting on with her riding, pony care and handling, and her confidence and enjoyment of the whole experience. Providing the pony and the equipment is only a start; continuing parental interest, guidance, and support are what make it work. Here are some things you might do for your child:

- **Read this book along with your child,** and help her learn and follow good horsemanship and safety practices.
- **Include your child in discussions about riding, Pony Club, and getting a pony.** It can help her learn about being prepared and organized and how to budget time and money. Be frank with your child about how much you can afford to spend for essentials, optional items, and special events. It is reasonable to expect your child to work to earn "nice to have" extras and optional activities. (Some clubs raise funds to defray the cost of special events like clinics.) You may want to set up a calendar and help your child plan time for stable chores, riding, Pony Club, and special events, as well as her non-riding activities, schoolwork, and other responsibilities.
- **Start out with the right pony.** If you are new to horses and riding, please don't start out by buying a pony. Read the later section on choosing a suitable pony, and above all, get expert advice—preferably from the instructor who will teach your child.
- **Get the right equipment.** You do not need to buy an expensive show outfit, but your child must have safe and suitable clothing and equipment. Often, good used equipment is a better buy than very cheap new tack. Ask your Pony Club instructor for help in choosing the right equipment, making sure it fits both child and pony, and checking it for safe condition. Many Pony Clubs and USPC Riding Centers have a used clothing and equipment exchange.
- **Enforce safety!** Insist that your child wear a properly fitted ASTM/SEI safety helmet (with the chin-strap fastened) *whenever she is on a pony.* This rule can prevent a serious head injury or even save your child's life! Some instructors insist that D Level members wear their helmets whenever they are around the horses. Don't let your child work around a pony or in the stable in sandals, sneakers, or bare feet. (Set a good example by following the rules yourself; don't visit the pony or enter the stable wearing sandals, etc.)

- **Spend time with your child as she works with her pony, and give her hands-on help and supervision.** Learn the basics of leading and handling a pony safely, and be aware of how well your child follows the safety rules she has been taught. Lead the pony while your child is learning to stop, steer, and control him, then be on hand to watch once your child is able to ride on her own. If your child's instructor suggests that she practice certain things, you can encourage this practice at home.
- **Check on the pony's health, well-being, and care daily.** Check his water supply, that he is being fed the right amount, that his stall is clean, and that care and chores are being done properly and on time.
- **Help by providing a regular source of feed, veterinary care, shoeing, and equipment repairs as needed.** Children can't drive to the feed store, pay a vet bill, or replace a broken stirrup leather by themselves. They must be able to count on parental support for basic essentials for the pony, for emergency help (like calling a veterinarian), and for repairs and maintenance that require adult help.
- **Insist on consideration for the pony.** In their enthusiasm, children sometimes forget to give the pony a rest. They may overdo things that are fun for them but hard on the pony. When children get frustrated, they may make a mistake and lose their temper. If you suspect that the pony is being mistreated, whether through thoughtlessness or ignorance, you *must* intervene.
- **Downplay competition.** Some children (and some parents!) can get carried away and put too much emphasis on competition—passing ratings as quickly as possible, qualifying for competitive rally teams, winning, and achieving at any cost. This can undermine the fun, sportsmanship, and spirit of cooperation that Pony Club is all about, and it can ruin the whole experience of riding and Pony Club. Try to help your child discover other important values like fun, friendship, learning at her own pace, and reaching her own personal goals while enjoying the relationship with her pony—not just winning or passing ratings for their own sake.
- **Be a good communicator.** If a "people problem" arises (with an instructor or other adults, or with other children), don't jump to conclusions—try to get the facts first. (Children may not understand a situation or may bring home a different version from what is really occurring.) Taking time to understand a

problem and then addressing it clearly and in a positive way often works wonders.

Get Involved in Pony Club

Pony Clubs can exist only with the involvement and commitment of parents of members and other volunteers of all ages. The more you put into Pony Club, the more your child is likely to get out of it. For example, as a parent, you might consider the following:

- Providing food or beverages at meetings or rallies.
- Painting or setting up jumps; building cross-country fences.
- Providing transportation for a field trip.
- Providing horse/pony transportation to a rally.
- Helping with fund-raising projects.
- Chaperoning field trips or out-of-town rallies.
- Helping prepare and maintain the grounds for your local Pony Club meeting place.
- Running unmounted meetings or mounted meetings; arranging for a speaker or instructor.
- Acting as chairperson for a rally or other club activity.
- Working at a rally as a coach, chaperone, organizing secretary, fence judge, or other helper.

You may become interested in taking a more active role in organizing and helping with your local club, or in helping to organize Pony Club activities.

Choosing a Suitable Pony for the D Level Rider

When you are looking for a pony for a novice rider, you should have an experienced horse person as an adviser (preferably your child's riding instructor). Determine how much you can afford to spend, and then consult with your adviser about what kind of animal you can expect to find in your price range.

A novice rider needs a good beginner's pony, even though she will probably move on to another mount someday. She may outgrow the pony physically as she gets taller, and she may need to move up to a more advanced mount as she becomes a better rider. Don't buy a pony who is too advanced (or one who is too green, or inexperienced) for your child at this stage in the hope that she will "grow into it." This very dangerous situation often results in a child being over-mounted, frightened, and put off riding forever, and in the pony being ruined. If you choose a good pony who is suitable for D Level work, there will always be new riders who need this kind of pony when your child is ready to move on to a more advanced mount.

Temperament and Manners

The most important qualities in a beginner's pony are temperament, manners, and suitability for a child. The first pony can make or break a child's confidence, enjoyment of riding, and ability to learn.

Look for a pony who is friendly, quiet, and unflappable. He should be easy to handle and willing to do what he is asked. He must not have any bad habits like nipping, kicking, or aggressive behavior, and he should not be easily frightened or upset. A beginner's pony must be able to tolerate some mistakes while his young rider is learning. If he is too quick and sensitive, or if he is nervous, spooky, or too eager to go, he will be easily confused and upset and will be difficult, if not dangerous, for a beginning rider to control. Avoid ponies who are very stubborn, willful, or irritable; even if they are safe, they will be no fun to ride.

Don't accept a pony with a bad habit or a questionable temperament in the hope that he can be retrained. Training will not change a pony's basic nature. If he is quick and sensitive, after training he may be well trained, but he will always be quick and sensitive. Retraining a problem pony is a long process that requires an experienced rider, and it is not always successful.

Age, Experience, and Training

The less experienced the rider, the more experienced the pony should be. A pony for a D Level rider should be a mature "solid citizen" who knows his job well, not a young, or green, pony! Young ponies, no matter how gentle, are still maturing and must have their training confirmed under an experienced rider. They can be confused and upset by an inexperienced rider, and will become difficult to ride and handle. Both pony and rider may have a bad time and be unsafe.

A pony for Pony Club work should be at least 5 years old (7 to 10 is better), and older ponies are often the best mounts for beginners. Many ponies are sound and useful well into their 20s and even beyond.

A good Pony Club pony should ride quietly at the walk, trot, and canter, in a ring and outside, alone and in a group of ponies. He should go quietly and easily over ground poles and low jumps (up to about 2 feet, 6 inches). It is easier to learn good riding from a pony who responds correctly to the aids. Because he will be handled by children, his ground manners are most important: he must be easy for a child to catch, lead, groom, and handle. Since your child will want to take her pony to mounted meetings and other events, it is important for the pony to be easy to load in a trailer, to unload safely, and to stand quietly when tied.

Size

A horse or pony should be of a good size to carry his rider easily and safely, and for your child to ride and handle. For security, your child's feet should reach at least halfway down the pony's sides, and the pony should not be so wide that it is uncomfortable for your child to get her legs around it. The child's feet should not hang below the pony's barrel, and pony and rider should be in proportion to each other.

A small child mounted on a too-large horse will have difficulty keeping her balance and being secure in the saddle, and mounting and dismounting without help. The long gaits and big movement make it harder to stay in balance with her mount, and the speed of the gaits and big movement of a jump may be frightening. It will also be very hard for a small child to safely groom, saddle, and care for a horse who is too big for her.

A child who is too large for a pony often feels insecure and top-heavy, as if she might topple forward over the pony's head. If the rider is too heavy for the pony, she will have balance problems and the pony may develop foot and leg trouble or a sore back.

Health and Soundness

The pony must be healthy, sound, and strong enough to do the kind of work you want of him. A lame pony or one with chronic problems can be a heartbreaking and expensive disappointment. Your veterinarian should examine any pony you are seriously considering buying (called a prepurchase examination). She will check the pony's general health and soundness. This should include a blood test (called a Coggins test) for equine infectious anemia. This test (and certain other vaccinations) is required by most stables, Pony Clubs, and USPC Riding Centers before you can bring your pony to mounted meetings.

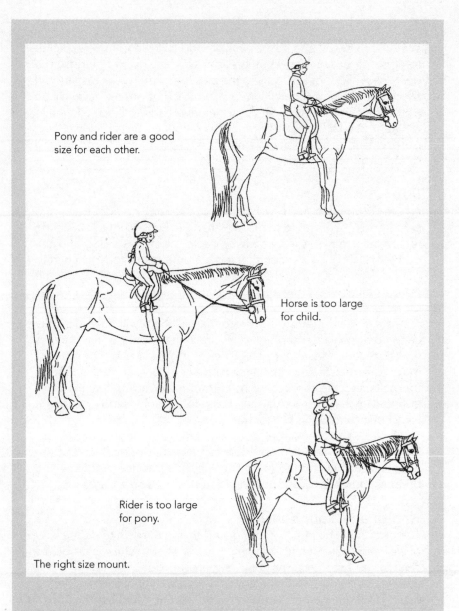

Pony and rider are a good size for each other.

Horse is too large for child.

Rider is too large for pony.

The right size mount.

Although perfect soundness is always desirable, a pony for D Level Pony Club work should not have to pass the kind of soundness tests expected for a race horse or a three-day eventer. He should be sound for riding lessons, ring and trail work, and low jumping. Some good, useful ponies have blemishes (like a scar or evidence of an old, healed injury), or a mild chronic condition that poses little or no problem with good management. Your veterinarian is your best adviser. Be sure she evaluates the pony in light of the work you plan to do with him and how you will keep him.

Gaits, Movement, and Jumping

A pony with good gaits will make your child's riding easier and more enjoyable. He does not have to move well enough to win in the show ring, but he should move freely, with steady and even gaits that are comfortable for your child. Ponies should walk, trot, and canter. Those who perform a pace, running walk, or other special gaits are less suitable for beginners.

Ideally, the pony should be a steady, experienced jumper who will jump quietly and easily over a variety of obstacles up to about 2 feet, 6 inches high in the ring and outside. However, a quiet, willing pony who is well trained on the flat but inexperienced in jumping would be preferable to an experienced jumper who is excitable or too strong for a beginning jumping rider.

Sex

Mares and geldings are equally suitable. Some mares may be irritable around other ponies for the few days they are in season each month, but a quiet, well-trained mare should not be hard to manage. Stallions, no matter how well trained, are not safe for D Level children to ride or handle, especially in a group. They cannot be brought to Pony Club mounted events.

Conformation and Breed

In a Pony Club mount, "handsome is as handsome does." Good conformation is always desirable, but sound, functional conformation is more important than show-ring quality. Some conformation points to consider are the structure and straightness of the legs; the strength of the back and hindquarters; the pony's balance and proportions; and the length, shape, and balance of his neck and head. Conformation defects that can lead to performance or soundness problems (such as poor feet or crooked legs) are more important than "pretty" points, like the size of the ears, the shape of the head, or color. Ask your Pony Club instructor or an experienced horse person to evaluate a pony you are considering, but emphasize the pony's real purpose—don't put conformation ahead of health, safety, and temperament.

A good Pony Club mount can be of any breed or combination of breeds. This is a matter of personal preference. It is more important to find a pony who suits your child than to insist on a particular breed of pony.

Trying Out a Pony

When you are looking for a pony, it's important to have an experienced horse person along (preferably your child's riding instructor).

The first thing to observe about a pony is how he behaves in his home environment. How does he act in his stall, in a pasture, during grooming and tacking up? Can your child catch him, lead him, pick up his feet, and tack him up (with assistance)? Does your child feel confident with him or intimidated by him?

Watch the pony as he is led in a straight line toward you and away from you. Does he travel straight and freely, or does he move crookedly?

Have someone else ride the pony first while you, your child, and an experienced horse person watch. How does the pony behave during mounting and as he is ridden? Does he move freely and evenly? Does he seem to respond easily to the rider's aids, showing good manners and a calm, pleasant attitude, or does he resist or act up? How does the rider's experience compare with that of your child? If the pony is of a suitable size, you may want to ride him yourself or have your child's instructor ride him before you put your child on him.

The real test of a pony is how well he performs for a child. This is a perfectly matched pair!

The real test of a pony's suitability is how he performs for your child. It may be a good idea to keep the pony on a lead line or a longe line until you are sure that your child is confident and in control. She should try walking, stopping, and turning before moving on to a faster gait. See if the pony is quiet and easy to ride on loose reins as well as on contact, and if he will stand quietly with the reins relaxed. If your child has experience in jumping, try the pony first over ground poles and work up gradually to the size jumps she and the pony are comfortable with. Try the pony in a ring and outside, alone and with other ponies.

Some owners will permit you to take a pony on trial for a week or longer, but this is a rare privilege, as a pony could be ruined in a short time in the wrong hands. Sometimes you can lease the pony for a month or so, which amounts to a trial period. If not, you may want to return for a second trial ride. In any case, you should insist on a veterinary examination (and an evaluation by your child's riding instructor) before accepting the pony. Take plenty of time to decide, because the pony will be your child's companion for a long time, and you want to find the right one.

PART II

Learning to Ride

2

Basic Riding on the Flat

This chapter introduces you to the basics of riding: how to mount and dismount; how to sit and hold the reins; how to start, stop, and turn a pony; and how to ride and control his safely at a walk, sitting trot, and posting trot. These are simple to learn, but it's important to start out right for your own safety, to be fair and kind to your pony, and so you can have fun while you are learning to ride.

Safety for Beginning Riders

Safety is important at any level, but especially so when you are starting out. If you learn how to do things the safe way and make it a habit, there is less chance of accidents or injuries to you, your pony, or other people. This lets you enjoy your riding without unnecessary risks that can spoil your fun.

Here are some important safety rules for *all* riders, not just beginners:

1. Dress safely for riding:
   - ASTM/SEI-approved safety helmet (properly fitted, with chin-strap fastened).
   - Riding shoes or boots with a hard, smooth sole and a definite heel.
   - Long pants that don't wrinkle, rub, or bind.

- Shirt or sweater that tucks in.
- No loose scarves, pins, or barrettes in hair; earrings, bracelets, rings, or waist packs. No candy or gum in mouth while riding.

2. Ride only with supervision in an enclosed ring until your instructor says you are ready to ride safely by yourself.

3. Ride a pony who is suitable for you and who you can handle and control safely.

4. Have a responsible person check your tack before you mount (both sides of the saddle and bridle).

5. Keep a safe distance (at least one pony length) between your pony and any other pony.

6. Run your stirrups up whenever you are not mounted. Keep the reins from dragging on the ground.

7. Pay attention to your pony and how he is feeling and acting. Always take good care of your pony after you ride him.

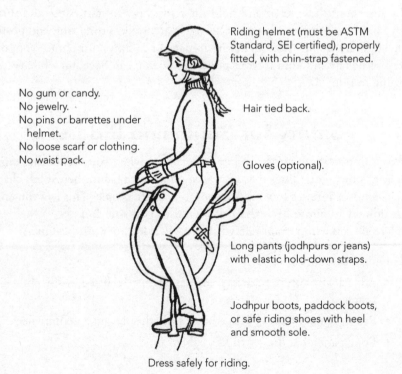

Riding helmet (must be ASTM Standard, SEI certified), properly fitted, with chin-strap fastened.

No gum or candy.
No jewelry.
No pins or barrettes under helmet.
No loose scarf or clothing.
No waist pack.

Hair tied back.

Gloves (optional).

Long pants (jodhpurs or jeans) with elastic hold-down straps.

Jodhpur boots, paddock boots, or safe riding shoes with heel and smooth sole.

Dress safely for riding.

Mounting and Dismounting
How to Do a Tack Safety Check

Always do a safety check before mounting. Follow these steps:

1. Put the reins over the pony's head, and always hold on to them or slip your arm through them as you or someone else does the safety check.

2. Starting on the *right* side, check that the saddle pad is straight and that the girth is buckled correctly.

3. Pull down the right stirrup.

4. Check the right side of the bridle. All buckles should be fastened properly, with nothing twisted.

5. As you go to the *left* side, check the left side of the bridle.

6. Check to be sure that the girth is tight enough and that the saddle pad is straight.

7. Pull down the left stirrup.

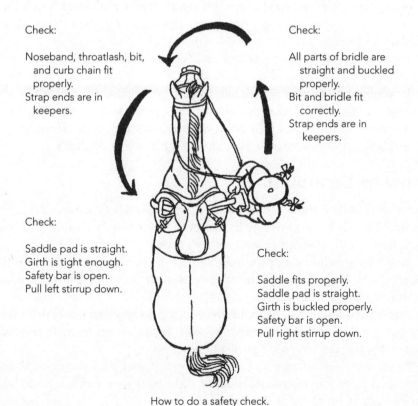

Check:

Noseband, throatlash, bit, and curb chain fit properly.
Strap ends are in keepers.

Check:

All parts of bridle are straight and buckled properly.
Bit and bridle fit correctly.
Strap ends are in keepers.

Check:

Saddle pad is straight.
Girth is tight enough.
Safety bar is open.
Pull left stirrup down.

Check:

Saddle fits properly.
Saddle pad is straight.
Girth is buckled properly.
Safety bar is open.
Pull right stirrup down.

How to do a safety check.

How to Check Stirrup Length

Put your knuckles (in a fist) against the stirrup bar and stretch the stirrup leather along your arm. The stirrup iron should just reach your armpit. Make sure both stirrups are the same length before you mount.

How to Mount

Stand next to your pony's left shoulder, facing the tail. Hold both reins in your left hand on top of his neck, with the reins snug enough so that he won't walk off. Put the extra loop of rein (called the *bight*) on the far side. With your right hand, take the back of the stirrup iron and turn it toward you. Put your left foot all the way into the stirrup with your toe down, so you won't poke the pony in the ribs with your toe.

Put your right hand on the pommel (the front of the saddle) or in the middle of the seat. Don't put your hand on the cantle (the back of the saddle), as this can pull the saddle over. Turn so you are facing the pony's side, spring up from your right foot, and stand for a moment with both legs together and your weight on your hands.

Swing your right leg over the pony's rump. Be careful not to kick him. Catch your weight on your knees and sink *gently* into the saddle. Never come down hard on his back!

Put your right foot into the stirrup and take your reins in both hands. Don't let your pony move off until you are ready.

If you are short or your pony is tall, you can get help from someone or stand on a step, a mounting block, or a hay bale. You can also let the left stirrup down so it is easier to reach, and then put it back up once you are mounted. (Don't try to climb on from a fence or from anything that might tip over.)

How to Dismount

Put both reins (and crop) in your left hand, with the end of the reins (the bight) on the right side of the pony's neck. Take both feet out of the stirrups. Put your right hand on the pommel or on the pony's neck.

Lean forward and swing your right leg over the pony's rump, making sure it doesn't touch his rump. Turn and slide down with your side against the pony, so that you land facing forward.

After dismounting, take the reins over your pony's head and run both stirrups up, being sure to always hold on to the reins. If you are not going to remount right away, you can loosen the girth a hole or two.

Never dismount by swinging your leg forward over your pony's neck. You have to let go of your reins to do this, and if the pony moves off you could land on the back of your head.

The stirrup should just reach your armpit. Make sure both stirrups are the same length before you mount.

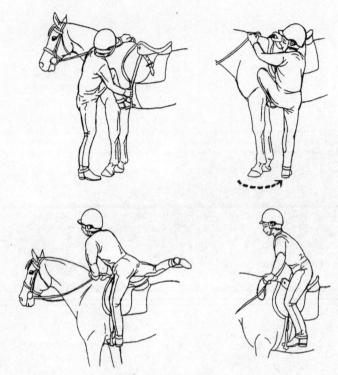

Steps in mounting.

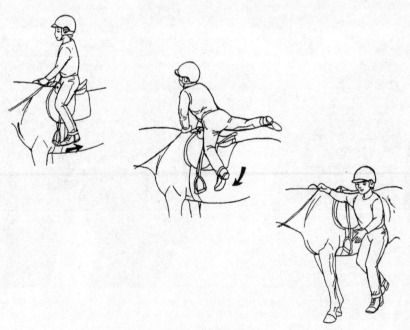

Steps in dismounting.

Basic Position and Balance

The way you sit makes all the difference to your riding. A good riding position makes it easy for you to stay on your pony and ride in balance and is comfortable for you and for your pony. Sitting incorrectly makes it harder to ride, puts you out of balance, and can make both you and your pony stiff and uncomfortable. It takes time and practice to learn to sit the right way, but it is worth it.

Good riders ride by balance, not by muscle grip. This is called the *Basic Balanced Seat.* When you ride with good balance, your body can relax and move easily with your pony, and it is easier to ride with confidence and control. At first you will have to think about your position and correct it when it goes wrong, but with practice it will become an automatic habit.

Seat

Sit on your *seat bones*, deep in the center of the saddle. To find your seat bones, rock your seat a little and you will feel two bones like the rockers of a rocking chair. Do not sit on the front of your seat or on your buttocks.

Sit deep and tall in the saddle. If you take a deep breath, you will feel your back get taller and more relaxed and your seat get deeper. Let your legs hang down long and relaxed, and let your head balance up over your shoulders. Sit evenly in the middle of the saddle, not off to one side.

Stirrups and Feet

When your legs hang down loosely out of the stirrups, the bottom of the stirrup irons should touch just below your ankle bones. If your stirrups are too long, you will bounce and dangle your legs. If the stirrups are too short, they will push your legs forward and your seat backward.

Your stirrup should be under the ball of your foot, and your heels should be down (this will take some practice). Your toes should point out a little (about as much as your knees). They should not be turned in or stick way out.

Dropping and Picking Up Stirrups

1. To *drop* your stirrups, slip your feet out.
2. To *pick up* your stirrups, turn your toes in and slip your feet into the irons without looking down at your stirrups or using your hands to help. Practice until you can pick up your stirrups quickly at a halt and then at a walk.

Legs

Your legs should hang down so that they lie gently against the saddle and the pony's sides. They should not grip or pinch the saddle (this makes you stiff), but they should not stick out, either. The inside of your calf should be lightly touching your pony's side. Your toes should be just under your knees, not out ahead of them. Your feet should hang underneath your seat.

Head and Eyes

Your head is quite heavy; it controls your balance. If your head tips down or to the side, it throws your balance off, and your pony will feel it and may think he is supposed to stop or turn. Your eyes steer your head. If you look up and out over your pony's head, it helps your head (and the rest of you) stay in balance. Keep your head up and look where you want your pony to go.

Shoulders, Arms, and Hands

Let your shoulders hang down wide and relaxed. Your arms hang down under your shoulders, close to your ribs. Keep a gentle bend in your elbows. Do not stick your forearms stiffly out ahead of you or poke your elbows out to the sides. Keep your hands low, with your forearms and knuckles pointing toward the pony's mouth.

Here are some tips for good position and balance:

- When you take a deep breath, it relaxes your seat and back and helps you sit up tall without making you stiff or sloppy.
- Look at a "target"—something at eye level in line with where you are going. Turn your eyes and find a new target whenever you turn your pony. This helps balance your head and "aims" your pony where you are looking. Never look down.
- Don't grip with your knees or thighs. Let them lie relaxed against the saddle. This helps them move with your pony and take up the bounces.
- To find your balance in the saddle (at a halt), try a teeter-totter exercise. Tip your body (from the seat bones up) back a little and forward a little until you feel yourself straight up and down in the middle of the saddle, sitting on your seat bones.
- Let your feet rest on the stirrups without pushing against them. Try to keep your heels back and down, not forward.
- To help remember the best length for your reins, you can put a rubber band or a piece of tape on your reins at the spot where you should hold them.

Good balanced position:

Eyes up.
Arms hang beside ribs.
Knees and ankles relaxed.
Head balanced.
Back straight.
Balanced on seat bones.
Feet and legs under body.
Heels down.

Problem positions:

WRONG
"Slumping."
Head and eyes down.
Round back.
Sitting on buttocks.
Rider out of balance.
Arms out ahead of body.
Knees pinching.
Heels up, toes down.

WRONG
"Chair seat."
Back straight, but feet
    and legs ahead.
Rider out of balance
    backward.
Knees tight.
Heels level.

WRONG
"Perching."
Too far foward.
Stiff, hollow back.
Sitting on front of
    seat (crotch).
Knees tight.
Legs too far back.
Heels level or up.

The Balanced Seat.

A balanced position. This rider's feet and legs are under her body, and you can draw a vertical line through her ear, shoulder, seat, and foot.

Incorrect "chair seat" position. Although she is sitting up straight, this rider's legs and feet are ahead of her seat, putting her out of balance.

Hands and Reins

Your hands hold the reins, which are attached to the bit in your pony's mouth. The bit gives signals to tell your pony what you want him to do. Holding your reins correctly helps you use your hands gently and clearly and avoids hurting your pony's mouth or confusing him.

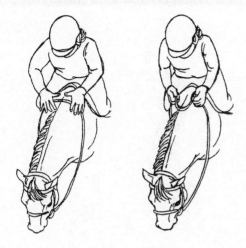

How to pick up the reins.

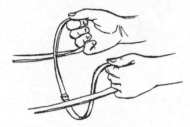

RIGHT
How to hold the reins.

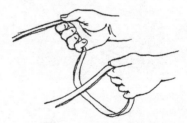

WRONG
Holding reins "upside down."

Holding the reins.

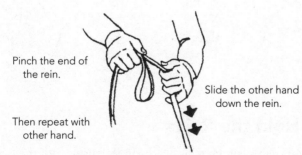

Pinch the end of the rein.

Then repeat with other hand.

Slide the other hand down the rein.

How to shorten the reins.

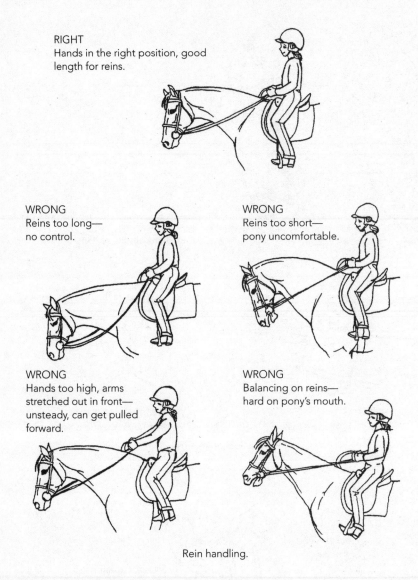

RIGHT
Hands in the right position, good
length for reins.

WRONG
Reins too long—
no control.

WRONG
Reins too short—
pony uncomfortable.

WRONG
Hands too high, arms
stretched out in front—
unsteady, can get pulled
forward.

WRONG
Balancing on reins—
hard on pony's mouth.

Rein handling.

How to Hold the Reins

To pick up your reins, lay the reins neatly on the mane with the buckle on top of your pony's neck. Put your thumbs together, palms down. Pick up the reins and turn the ends of the reins forward, with your thumbs on top. The rein may go between your little finger and your ring finger, or all your fingers may be around the rein. Your hands should be closed in a soft fist, not with open fingers (which can let the reins slip), or with tight, hard fists. The tail of the reins, or bight, comes out the top of your fist and flips over the front of your fingers. The bight should be inside the reins, on the right side of the pony's neck.

Shortening and Lengthening the Reins

To make your reins shorter, hold the tail end of your left rein with your right hand while you slide your hand down the rein. Then hold the tail end of the right rein while you slide your right hand down the rein. Put your thumbs on the ends of the reins so they won't slip.

To make your reins longer, open your fingers a little and let the reins slide through.

Proper Length of Rein

Keeping the reins at just the right length takes some practice, but it makes a big difference in how easy it is to ride and control your pony. Your reins should be long enough so that you can keep your hands over your pony's withers with your elbows bent. When your pony is going along as he should, there should be a gentle sag in the reins, but you should be able to tighten them by squeezing your hands into fists.

If your reins are too short, your pony will be unhappy and may pull or toss his head. You may also get pulled forward. If they are too long, your pony will not pay attention and it will be hard to stop or turn him.

Learning to Control Your Pony

When you first begin to move, just relax and let your body get the feel of the pony's movements. Someone should lead your pony until you have found your balance, are comfortable at the walk, and have learned how to control your pony. The walk is a four-beat gait (it sounds like "one, two, three, four" or "clip, clop, clip, clop"). It is quite smooth and easy to ride. Try to relax and let your body move easily with the motion of the walk.

Basic Control: The Aids

Ponies can't understand human talk the way we can, but we must have some way to communicate with them. The *aids* are the signals you use to help your pony understand what you want him to do. They are your legs, your hands, your seat, and sometimes your voice. Since a pony is trained to obey certain aids, you have to learn how to give the proper aids so he can understand you and do what you want. If you don't give him the right aids at the right time, he will be confused.

The simple aids are:

- **Legs.** A short squeeze of both legs (using the calf muscles) or a nudge with the heels means to go forward. A squeeze with one leg means to turn that way.
- **Hands.** Your hands hold the reins, which are attached to a metal bit in the pony's mouth, so use them smoothly and gently. Both hands squeezing backward (like squeezing water out of a sponge) means to stop or slow down. One hand moving out to the side means to turn that way. To let the pony move forward, both hands must relax.
- **Seat.** Your pony can feel your seat through the saddle. When you relax your seat and sit up deep and tall, it tells her to slow down or stop. When you look to one side and turn your head and your body, she knows she should turn the way you are looking.
- **Voice.** Your voice is used only to help out the other aids and not used instead of them. A low, gentle "Whoa" or "Easy" can help calm down a nervous pony, and a short "cluck" sound may help get a lazy pony to move on. Remember to praise your pony with a "Good boy" and a pat on the neck when he does what you want.

Aids should be short, like a heartbeat. You use an aid and then relax it right away; a long, hard pull or squeeze annoys and confuses the pony. If your pony doesn't pay attention, give him another short aid, a bit stronger, but not longer. Sometimes it may take four or five aids before he understands and starts to obey you. As soon as he begins to obey, ease up on your aids.

Learning to Walk On, Stop, and Turn

To Walk On
First, look ahead where you want to go. Make sure your reins are short enough so that you can just feel your pony's mouth. Squeeze your legs against your pony's sides once to make him listen, then give him two short nudges with your legs to tell him to walk on. Let your hands go forward a little to "follow" his head as he starts to walk.

To Stop (or Halt)
To stop your pony, take a deep breath and sit tall with your shoulders back. Close your legs in against your pony's sides and keep your heels down, then stop following with your arms and hands, and squeeze your fingers several times as though squeezing water out of a sponge. Squeeze as strongly as you have to in order to make it work. Let your hands and legs ease up as he stops.

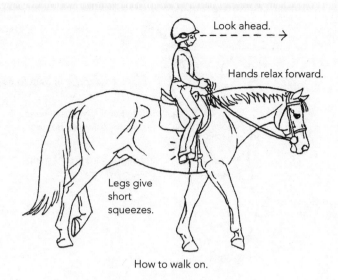

Look ahead.

Hands relax forward.

Legs give short squeezes.

How to walk on.

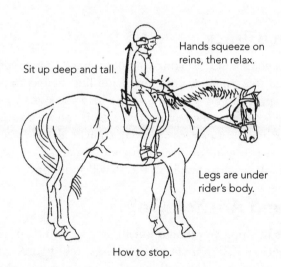

Sit up deep and tall.

Hands squeeze on reins, then relax.

Legs are under rider's body.

How to stop.

To Turn

First, look in the direction you want to turn. Sit up tall, turn your seat a little bit, and take your hand out to the side (away from the pony's neck). This asks your pony to turn his head and shows him where to go. Your other hand must ease up enough to let him turn. Use both legs to keep him going, and let your outside leg (the one you are turning away from) slide back a little. This helps to control his hindquarters so it doesn't swing sideways in the turn.

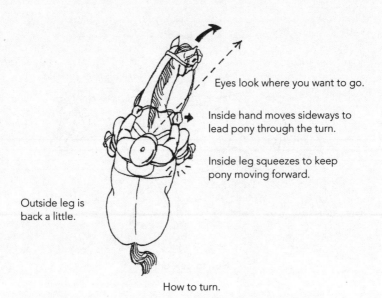

Eyes look where you want to go.

Inside hand moves sideways to lead pony through the turn.

Inside leg squeezes to keep pony moving forward.

Outside leg is back a little.

How to turn.

Riding on a Track

When you ride, you should be taking your pony exactly where you want him to go. This is called *riding a track*. Look ahead and find a target to ride your pony toward. (This target should be in line with where you want your pony to go, and at your eye level, not down on the ground.) If you keep your eyes on your target, it is much easier to steer your pony straight along a track. When you reach a corner or you want to turn, turn your eyes and look for a new target. Your body will follow where you look and so will your pony.

Which Hand Are You On?

When you ride in a ring you should usually stay *on the rail*, or ride on a track close to the fence, unless you are making turns, ring figures, or doing other exercises. If you are riding to the left (your left hand is toward the center of the ring), this is called riding *on the left hand*. Riding to the right (right hand toward the center) is called riding *on the right hand*.

Inside and Outside

Inside means the side toward the center of the arena or the inside of a turn or circle. *Inside* can refer to your inside leg, hand, rein, or the side of your pony. *Outside* means the side toward the rail of the arena, or on the outside of a circle or turn.

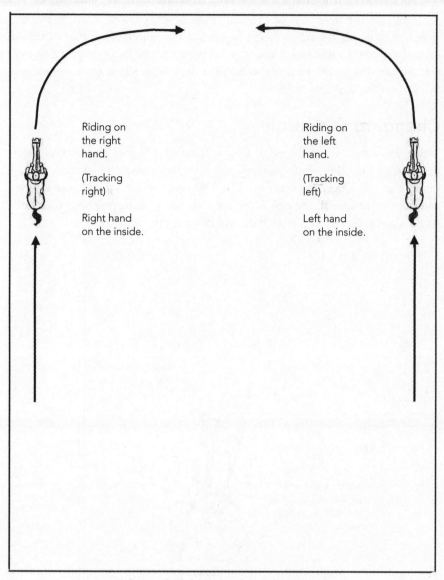

Riding on
the right
hand.

(Tracking
right)

Right hand
on the inside.

Riding on
the left
hand.

(Tracking
left)

Left hand
on the inside.

Riding on the left hand and on the right hand.

Keeping Your Pony on the Rail

Many ponies like to cut their corners and come into the center of the ring. To keep your pony *on the rail* (close to the fence), look ahead where you want him to go. Next, squeeze or nudge with your inside leg (the leg toward the center of the ring) as you steer him out toward the rail with both hands. If you pay attention, you can tell when your pony is beginning to cut a corner or lean in toward the center. It is much easier to keep him where he is supposed to be if you correct this before he gets too far into the center. With some ponies, you will have to be alert and firm!

Changing Direction

When you turn and go the other way, it is called a *change of direction*. Before you change direction, your pony should be walking straight, next to the rail. Look in the direction you want to turn. Turn your eyes, your seat (just a little), and your hand toward the new direction, and use your legs to keep your pony going. As you return to the rail, you will be going the other way.

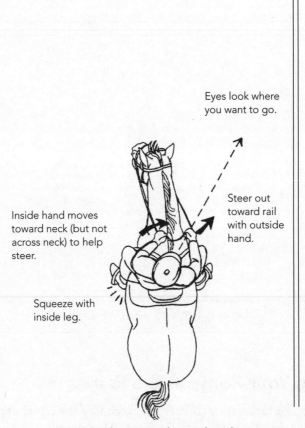

Eyes look where you want to go.

Steer out toward rail with outside hand.

Inside hand moves toward neck (but not across neck) to help steer.

Squeeze with inside leg.

How to keep pony close to the rail.

There are two ways to change direction:

- **Ride a reverse.** Turn off the rail, beginning a medium-size circle. When you are halfway around the circle, ride in a straight line back to the rail.
- **Turn across the arena.** Ride to a letter or marker and turn straight across the arena. (Look at the marker to aim your pony straight.) When you reach the other side of the arena, turn along the track in the new direction.

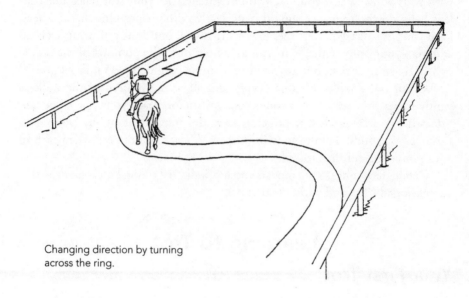

Changing direction by turning across the ring.

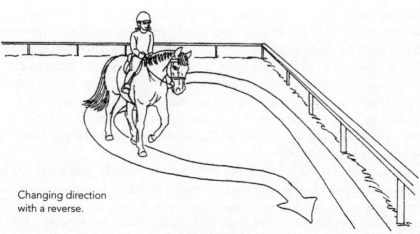

Changing direction with a reverse.

How to change direction.

To practice turning and changes of direction, it helps to set up cones or other markers to steer around and help you remember where to turn. Make your turns and reverses large enough so your pony can keep moving easily.

Riding without Stirrups (at a Walk)

Riding without stirrups at a walk helps you relax, sit comfortably, and move with your pony. When you ride without stirrups, let your seat relax and your legs hang down. Your legs should hang softly without gripping at the knees; keep your legs relaxed. Your toes may hang down, but don't pull your heels up and grab your pony with them. You may hold onto the pommel of the saddle or a safety strap at first, but as you become more confident you may let go.

As your pony walks, breathe deeply and allow the motion of the walk to gently move your seat. If someone (your instructor) leads your pony, you can ride with your eyes closed, noticing how the movement of the pony goes through your body. Think "go with the flow!" See if you can tell when each of your pony's feet hit the ground.

To really feel your pony's movement at a walk, try riding bareback or with a bareback pad (the kind without stirrups).

Learning to Trot

Your First Trot

When you are comfortable and can ride with good balance and control at the walk, you may learn to trot. A *trot* is a two-beat gait (it sounds like "one, two" or "clip, clop"). It is a little faster and more bouncy than the walk. Someone should lead your pony at first, or your instructor should control your pony with a longe line, until you get your balance and can control your pony in a trot. Hold on to the pommel of the saddle or a neck-strap (a spare stirrup leather that is put around your pony's neck for you to hold on to), so that your hands won't bounce up and down and hurt your pony's mouth or make you lose your balance. At first, try a short, slow trot (just a few yards) several times, instead of trotting too long or too fast.

The aids for the trot are the same as for walking forward. Shorten your reins a little, squeeze with your legs once to make your pony listen, then give two short squeezes or nudges—or as many as it takes to get your pony to trot. Be careful not to pull back on the reins, or the pony won't trot. If you don't hold on to the saddle or neck-strap and your hands bounce around, you will jerk on the pony's mouth and she may stop short.

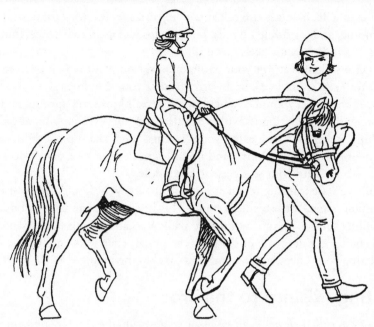

Riding a trot for the first time.

When you ride the trot, it helps to breathe deeply, relax, and sit up tall. Keep your shoulders back and let your legs hang down. Let your knees, hips, and ankles be soft and springy to take up the bounces.

When you get used to trotting, you can put the reins in one hand and hold the pommel of the saddle with the other. Be sure to keep the hand that holds the reins down low against the pony's neck, so that it doesn't bounce and jerk. You can pull on the pommel to get your seat deep into the saddle. When you can keep your seat deep and your rein hand still and quiet, you can try letting go of the saddle and holding the reins in both hands. But if you start to bounce or lose your balance, catch the pommel quickly so you don't hurt your pony's mouth. Practice with short, slow trots until you are quite comfortable sitting at the trot. It's a good idea to practice trotting on a longe line with an instructor controlling your pony while you learn to sit and go with the movement of the trot.

Half-Seat (2-Point Position or Jumping Position)

Half-seat is a balancing position in which you are half-sitting and half-standing, not standing all the way up. It is also called *2-point position* because your two "points" (your legs) are touching your pony but your third "point" (your seat) is off the saddle. Half-seat is also called *jumping position*. It is used for posting trot, for jumping, and for riding up hills. It also helps you learn to balance, find your "springs," and keep your heels down.

To get into half-seat, tilt your body forward from your hips (not from your waist). Your seat should sink backward a little as your shoulders go forward, just over your knees. Let your heels sink down and your knees stay springy, and keep your weight on your thighs, with your head up and eyes looking ahead. Let your hips, knees, and ankles be your "springs" and take up the bounce and movement of the pony. Don't stand up or lean out over your pony's neck. You should balance with your seat close to the saddle.

While you are learning to balance in a half-seat, you should rest your hands on the pony's neck or use a neck-strap. This keeps your hands from bouncing and pulling on her mouth by mistake while you are getting your balance. As you get better at riding in half-seat, you can practice at a walk and then at a slow trot, letting your knees, ankles, and hips take up the bounces.

Posting (Rising) to the Trot

Posting (also called *rising*) is an efficient way to ride the trot. In a posting trot, you let your pony lift you up with one bounce and sit down with the next. This is easier on her back and less tiring for you than sitting the trot, especially when trotting faster, for long distances, or riding a pony with a bouncy trot.

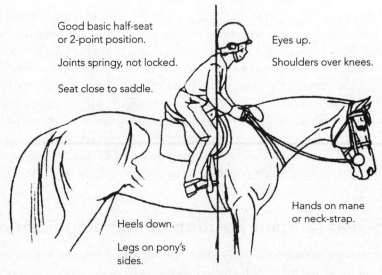

Good basic half-seat or 2-point position.

Joints springy, not locked.

Seat close to saddle.

Eyes up.

Shoulders over knees.

Hands on mane or neck-strap.

Heels down.

Legs on pony's sides.

Half-seat or 2-point position.

To learn to post, or rise, to the trot, you will need good balance and control at the trot first. At a steady trot, count with your pony's rhythm: "One, two; one, two; one, two . . ." You will feel him lift or push you up with every other bounce (on "one"). You sit back down on the next step (on "two"). When you are balanced just right and catch her rhythm, it feels like you are "with" him perfectly and posting is easy. Remember, the bounce of your pony's trot does all the lifting—don't try to lift yourself up and down. You should only post as high as he lifts you, which is usually very close to the saddle, not standing up high. When you are learning to post, keep your hands on the pony's neck or hold a neck-strap so your hands don't bounce and jerk his mouth or make you lose your balance. Keep your eyes up and look ahead, and let your heels sink down. It is easier to post if your pony trots steadily along the rail than if he slows down, speeds up, or cuts into the center. It may be easier to practice your posting in a longe lesson, with your instructor controlling your pony. To help you feel her rhythm, you can count, hum, or sing along with his trot. To help your balance, you can practice half-seat at a walk or at a slow trot.

When you post the trot, keep your heels down and your legs close to the pony, with springy knees and ankles. Be careful not to pinch with your knees or let your heels come up (this will take some practice). Don't try to stand up high by pushing against the stirrups. This can make you post too high, which makes it hard to keep your balance. If you can find the right balance and rhythm, the bounce of the trot will lift you up and makes it easier to post with your pony's trot.

Let your pony lift you up on one beat.   Then sit down for the next beat.

Posting trot.

Improving Control

Transitions (Changes of Gait)

A *transition* is a change. When you walk on from a halt, or trot from a walk it is called an *up transition*. When you slow down from a trot to a walk or from a walk to a halt, it is called a *down transition*.

Transitions should be smooth and gradual, so they are easy on you and your pony. He will take several steps to slow down from a trot to a walk or to stop. You and your pony should be in balance during transitions, so that you feel secure and your pony can go forward, stop, or turn easily.

To make a good transition, you must prepare your pony by sitting up deep and tall, closing your legs on his sides, and having your reins short enough to feel her mouth. This tells him to get ready. Ask for up transitions with short squeezes or nudges of your legs (being sure to look ahead and to relax your hands to let him go forward). For down transitions, sit deep and tall, take a deep breath, keep your shoulders back, and give short squeezes with your hands on the reins. Remember to ease up on the pressure as soon as your pony starts to obey your aids.

Speed Control at the Walk and Trot

Sometimes you may want your pony to go faster or slower in the walk or trot without changing to another gait. This is called *rating*, or controlling speed in a gait.

To go faster, give short squeezes or nudges with your legs in rhythm with your pony's walk or trot. (If you are posting, squeeze or nudge when you sit and relax your legs back to normal when you go up.) Your hands must let him stretch his neck out more in order to move faster.

To go slower, sit deep and tall, take a deep breath, and keep your shoulders back while you give short squeezes on the reins in rhythm with your pony's walk or trot. If you're riding at a posting trot, squeeze your hands on the reins (especially the outside rein) when you sit, and relax back to normal when you go up. Keep your legs closed on your pony's sides so that he slows down rather than stops.

Getting the Best from Your Pony

Each pony is special and a little different from every other pony. Your pony should be trained to obey proper aids, but you will have to learn how to give the aids in the best way for him. Some ponies are quite sensitive and respond quickly to a soft, light touch of your hands or legs. They may get upset if you use your aids too hard or too quickly, or if you are not smooth and quiet with your aids. Other ponies are a bit lazy. They need a "wake-up call" (like a strong squeeze or a firm nudge of your legs) to get them to pay attention when you give them an aid, and you may have to use your aids more firmly.

Always use the lightest aids that will get the job done. Start out with a light aid, then make the next one stronger if you have to. If you start out with strong, hard aids, it can upset your pony and make him difficult to ride.

When your pony does something good (like respond to your aids), you must let him know by rewarding him. Always thank your pony by relaxing your rein or leg pressure when he first starts to respond. You can also stroke his neck or shoulder and say, "Good boy," when he does well. Stroke his neck gently, don't slap him! When you are standing still for a while, don't hold him with a tight rein, but give him a little slack in the reins so he can relax his mouth and his neck. (However, he must behave and not move around, eat grass, or bother other ponies.)

Some ponies want to have their own way. They will try to find out if they can ignore your aids and do as they please, and if you will give up. If a pony acts stubborn, you must not lose your temper, but you should not give up, either. He might be confused because you made a mistake in using your aids. Try again, giving a very clear, correct aid. If he still does not do what you ask, give the aids again several times, a bit stronger each time. Be as strong as you have to until he obeys, but remember that getting angry or losing your temper doesn't work and is unkind to your pony. Remember to reward him with a pat and a "Good boy" as soon as he starts to obey you.

If you are having trouble with your pony and you find yourself starting to get upset with him, *stop, dismount, and take time to calm down.* Don't try to ride a pony when you are upset or angry, and *never* lose your temper with him. Instead, ask your instructor for help with the problem.

Common Problems for Beginning Riders

The Pony Pulls

Some ponies pull on the reins with a jerk. This can hurt your hands, especially if the reins get pulled through your fingers; or if you are leaning forward, you could get pulled down onto the pony's neck.

The reason most ponies pull is because somebody has pulled on their mouth and hurt them, or because you are holding the reins too short. This can happen if your hands bounce or if you grab the reins for balance. If you have trouble with your balance, put your hands on your pony's neck or hold a neck-strap so you won't pull on the reins by mistake.

Drop your seat bones deep into the saddle and sit up deep and tall with your shoulders back so you won't be pulled forward. Keep your fingers closed on the reins and your thumbs on the end of the reins so they can't be pulled through your fingers. Give your pony enough rein so that he can relax his neck and his

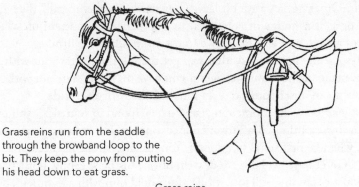

Grass reins run from the saddle
through the browband loop to the
bit. They keep the pony from putting
his head down to eat grass.

Grass reins.

mouth, especially when he is standing still. When you use your hands to turn, slow down, or stop your pony, use short, gentle squeezes, not long, hard pulls.

It also may help to wear gloves when you ride.

The Pony Eats Grass

If your pony tries to eat grass while you are riding, he may put his head down suddenly and give you a jerk. If you let him eat grass when he should be working, he will want to eat instead of work, and he may get stubborn about it.

To keep him from eating grass, sit up deep and tall and keep your shoulders back. If he puts his head down to eat, keep your seat down in the saddle and your elbows bent, and hold the reins firmly. This makes him pull on his own mouth instead of pulling you forward.

If your pony gets his head down and will not stop eating, pull sideways and up instead of straight back. Use your legs to make him move on. You may have to tap him with a crop to get his attention.

In lessons only, a pony who is very stubborn about eating grass may have to wear a special check rein (called *grass reins*). **Caution:** Never use grass reins on a pony when jumping or going over ground poles. Grass reins are not allowed to be used in competitive rallies.

Improving Your Seat

Your *seat* means the way you sit, your balance, and the way you use your body when you ride. A good seat helps you stay on your pony, makes you more comfortable, and makes it easier for your pony to carry you.

A good seat is relaxed and supple, not tight and tense. It comes from balance, not from gripping with your muscles. An *independent seat* means that you can ride securely without using your hands for balance or to hold on. It also means that you can move one part of your body (like your arms) without making other parts of your body (like your legs or seat) move out of position. Without an independent seat you will get bounced around, and you might grab the reins to keep your balance. Bouncy, unbalanced riders; tight, tense riders; and riders who grab the reins for balance are hard on their ponies, even though they don't mean to be.

To develop an independent seat, you must get used to riding in good balance and position, and let your body go with your pony as he moves. This takes practice, but it helps you ride better.

Before You Move Off: Girth and Stirrup Check

As a more experienced rider, you should be able to check your girth and stirrups yourself (but if you aren't sure if they are right, ask your instructor). You can learn to tighten the girth and adjust your stirrups while you are mounted. This takes less time than dismounting to do it.

Even though you should always check your girth before mounting, you should recheck the girth 5 or 10 minutes after you start to ride. It often gets looser as your pony warms up. *Always* recheck it before you jump. After you dismount, let your girth out one or two holes while you cool your pony out.

Before you start to fix your girth or stirrups, stop your pony and put your reins in one hand, short enough to control your pony. If you are with a group of riders, ask them to wait for you (if on the trail), or move to the center of the ring, out of the way.

- **How to adjust the girth while mounted:** Keep your left foot in the stirrup. Put your left leg up over the knee roll and lift the saddle flap. Take the end of the billet and pull up. It is easier to slip the buckle tongue into the next hole if you keep your finger on the tongue.

- **How to adjust the stirrups while mounted:** Keep your feet in the irons but relax the pressure on the stirrup, and turn your knee out so you can reach the buckle. Pull on the end of the strap so that the buckle slides out where you can hold it. With your finger on the tongue of the buckle, you can slide the buckle up toward the stirrup bar (to shorten the leather), or down (to make the leather longer). When you are finished, pull on the end of the leather to slide the buckle up under the saddle skirt. Put the end of the stirrup leather through the keeper.

How to tighten the girth while mounted.

How to adjust a stirrup while mounted.

To be safe, keep your feet in the irons and use only one hand to fix your stirrups while holding the reins in your other hand. This way, you still have your feet in the stirrups and control of your pony if he should move while you are fixing your stirrups.

Warming Up and Cooling Down

Both ponies and their riders need to warm up and loosen up their muscles before they are ready to work well. This protects the muscles from strains and injury and gets them ready to do their best. Riding a pony too hard or fast without warming him up properly is unkind and can cause injuries. A good warmup takes at least 15 minutes of walking and trotting. This is a good time to do rider warmup exercises, too.

At the end of a ride, a pony may be hot, tired, and breathing hard. He needs to cool down and his temperature and heartbeat need to return to normal before he can be put away safely. You can start the cooling-down process by riding at a walk for the last 10 minutes of every ride. When you dismount, loosen the girth, give him a drink of water, and walk him around until he is breathing normally. A pony should always be checked over and put away cool, dry, and comfortable after he has been ridden. This may require hosing, sponging, scraping, or rubbing him dry; walking until he is cool; and other care. (For more about cooling out your pony, see chapter 6, "Taking Care of Your Pony.")

Balance and Suppling Exercises

At first, you may get sore muscles after riding because your muscles are not used to the work. The exercises in this section warm up your muscles and make them stronger and more supple so you won't get so sore. They will also help your balance, confidence, and control of your hands and legs. They are fun, too, and they will make you a better rider!

Always do a new exercise first at a halt with someone holding your pony and watching out for you while you learn the exercise. Start gently and slowly to let your pony get used to it. Later you can do exercises at a walk while someone leads your pony, or during a longe lesson, with your instructor controlling the pony on a longe line.

When your feet are out of the stirrups during some exercises, you can cross your stirrups in front of the saddle to keep them out of your way so they won't bump against your pony's sides. (If you pull the stirrup leather buckle out about 6 inches from the stirrup bar, you can fold the stirrup leathers flat as you cross them over.) When you do exercises with your hands off the reins, tie a knot in the end of the reins to make them shorter so they will lie on the pony's neck where you can reach them. This also keeps them from hanging too low where your pony could step on them.

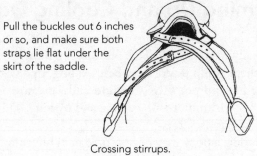

Pull the buckles out 6 inches or so, and make sure both straps lie flat under the skirt of the saddle.

Crossing stirrups.

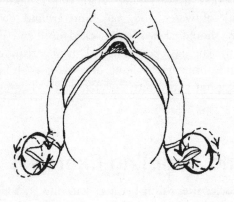

Foot circles: do them both ways.

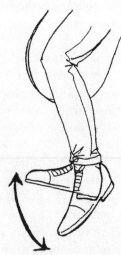

Ankle stretches: point toes down, then up.

Foot and ankle exercises.

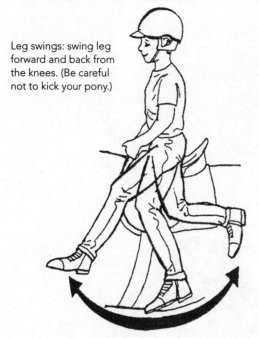

Leg swings: swing leg forward and back from the knees. (Be careful not to kick your pony.)

Leg exercises.

- **Foot circles and ankle stretches.** These keep your ankles supple and help keep your heels down.

  1. With both feet out of stirrups, draw circles in the air with your toes. Circle both feet one way, then the other.

  2. Point your toes down toward the ground, then point them up as high as you can. Repeat several times.

- **Leg swings.** These relax your knees and loosen the muscles in your lower legs. With feet out of stirrups, swing one leg forward and the other leg back, from below your knees. Then swing the other leg forward and back. Let your toes hang down to relax your legs. Be careful not to kick your pony.

- **Poll and croup touches.** These are good for suppleness and for confidence. Try to keep your legs in position even though your upper body and arms move.

  1. With feet in stirrups, reach forward with one hand as far as you can along your pony's mane, and try to touch her poll. (Don't touch his ears—he may not like it.) Your other arm stays behind you. Then sit up.

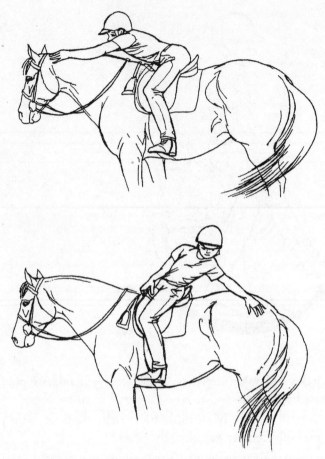

Touching poll and croup.

2. Sit deep and tall in the saddle. Stretch one arm up over your head. Lean back, reach around behind you, and pat your pony as far back on his croup as you can reach, near his tail. Your other arm stays in front of you. Then, sit up without using your hands to pull yourself up.

- **Around the world.** This is good for balance and confidence, and besides, it's fun! You must have a helper to hold your pony and watch out for you while you are learning this exercise.

    1. With feet out of stirrups (stirrups crossed over), swing your right leg over your pony's neck and sit sideways.

    2. Then swing your left leg over his rump and sit backward.

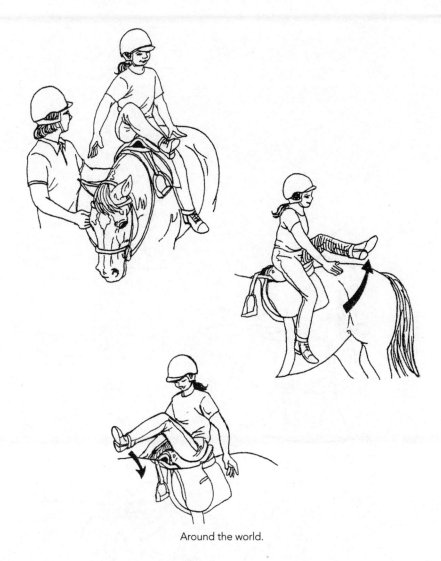

Around the world.

3. Swing your right leg over the rump and sit sideways.

4. Now swing your left leg over the neck and you're "home." Then try it the other way. How fast can you do it?

When you can go "around the world" using your hands, try it "no hands" with your arms folded. You can have around the world races (with hands or no hands).

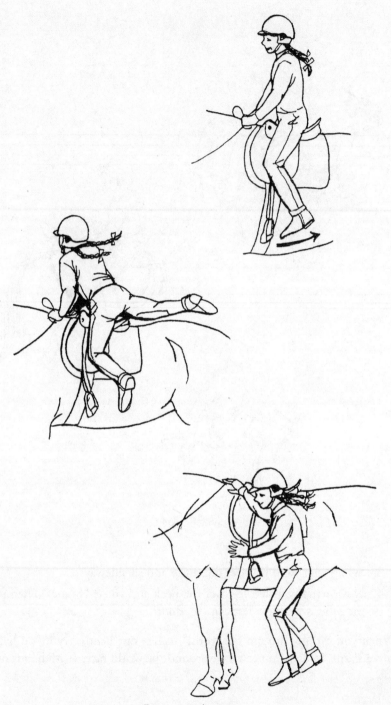

Emergency dismount.

Emergency Dismounts

An emergency dismount is the fastest safe way to get off a pony. You could use it an emergency, any time you need to get off quickly, or just for fun and practice. Here's how to do it:

1. Take both feet out of the stirrups.
2. Put both hands on your pony's withers, lean forward, and swing your legs back and up to clear the saddle and the pony's rump.
3. As you swing off, turn so that your side is next to the saddle (not your stomach) and you are facing forward beside your pony. If you don't, you could lose your balance and sit down when you land.
4. Land with your knees bent, holding the reins in one hand.

When you practice emergency dismounts, have somebody stand by to help you at first. As you get better, try faster dismounts. When you can do emergency dismounts easily at a halt, you can practice them at a walk.

Caution: Just because you have learned emergency dismounts, don't try to jump off your pony whenever things go wrong. It is usually best to try to stay on and get back in control. Emergency dismounts are for dismounting quickly on purpose, or to land on your feet in case you begin to fall off.

Falls

If you ride very much, sooner or later you may take a spill. Most falls are like tipping over on a bicycle—no fun, but not serious. Sometimes you just slip off and land on your feet. If you should fall, try to remember to fold up your arms and legs, fall as relaxed as you can, and don't try to hang on to the reins. Falling like this means you are less likely to get hurt.

If a rider falls and you are there to help, don't move the rider. Keep him lying still until you are sure there is no injury or until further help arrives.

Longe Lessons

For a longe lesson, your instructor controls your pony on a circle using a longe line. You can work on your seat, balance, and suppleness without having to control your pony. A longe lesson is a good time to practice exercises, to learn to sit better, and to work on your position.

Your pony must be trained to work on a longe line. Your instructor should try out your pony to see if he is ready for longe lessons. He will need a longe

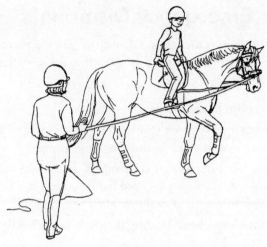

Longe lesson.

line, a longe whip to give signals, side reins for control, boots or bandages to protect your pony's legs, and a special longe cavesson, which works on the pony's nose instead of his mouth. Your instructor will check the longeing equipment and longe your pony for a few minutes to get him ready before you start your lesson.

First, you must get used to the feeling of riding in a circle. You will not need the reins, so they are tied up out of the way. You may hold a neck-strap or the saddle. (Put your outside hand on the pommel and your inside hand behind you, on the cantle.) When you are comfortable at the walk, your instructor may ask you to drop your stirrups and cross them over. You can practice balance and suppling exercises until you can ride easily with no hands and without stirrups at a walk.

Next, your instructor will have you hold the neck-strap or the saddle while you try a slow trot. Holding the pommel with your outside hand helps you stay deep in the saddle; it also turns your shoulders to follow the track of the circle. As you get better at trotting, you can do exercises to help your seat and your balance. Eventually, you will be able to trot with no stirrups and no hands. You can also practice posting the trot (with stirrups).

Longe lessons are hard work for a pony because working on a circle is harder than ordinary riding. He should have a break, a chance to stretch his neck, and a change of direction now and then to rest his muscles. A longe lesson should not last too long (about 20 minutes is plenty).

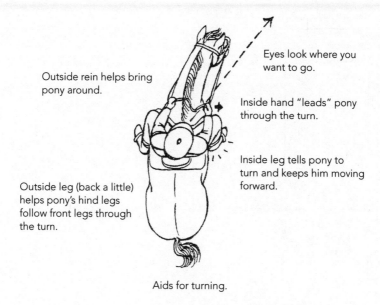

Eyes look where you want to go.

Outside rein helps bring pony around.

Inside hand "leads" pony through the turn.

Inside leg tells pony to turn and keeps him moving forward.

Outside leg (back a little) helps pony's hind legs follow front legs through the turn.

Aids for turning.

Turns, Reverses, and Circles

When you first started to ride, you learned simple turns and changes of direction. Now you can ride with better control, riding turns, circles, and reverses at the trot as well as at a walk.

Turns

When you ride through a turn, remember to do the following:

- Use your *eyes* to look where you want your pony to go.
- Use your *inside leg* to keep your pony moving and to keep him from cutting the corner.
- Use your *inside rein* to ask your pony to bend around the turn.
- Use your *outside rein* to help bring your pony around the turn.
- Keep your *outside leg* back a little to keep your pony's hind legs from swinging out on the turn.

The following sections look at some ways to practice turns.

Riding through Corners

To make smooth, even turns at each corner of the ring, you must ask your pony to go straight along the rail and into the corner. (Many ponies like to cut

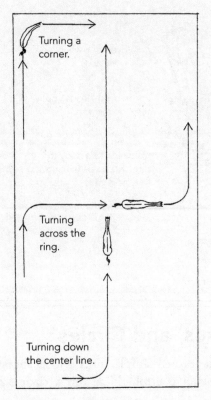

Turning a
corner.

Turning
across the
ring.

Turning down
the center line.

Turns.

Bending cones in line.

corners, so be ready and keep yours close to the rail.) As you ride through the corner, turn your head and look through the turn. Use your inside leg close to the girth to ask your pony to go deep into the corner and bend around the corner. You can put cones or markers in the corners of the ring to keep you on the track as you ride through the corners.

Turning across the Arena

To change direction by turning across the ring, ride down the track to the center marker and turn straight across the ring. Ride straight toward the other side, then turn in the new direction when you reach the track.

Reversing with a Half-Circle

A *half-circle* is one way to reverse or change direction. To ride a half-circle, pick a spot along the rail (like a letter or a marker), and begin to ride a circle. When you have made half a circle, ride back to the rail on a diagonal line (a slanting line). A half-circle looks something like an ice-cream cone. You ride the round part (the "ice cream") first, then the diagonal line makes the "cone."

Circles

Circles are good practice for you and your pony. They help you learn good control, and they help your pony with his balance and make him supple and easier to ride. At first, your circles should be quite big. Small circles make it too hard for your pony to keep going and to balance well.

A circle should be round like an orange, not long like a bathtub or uneven like a pear. It should have a clear starting point and always begin and end at the same point.

To ride a good circle, you need to *look ahead* on the circle and use your *inside leg* to keep your pony going. Your outside hand and rein control the pony's speed and the size of the circle.

At first, make your circles big enough so your pony can keep moving forward easily (about 60 feet across is a good size). When you can make good round circles of 60 feet or 66 feet, you can ride smaller circles (about 30 feet across) in the corners. It is harder for your pony to balance well and keep moving forward on a smaller circle, so you will have to think ahead and use your aids clearly.

Bending Cones in a Line

For turning practice, you can ride through *bending cones* (three to five cones or markers set in a line about 25 feet apart) in a gentle zigzag. If you ride to the

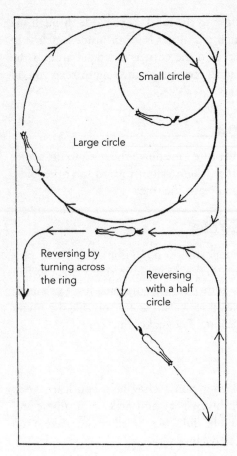

Circles and reverses.

outside of the first cone, the turns come out right. Sit up deep and tall and turn with a slight swivel of your seat and body; help with your legs and reins. You may feel your pony become supple and better balanced as he turns smoothly through the bending cones. He may get so good that he will turn mostly by body language and hardly need the reins at all.

Posting on the Correct Diagonal

What Is a Diagonal?

Diagonal means opposite corners. When a pony trots, his legs move in diagonal pairs. The left front and right hind legs move together; they are called the *left diagonal*. The right front and left hind legs move together; they are called the *right diagonal*.

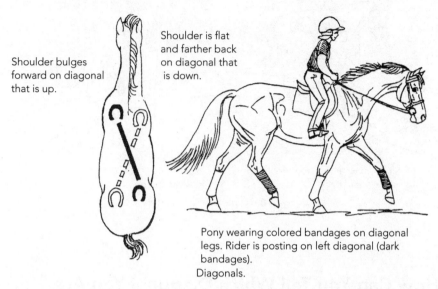

Top view of diagonals:
Left diagonal: L F and R H
Right diagonal: R F and L H

Shoulder bulges forward on diagonal that is up.

Shoulder is flat and farther back on diagonal that is down.

Pony wearing colored bandages on diagonal legs. Rider is posting on left diagonal (dark bandages).
Diagonals.

It is easy to see the diagonals moving at a trot if your instructor puts different-colored bandages on each diagonal pair of your pony's legs.

What Is Posting on a Diagonal?

When you post or rise to the trot, you go up and down with one diagonal. When a pony is turning or going around a ring, you should post on the *outside* diagonal. This means that when you are riding to the *right*, you rise when the *left front and right hind* legs go up, and you sit when they go down. (When you ride to the left, you rise when the right front and left hind legs go up, and sit when they go down.) If you watch a rider posting on a pony who is wearing different-colored bandages on each diagonal pair of legs, it is easy to see which pair of legs the rider is going up and down with.

Why Should You Post on a Certain Diagonal?

It is easier for your pony to balance around a turn if you post on the outside diagonal. This means you rise and sit with the outside front leg and the inside hind leg.

The legs of the diagonal you are posting on work harder. You should change direction (and diagonals) every now and then to give your pony's muscles a rest.

Sit down when outside shoulder
is down and back.

Rise when outside shoulder is
forward and up.

Posting on the correct diagonal on a turn.

How Can You Tell Which Diagonal You Are Posting On?

To learn how to tell which diagonal you are posting on, you must be able to keep your pony at a steady trot along the rail without breaking into a walk. If she stops trotting, it will interrupt the diagonals, making it hard for you to learn this. You may need some practice or some help from your instructor.

Here's how to tell which diagonal you are posting on:

1. Start a steady posting trot along the rail.
2. As you sit, quickly glance down at the pony's outside shoulder. (Take a quick peek each time you sit, but don't ride along staring at the shoulder for a long time.)
3. If the outside shoulder is back when you sit, you are on the correct diagonal. If you find the shoulder is forward when you sit, you are on the wrong diagonal.

To help you check the shoulder, you can stick a piece of colored tape on the bottom of the shoulder. It is easier to see if the tape is forward or back. Check the *outside* shoulder (next to the rail, not the one toward the center of the ring). It may help you remember if you say "Rise and fall with the leg near the wall."

As you get used to posting on the correct diagonal, you will be able to feel when you are on the correct diagonal and when you are on the wrong one.

How Do You Change Diagonals?

When you change directions at the trot, you must change diagonals. There are different ways to change diagonals, but here is the simplest way:

1. As you post to the trot, say "Up, down, up, down" as you rise and sit with the rhythm of the trot.
2. To change diagonals, say "Up, down, up, down, down, up." Sit down for one extra beat (two "downs"), and then go on posting.
3. If you sit for two beats, you will change diagonals. If you sit for three beats, you will stay on the same diagonal.

When you change diagonals, keep your eyes up and look ahead. Don't look down as you change your diagonal, but you can take a quick check afterward to see if you have changed it correctly.

When you change direction at the trot, you should change diagonal at the center of the ring. This prepares your pony to turn in the new direction.

Learning to Canter

As your seat, balance, and control improve, you will be ready to learn to canter. The canter is a three-beat gait; it sounds like "one, two, three." It has a rocking motion like a merry-go-round, but a bit faster. The rocking motion makes it fun to ride!

To canter safely, you must have good balance and control at a trot (both sitting trot and posting trot). You must know how to ask your pony to canter, how to ride the canter, and how to come back to a trot and then a walk after cantering. You should learn to canter on a pony who is well trained and easy to canter.

Aids for Canter

When your pony starts to canter, it is called a *canter depart*. To canter, you must follow these steps:

1. Prepare to canter:
   - Sit deep and tall. Have your reins short enough to control your pony, but not tight or pulled back.
   - Wake up your pony with leg squeezes so that he wants to go faster, but keep him to a fast walk or a slow sitting trot. (A canter takes more energy, but if he trots fast or if you are posting, he won't be ready and

will just trot faster instead of canter.) Do not post, or he will think you only want to trot faster.

2. Give the signal for a canter depart:

- Put your *outside leg* (the one next to the rail) back a couple of inches and squeeze or nudge your pony's side. If he is lazy, you may have to use your leg quite firmly, and you may also have to cluck to your pony or say "Canter!"
- Relax your hands to let him begin cantering.

Be careful not to pull back on the reins as he starts to canter. Keep your hands down on your pony's neck or hold a neck-strap.

Riding the Canter

As your pony canters, it may feel like you're on a rocking horse or a merry-go-round, but moving faster. To ride the canter, you must sit down; don't stand up, lean forward, or bounce, which can put you off balance and might make your pony go too fast. It helps to sit deep and tall and remember to breathe. Relax as much as you can and let your seat rock easily with your pony. You may even feel like you are leaning back a little to keep your seat in the saddle.

You may need to use your legs and seat to keep your pony going in the canter. Give a leg squeeze or nudge with every stride as your seat sinks down in

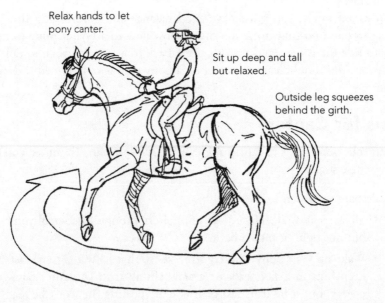

Relax hands to let pony canter.

Sit up deep and tall but relaxed.

Outside leg squeezes behind the girth.

Aids for a canter depart.

the saddle. You can also give a little push with your seat (like swinging in a swing) at each stride. Keep your hands down low and quiet, hold a neck-strap or a safety strap if necessary, and be careful not to accidentally pull back on the reins. That will make your pony stop cantering and can confuse him. Look up and ahead to where you want your pony to go, and remember to guide him around the corners and keep him close to the rail. If you let him cut the corners or come into the middle of the ring, he may break down to a trot or become hard to steer.

To come back to a trot and to a walk, do the following:

1. Take a deep breath and sit deep and tall.

2. Squeeze and relax your hands on the reins as firmly as you have to until your pony slows down and begins to trot. Use a quiet voice command, "Whoa," if you need to.

3. When your pony trots, post for a few steps and then sit deep and tall again, breathe and squeeze with your hands to ask him to walk.

Remember to thank your pony with a pat and a "Good boy!"

Leads at the Canter

What Is a Lead?

When a pony canters, his front and hind legs on one side reach out ahead of the other, like a person skipping. If his left legs are ahead, he is on the *left lead*. If his right legs are ahead, he is on the *right lead*.

Sitting down to the canter.

It is easy to see which lead a pony is on if your instructor puts different-colored bandages on your pony's front legs. Watch to see which front leg reaches farther in front as he canters around a turn.

Why Should a Pony Canter on the Proper Lead?

When a pony canters around a ring or on a turn, he should be on the correct lead. His *inside* legs must be ahead, so he can balance safely around the turns. If her outside legs are ahead, he is on the wrong lead. (You can try this yourself if you skip with one leg in front of the other. It is easy to turn toward the leg that you are leading with, but if you turn the other way, your legs cross and you can't balance as well.)

How Can You Tell Which Lead Your Pony Is Cantering On?

Your pony must be in a steady canter, and you must be sitting up deep and tall. Here's how to tell which lead your pony is cantering on:

1. Take a quick peek at your pony's *inside* shoulder (the one toward the center of the ring). You may see the tip of his toe coming out in front of the shoulder. If you see his toe, he is on the correct lead.
2. Take a quick peek at *both* shoulders. When a pony is on the inside lead, the outside shoulder moves first and shorter, and the inside shoulder moves second and longer.

Caution: Just take a quick peek. Don't ride along with your head down looking at the shoulders or lean forward to look. That could put you off balance. With more experience in cantering, you will be able to feel the difference between a correct lead and a wrong lead.

How Do You Ask a Pony to Canter on the Correct Lead?

When you give your pony the correct aids for a canter depart, it tells him to take the correct lead. Most ponies are trained to take a left lead when you use your right leg a little behind the girth, and to take a right lead when you use your left leg behind the girth. Some ponies are trained to other signals. Your instructor will tell you if your pony needs other aids or signals.

If a pony can see that he is about to make a left turn, it makes sense to him to take the left lead. If he is thinking about turning right (perhaps because he wants to go back to the barn or toward other ponies), he may want to take a right lead. Giving him the correct canter aids just before a turn makes it easier to get the lead you want.

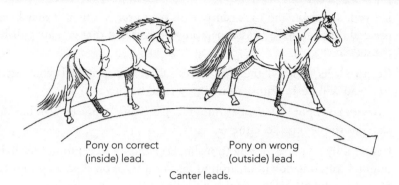

Pony on correct
(inside) lead.

Pony on wrong
(outside) lead.

Canter leads.

Front leg on
lead side comes
out in front of
shoulder.

Leading shoulder
is forward.

Other
shoulder
is back.

LEFT LEAD

RIGHT LEAD

How to identify the canter lead.

Some Tips about Cantering

- Remember that cantering is hard work for your pony, even if it's fun for you. Give him a break now and then, and don't overdo it.
- At first, canter only for short distances. Don't try to canter too long or too fast.
- If your pony gets into a fast trot, slow down and start over. He can't start a good canter from a fast trot.

- Let your seat relax and rock gently with your pony's canter. It may help to pretend that you have saddle soap on your seat and that you are polishing the saddle.

- Keep your legs relaxed and your knees and ankles springy. If your legs get stiff, you will push against your stirrups and bounce.

- Go with your pony's balance around turns. Don't lean way over, but don't lean out to the outside, either.

- Canter only on good footing (not slippery) and on level ground or slightly uphill. Cantering downhill, around sharp turns, or on slippery ground can get your pony off balance and is not safe.

Better Riding

As you gain experience and advance in your riding on the flat, you will progress to techniques and skills that help you ride better and with greater ease. This also prepares you for new and challenging riding activities, and for getting the best from your pony.

More Balance and Suppling Exercises

You have already learned some basic rider suppling and balance exercises at the halt and the walk. Now you can add more mounted exercises, and even do some at the trot. A longe lesson is a good way to practice these exercises.

The following sections show you some new exercises.

Toe Touching and Opposite Toe Touching
These exercises make your waist supple, strengthen your core muscles, and teach you to keep your legs in position while your upper body moves.

- **Toe Touching:** Start with both hands straight up over your head. Bend down and touch both toes, then sit up straight again. Keep your feet and legs in position. (If you can't reach your toes, just touch your ankles, or as far down as you can reach.)

- **Opposite Toe Touching:** Start with both arms straight out from your shoulders. Twist to the left, then bend down and touch your right hand to your left toe (or as far down as you can reach). Sit up again, then twist the other way and touch your left hand to your right toe. Try to keep your legs in place, and don't let your heels come up or your legs swing back when you bend down.

Touching toes.

Touching opposite toe.

Lying Down and Sitting Up, Forward and Backward

These exercises make your muscles stronger, strengthen your core muscles, and teach your legs to stay in position even when your body and arms move. This improves your riding position.

- **Lying Forward and Sitting Up.** Put your arms behind your back. With feet out of the stirrups (stirrups should be crossed over), lean forward until your chest touches your pony's neck. Try to sit up without using your hands. Keep your legs in position while you lean forward and sit up.

- **Lying Back and Sitting Up.** With your feet out of the stirrups, lean back slowly until you are lying down on your pony's back. Let your arms hang

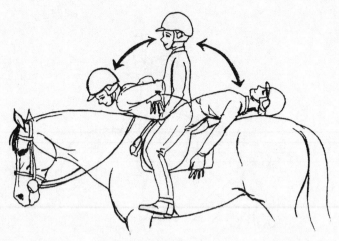

Lying forward and sitting up, lying backward and sitting up.

by your sides. Try to sit up without using your hands, keeping your legs in good position.

Stirrup Standing and "Airplane" Exercises

These exercises get your heels down and make your legs stronger. They also help your balance and position.

- **Stirrup Standing.** With feet in the stirrups, lean slightly forward to find your balance, then stand up. Rest your hands on your pony's neck or hold a neck-strap. Let your knees relax so your weight can go down past your knees into your feet, and let your heels sink down and back. Stay up while you count to five, then gently sink back down, leaving your heels down and your lower leg in position.

    At first, do this exercise for five seconds or so at the halt, then at the walk and the trot. Then begin staying up longer—while you count to ten, twenty, or more. When your pony trots, you will feel him "bounce" your heels down with each step.

    Remember that this is an *exercise*, not a position for regular riding or jumping. Don't get this exercise confused with half-seat or jumping position.

- **"Airplane" Exercise.** This is a half-seat with no hands, with your arms straight out from your shoulders. Don't stand up too high or lean too far forward. Just find the balance point where you can stay up without gripping with your knees. Start with two or three short airplanes at a halt; then work up to ten. You can also practice airplanes at a walk and trot on the longe line.

Stirrup stand.

Airplane exercise.

Shoulder Circles and Drops

These exercises loosen up your shoulder muscles and teach you how to keep your shoulders back and down. It helps to take a deep breath as you do them.

1. Move both shoulders in a circle: forward, up, back, and down.
2. Lift both shoulders up toward your ears, then let them drop back and down behind your ribs.

Shoulder circles and drops.

Drop your shoulders whenever you need to sit up deep and tall or stop your pony. This keeps you from leaning forward and keeps your arms from getting pulled forward.

Arm Circles

These loosen up your neck, back, and shoulders, and teach your legs to stay in position while your arms are moving. They also teach you to ride "automatically," without having to look at what you are doing.

Start with the reins in one hand. Stretch the other arm straight up over your head. Move it slowly in a big circle. Turn your head and watch your hand as it goes around. Be careful not to pull on the reins with your other hand. Circle your arm in both directions, then switch and do it with the other arm.

You can do this exercise on a longe line, while somebody leads your pony, or while you ride with the reins in one hand.

Finding Your Center for Balance and Control

Your *center* is your balance and control point. When you can feel your center is in the right place, it makes it easier to sit deep and tall and to keep your balance. It also helps your pony to pay attention to your balance and your aids.

To find your center, put one hand over your belly, just below your belly button. Put the other hand on the back of your seat, behind it. Your center "floats" between your two hands. If you are a little bit tense or if you are leaning forward, it may be too far forward. Take a deep breath and think of your center floating back until it finds the middle. When it does, you may get a feeling that it sinks down. This helps your seat feel deeper and more relaxed and secure.

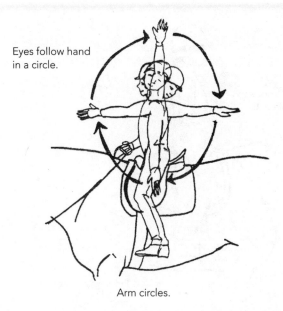

Eyes follow hand
in a circle.

Arm circles.

Once you have learned how to take a deep breath and find your center, you can use this any time you need to relax, sit deeper, or get your balance back. It helps to let your center sink down when you want to halt or make a transition down to a slower gait. It also can help you sit the trot and canter without bouncing.

"Teeter-Totter" Exercise for Balance

This exercise helps you find your best balance sitting in the saddle and know when you are out of balance forward or backward. It gets you balanced correctly on your seat bones. This exercise should be done at the halt.

With your feet out of the stirrups, find your center and sit deep and tall in the middle of your saddle. Tip your body forward from your seat bones, keeping your back long and straight and your head and neck in line with your back. Then tip backward. Tip forward and backward several times, a little bit less each time (this is the teeter-totter). Notice how it feels when you are too far forward and too far back. Let your "teeters" get smaller and smaller, until you end up sitting balanced, straight up and down, with your feet hanging down under your body.

Swivel Exercise for Turning

This exercise teaches you to keep your balance instead of leaning forward or sideways when you turn. It makes it easier for your pony to turn better, and gives you better control.

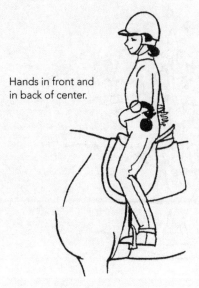

Hands in front and in back of center.

Finding your center.

Teeter-totter exercise for balance.

At a halt, with feet in the stirrups, take a deep breath and find your center. Put one hand on your belly and the other hand behind your seat.

Sit deep and tall and turn your body a little bit, deep inside between your hands, at the bottom of your center. Imagine a merry-go-round pole or a candy cane with spiral stripes running up through your center and out the top of your head, spiraling in the direction you are turning. Then come back to the center and turn the other way. You should make several short swivels, not try to hold one for a long time.

When you turn like this, you will feel that you sit up deep and tall and that your body swivels instead of leans forward or sideways. Your shoulders and chest turn, and your eyes can see where you are going.

Once you have tried this at a halt, do it at a walk. You may find that your pony listens so well to your swivels that he turns with almost no rein aids. This is fun to practice around a line of bending cones. When you can do this in the walk, you can also practice it in turns at the trot.

Riding the Sitting Trot without Stirrups

To ride a sitting trot well, you must be in balance, relaxed, and supple. (Your pony should trot slowly and smoothly. If he trots too fast, you will have a hard time sitting the trot.) Practice the suppling and balance exercises in this chapter (especially finding your center and the teeter-totter exercise) to help you get ready to sit the trot.

Swivel turns.

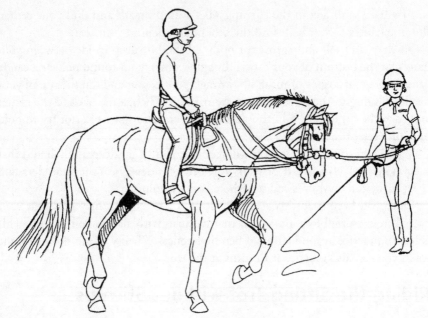

Riding a sitting trot without stirrups in a longe lesson.

The best way to learn to ride the sitting trot is in a longe lesson. Take your feet out of the stirrups, cross over your stirrups, and find your balance in the center of the saddle at a walk. Hold the pommel of the saddle with your outside hand and the cantle with your inside hand. Let your legs relax and hang down under your seat. Your instructor can start your pony into a slow, easy trot while you breathe, relax, and let your seat go with the motion. If you feel bouncy, use your hands to pull your seat down into the saddle. Don't grip with your legs or tighten your muscles. This makes you bounce and can make your pony go faster. The more you breathe deeply, relax, and keep your balance, the easier it is to let your seat go with your pony's trot.

At first, ride the sitting trot for just a little way, then come back to the walk. As you get better at it, you can relax your hold on the saddle and trot longer. Eventually, you will be able to trot no hands. When you are comfortable at a sitting trot without holding on, you are ready to take your reins and learn to keep your pony in a slow, steady sitting trot yourself. You can start out with the reins in one hand and the other hand on the pommel of the saddle, but be careful not to pull on the reins if you need to catch your balance.

Learning to Rein-Back (Backing Up)

The rein-back, or backing up, is not easy for a pony, so you must be careful when you ask him to do it. When a pony backs correctly, he steps backward by moving his legs in diagonal pairs. After backing, he should move forward again easily and promptly.

When backing, a pony should not stiffen his neck and back, throw his head up, back crookedly, or drag his feet backward. These are usually caused by a rider pulling too hard and making the pony confused and uncomfortable.

To ask your pony to rein-back, sit up deep and tall. Your reins must be short enough for you to feel his mouth, and your legs must be against his sides. Give him a short squeeze or two with your legs to wake him up and make him think of moving, then squeeze your fingers on the reins to keep him from moving forward. As he begins to step backward, relax your legs and hands to say "That's right, thank you." After he has made one step backward, use your legs to make him walk forward again.

Be gentle and patient when you ask your pony to rein-back. If you pull long and hard on the reins, or kick to go forward while pulling backward, he will get confused and upset. You must give him a clear idea of what you want him to do, then give him time to understand and to do it right. For now, only ask for one step backward, not several steps in a row. Once this is going well, you can ask for a couple of steps backward.

Ring Figures in a Dressage Arena

Ring figures are good for practicing control, and they help ponies to become more supple and easier to turn. You will need to know simple ring figures for riding lessons and for Pony Club dressage tests.

Dressage Arena and Letters

It is easier to learn to ride ring figures if you practice in a *dressage arena* or a riding ring with dressage letters. The letters give you a place to begin and end your ring figures and help you judge whether your figures are the right size. A practice ring should be twice as long as it is wide. A *small dressage arena* is 20 meters (66 feet) wide and 40 meters (132 feet) long, and the dressage letters are always in the same places. (A *large dressage arena*, 20 by 60 meters, is used for some competitions.) You can set up dressage letters in your riding ring by painting them on the fence or on the wall, or by setting up markers or plastic cones with the dressage letters painted on them. If you use dressage letters when you are practicing ring figures and ordinary flat work, it will be easier to learn dressage tests for Pony Club ratings and for competitions.

The following illustration shows a small dressage arena with the basic dressage letters.

20-Meter Circles

A 20-meter circle is a circle that is 20 meters, or 66 feet, across. It fits perfectly into a dressage ring, which is 20 meters wide. This is a good size circle for practice, and it also gets you ready for Pony Club dressage tests.

To learn to ride a 20-meter circle, it helps to mark out a space the right size with cones or other markers. If you set four cones on a square, 20 meters apart, your circle will fit perfectly inside.

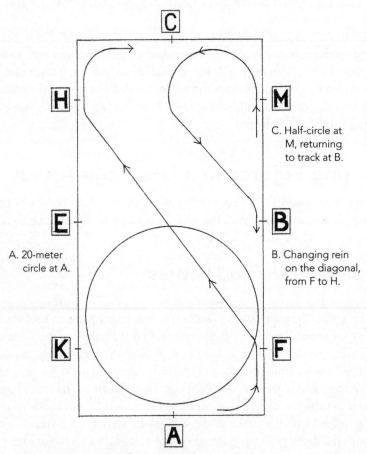

C. Half-circle at M, returning to track at B.

A. 20-meter circle at A.

B. Changing rein on the diagonal, from F to H.

Ring figures using dressage letters.

A circle should be round, like an orange, not flat on one side or uneven like a pear. To make a round circle, try looking one quarter of the circle ahead. When you are at one cone, look ahead to the next one. This will keep your circle the right size and even—not wide on one side and short on the other.

Riding the Clock

This is an exercise to help you make good circles. Set four cones or markers at the four quarters of the circle. The first cone represents 12 on the clock; the second is 3, the third is 6 and the fourth is 9. Ride around the circle to the right (clockwise), riding from 12 to 3, then 3 to 6, 6 to 9, and 9 to 12. Your eyes should look at the next marker on the "clock" (if you're at 12, your eyes look at 3). Try to ride each quarter of the clock just the same as the others. Don't let your pony cut in, bulge out, or make a corner—keep him on a smooth curve.

When you have practiced the clock exercise going to the right, ride to the left (counterclockwise), going "backward" around the clock (from 12 to 9, 9 to 6, 6 to 3, and 3 to 12).

The aids that you use to ride a circle are your legs, seat, and hands. Your *inside leg* stays in its regular position, close to the pony's girth. It tells your pony to keep moving and not to cut in. Your *outside leg* should be just a little bit farther back. It tells your pony's hind legs to stay on the track of the circle and not to swing out. Swiveling your *seat* tells him to keep turning. (If you lean sideways instead of swivel, he may cut in and make the circle too small.) Your *hands* help to keep him on the track. The *inside rein* asks him to look in the

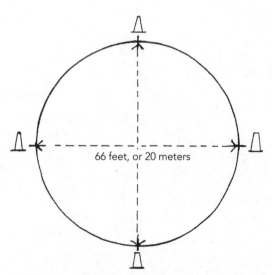

A 20-meter circle with cones set as quarter markers.

66 feet, or 20 meters

right direction, and the *outside rein* tells him not to go too fast or make the circle too wide. Your *eyes* are also important. They should look ahead on the circle to where you are going. Looking somewhere else (especially looking down) makes it hard to ride a circle.

Start at the walk, riding 20-meter circles in both directions. (Ponies are right-handed or left-handed just like people, so it is easier for your pony to make a good circle in one direction than it is in the other.) Then practice circles at the sitting trot and the posting trot. Remember to post on the correct diagonal (the outside diagonal), because this makes it easier for your pony to balance well on a circle. Finally, you can canter on a 20-meter circle. When you canter, your pony should be on the correct lead (the inside lead) because it is quite uncomfortable to be on the wrong lead on a circle of this size. Check your pony's lead. If he is on the wrong lead, come back to the walk and try again.

10-Meter Circles

A *10-meter circle* is 33 feet wide, or half the size of a 20-meter circle. Since a dressage arena is 20 meters wide, a 10-meter circle fits in the corner of an arena or along the wall, touching the track and the center line. Ten-meter circles require more balance and suppleness than larger circles, especially at the trot. Your pony can do them at the walk and trot. They are too small for cantering until your pony is more advanced.

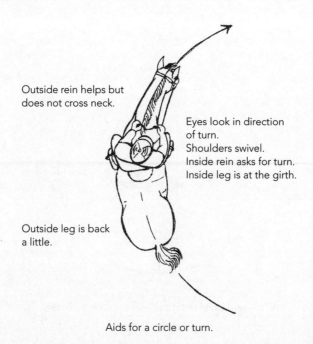

Outside rein helps but does not cross neck.

Eyes look in direction of turn.
Shoulders swivel.
Inside rein asks for turn.
Inside leg is at the girth.

Outside leg is back a little.

Aids for a circle or turn.

Half-Circle

To ride a *half-circle*, start by riding along the track to a letter. At the letter, begin a 10-meter circle (33 feet wide). When you reach the halfway point of the circle (at the center line), return to the track at the next letter, on a straight diagonal line, then continue along the track. You can do this at the walk or trot.

Changing the Rein on the Diagonal

Changing the rein means changing directions. When you are riding with your right hand toward the center, you are riding *on the right rein*, so when you change directions, you *change the rein*. Changing the rein *on the diagonal* is a way of changing directions with a long diagonal line. Here's how to do it:

1. Ride on the track of the ring, close to the rail.
2. Ride through the "short side" (the end of the ring), to the corner marker.
3. At the corner marker, turn and ride on a diagonal line, aiming toward the opposite corner maker. Look at the marker to aim your pony straight.
4. When you reach the rail at the next corner marker, stay on the track in the new direction. You should be in position to ride through the corner and the short side of the ring in the new direction.

If you are posting to the trot, remember to change your diagonal in the center whenever you change directions.

Turning Down the Center Line

The *center line* is an imaginary straight line down the center of the arena. Turning down the center line is a test of how well you can ride your corners and ride a straight line. If you ride deep into the corner and stay close to the rail, it is easier to turn at the right place so that you come out going straight down the center line of the ring. Remember to plan and turn a little before the center line; it takes your pony a while to turn and you want to end up on the center line and not past it. As you reach the other end, plan your turn so that you change direction and ride a good corner. If you are posting at the trot, change your diagonal at the center of the ring.

Turning Down the Quarter Line

The *quarter line* is an imaginary line that runs the long way of the arena, parallel to the long side and halfway between the center line and the track. You must look ahead and plan your turn to come out exactly right on the quarter line. It helps to look at something at the other end of the arena that is in line with the quarter line.

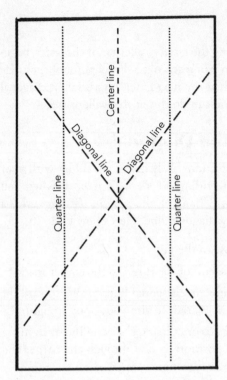

Center line, quarter line, and diagonal line.

Rating or Adjusting Speed in the Gaits

Increasing and decreasing your pony's speed in a gait is called *rating*. It is important to be able to ride your pony at the speed you choose and to keep him from breaking down to a slower gait or speeding up to a faster one without being asked to do so.

- **To increase speed in a gait,** use short squeezes or nudges with your legs in rhythm with the gait. In the walk, use *alternating leg aids* (one leg and then the other) in rhythm with your pony's steps, as if you were walking with him. In a posting trot, use your legs when you sit and relax them when you rise. In the canter, give a leg squeeze or nudge at every stride as your seat sinks down in the saddle. Your hands must relax just enough to tell your pony he may go faster, but don't let your reins get too long and sloppy.

- **To decrease speed in a gait,** give rhythmic short squeezes on the reins; don't use a long, continuous pull. In the posting trot, squeeze your fingers closed on the reins each time you sit, and relax them as you rise. If you post more slowly, your pony will slow his trot. To slow down in the canter, sit taller and give a squeeze on the reins each time your pony's head and neck rock upward. Your legs should be ready to keep your pony going so that she doesn't break down to a slower gait.

Passing other riders and being passed (at the trot) will give you practice in rating, or speed control. You will have to use your legs firmly to get your pony's attention and to make him trot fast enough to pass another pony. (For safety, pass wide—at least one pony length away.) When it is your turn to be passed, slow your pony's trot down and keep his head turned a little bit toward the pony who is passing her, to prevent him from kicking.

Understanding the Aids

Aids are the means by which you communicate with your pony and control him. *Natural aids* are the aids that are part of you: your hands, legs, seat, and voice; *artificial aids* are the aids that help out the natural aids, like crops and spurs.

Your aids are like a language that lets you talk with your pony by touch. When you use your aids very softly, it is like a whisper. Strong aids are more like a shout. Always start out with soft, light aids. If your pony does not pay attention, then you can use stronger aids. (Wouldn't you hate it if somebody yelled at you, when you could hear him just as well if he spoke quietly?)

Any natural aid (hands, legs, or seat) can be *active, passive,* or a *preventing* aid. An *active aid* is an aid that is asking your pony to do something (for example, a leg that is squeezing to ask him to move). A *passive aid* is ready, but is not asking (for example, a leg that is resting on the pony's side but relaxed, not squeezing). A *preventing aid* is one that tells a pony *not* to do something (for example, a short squeeze on the reins that says "No" when a pony wants to go faster).

Your voice can sometimes be used in conjunction with other natural aids (for example, giving a cluck as you use your legs to ask your pony to trot, or saying "Easy" to help calm him down and prevent a spook). However, good riders don't rely on voice aids very much because they can disturb other ponies and riders. Most of your communication with your pony should come from your legs, hands, and seat.

Simple Leg Aids

There are three different leg aids:

1. **Both legs (used in short squeezes or nudges)**—asks the pony to move forward or increase his speed.
2. **One leg in normal position near the girth**—asks the pony to move forward and bend or turn in that direction (left leg for left turn). It can also be used as a preventing aid, to tell the pony not to cut corners.

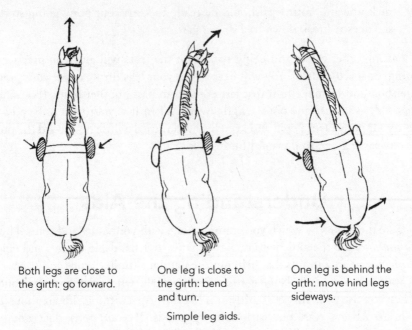

Both legs are close to the girth: go forward.

One leg is close to the girth: bend and turn.

One leg is behind the girth: move hind legs sideways.

Simple leg aids.

3. **One leg a little behind the girth (about 4 inches)**—asks the pony to move his hindquarters sideways. It can also be used as a preventing aid to tell the pony not to move his hind legs sideways.

Simple Rein Aids

There are four different rein aids:

1. **Both hands squeeze and relax; straight back**—asks the pony to slow down or stop. It can also be used as a preventing aid to tell the pony not to move forward.

2. **One hand moves slightly out to one side**—asks the pony to turn in a wide turn without slowing down. This is called a *leading rein* because it *leads* the pony into a turn.

3. **One hand squeezes and relaxes; straight back**—asks the pony to turn in that direction, in a tighter turn. This is called a *direct rein.*

4. **One hand presses inward against the pony's neck**—a preventing aid that asks the pony to stop going sideways. It is called a *neck rein* because it presses against the pony's neck.

When you use rein aids, remember to squeeze and relax your fingers and hands. Don't pull your hands backward. Give rein aids in short squeezes, not long, hard pulls.

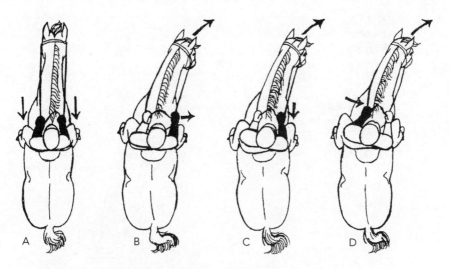

A. Both hands squeeze backward: slow down or stop.
B. Leading rein—one hand moves outward: turning.
C. Direct rein—one hand squeezes backward: turning.
D. Neck rein—one hand moves inward toward neck (but doesn't cross the
     neck): outside rein to help turn.

Simple rein aids.

Simple Seat or Weight Aids

There are three different simple seat or weight aids:

1. **Sitting up deep and tall** tells your pony to pay attention, to slow down or stop, or to fix his balance. Always do this when you need to slow down or stop.

2. **Swiveling** (turning your body a little, deep in your seat) tells your pony to turn the way you swivel. (It also turns your seat bones, so your pony feels it through his back.)

3. **Aiming your eyes where you want your pony to go** tells your pony to go straight or to turn, depending on where you are looking. This works because your head is quite heavy (about twelve pounds), so your pony can feel your head turn when you turn your eyes. Don't look down, or your pony will feel your head wobble. This tips your weight forward and upsets your balance, and he might stop.

You have to use the right aids or your pony won't understand what you want. When you use more than one aid together, they must help each other, not work against each other. *Clashing your aids* means using two aids against each other by mistake (like pulling to stop while kicking to go forward). This confuses and

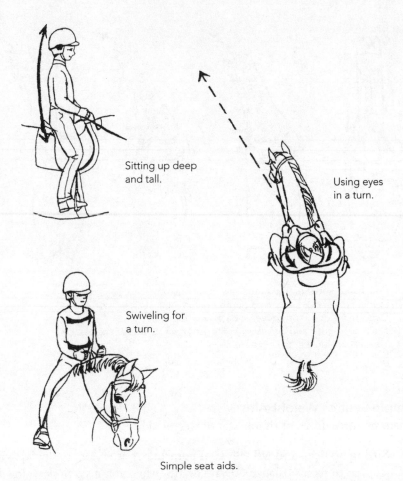

Sitting up deep
and tall.

Using eyes
in a turn.

Swiveling for
a turn.

Simple seat aids.

upsets a pony and makes him stubborn. When a pony doesn't do what you want
him to, it is usually because he does not understand your aids.

Aids must be used on purpose, not by accident. If you accidentally pull on
the reins, your pony will think you mean he should stop. If your legs bump his
sides, he might think you mean to go faster. Pulling, kicking, or giving aids by
accident can get a pony mixed up and very cross. After a while, he may become
hard to ride. That is why it is so important to learn to ride with your legs, seat,
and hands in good position, and to develop an independent seat.

Good Hands

Having *good hands* means that you can use your hands and reins to communicate
clearly but kindly to your pony what you would like him to do. This is especially

important because your hands connect (through the reins) to the bit in the pony's sensitive mouth. A well-trained pony responds to gentle but clear pressure, but it is confusing, upsetting, and painful for a pony if the rider makes mistakes with his hands and reins.

The first thing you need for good hands is respect for the pony's mouth and how the bit works, and to treat it kindly and carefully. You can hold a bit in your hands or even in your mouth and have another person use the reins to ask you to stop or turn as if you were a horse. Most people are surprised by how the bit feels!

Next, you need to ride with good balance and a secure *independent seat* so that you never need to grab the reins to catch your balance, which causes an accidental jerk or pull on your pony's mouth. It takes time and practice to develop a balanced, independent seat, and while you are learning you must protect your pony's mouth by using the right length of reins, holding the mane or neck-strap for some exercises, and not going faster than you are ready for.

At this stage, you should be riding with your reins at the proper length so that a slight squeeze will ask your pony to slow down, stop, or turn. You may also ride with semi-loose reins (a slight loop in the reins, allowing your pony to stretch his neck and relax his mouth). Learning to ride *on contact* will come at a later stage.

Here are some tips for developing good hands in basic riding:

- Adjust your reins smoothly and gently to the proper length, never with a jerk. Keep your reins even.
- Close your fingers around the reins with your thumb on the "tail" of the rein to prevent them from slipping. Don't ride with open fingers—this makes your hands stiff, and the reins will slip.
- When you want to slow down, stop, or turn, give short squeezes to the reins, as if you were squeezing a sponge. Don't pull backward with your fists, wrists, or elbows, and never jerk on the pony's mouth!
- Always thank your pony by relaxing your rein pressure when he begins to respond to your hands.
- When your pony walks or canters, his head moves forward and backward. Relax your arms, elbows, and shoulders and allow your hands to follow the motion of his head and neck.
- At a posting trot, a pony's head is steady, but the rider's body is moving up and down, so his elbows need to open and close to keep his hands quiet and steady. You can practice keeping your hands still during a posting trot by touching the tip of one finger (in each hand) to your pony's neck as you post.

- After your pony has worked, let him relax and stretch his neck by walking with a semi-loose rein. When you are standing still, allow your pony enough rein to relax his neck and his mouth.

- Do not try to "collect" your pony or "put him in a frame," even if you see other riders doing this. This will come at a higher level of riding. Trying to make your pony do this before you understand how to do it is unfair to him and can hurt his training.

Riding with Rhythm

Each of your pony's gaits has its own *rhythm*, or number of beats. (A *beat* is the sound made by one or more of the pony's hooves hitting the ground.)

- The walk is a four-beat gait that sounds like "one, two, three, four" or "clip, clop, clip, clop."
- The trot is a two-beat gait that sounds like "one, two" or "clip, clop."
- The canter is a three-beat gait that sounds like "one, two, three" or "da, da, dum."

A pony is much easier to ride when he moves with a steady rhythm instead of speeding up and slowing down or breaking into another gait without being asked to. When he finds his best working rhythm, it also helps him breathe evenly and use his muscles more efficiently, so he doesn't get tired as quickly.

To get your pony to move with a steady rhythm, you must notice the rhythm of his gait. You can count, hum, sing, or say something in a singsong voice along with your pony's steps. For the walk, count "one, two, three, four" or you could say, "bread-and-butter, bread-and-butter" along with your pony's steps. For the trot, try humming a song like "Jingle Bells" or counting "one, two, one, two" as you post. For the canter, try saying, "da, da, dum, da, da, dum" or singing "Row, Row, Row Your Boat" along with his strides.

Once you have picked up the rhythm of the gait, you can keep your pony steady by using your aids in rhythm. If he is too slow, use a brief leg aid at each stride (if you are posting, use your legs when you sit down and relax them when you rise). If he is too quick, give a squeeze and relax on the reins (especially the outside rein) at each stride. You may also enjoy riding to music, especially if the music has the right rhythm for your pony's gait.

Relaxation

Relaxation is important for your pony as well as for you. Relaxation doesn't mean being lazy or sloppy; it means being well loosened up, warmed up, and calm but confident, like a good athlete. This takes a good warm-up (see page 53) and a good mental attitude. Remember to breathe and stay supple, not stiff, as this makes for a better rider who can communicate with his pony.

The opposite of relaxation is tension, stiffness, and nervousness, which are not good for ponies or riders. Some ponies are naturally more relaxed and others become tense and nervous more easily. Ponies often get tense and nervous in a new situation, if they are confused or don't understand, when it is cold and windy, or if exciting things are going on. They are good at reading a rider's body language, and they can tell from the way your body, muscles, and breathing feel if you are tense or relaxed. A pony will pick up relaxation—or tension—from his rider.

One good way to teach your pony to relax is to use *breathing halts*. To do this, you start at a walk and take a deep breath, breathing in deeply so it feels as if the air flows down through your body and relaxes your seat. Breathe out, then say, "Whoa," and stop your pony, rewarding him with a pat, praise, and relaxed reins as soon as his feet stop moving. Then repeat the exercise: *Breathe, whoa, stop,* and *reward.* Your pony will soon learn that when you breathe out and relax your seat, he should relax and prepare to stop—he may begin stopping when he feels you breathe, even before you use the reins. This can become a *calm-down signal* for him, and it's a good thing to do any time you feel tense or nervous, too.

If your pony is especially tense or nervous, he may need:

- Less grain and more turnout time.

- A calm, quiet rider who can give him confidence, especially in a new situation. Sometimes you might need to have a more-experienced rider ride your pony, especially if you feel tense or nervous.

- Longeing or other groundwork before he is ridden (ask your instructor for help with this).

- A quiet walk with another calm, steady horse or pony who will act as a good example and help him settle down, especially in a new place.

- Working at a steady, rhythmic trot with large circles and ring figures for 10 minutes, until he becomes more relaxed and steady.

- Most of all, patience and calmness on the part of the rider.

3

Learning to Jump: From Ground Poles to Simple Courses

Jumping is just another part of riding, like trotting or cantering. It should be safe, simple, and fun. However, there are some things you must have or do in order to learn to jump safely. The most important is a good, knowledgeable jumping instructor!

What You Need for Safe Jumping

- **Pony.** Your pony should be experienced and quiet over low jumps. Jumping is hard work, so he must be sound, in good condition, and his feet must be properly trimmed or shod. It is not a good idea to try to learn to jump on a green pony (one who isn't experienced in jumping), as you can confuse each other. A pony who is lame, in poor condition, or very young (under 4 years old) should not be jumped.

- **Place.** A ring or field should have good footing. It should be fairly level, not too hard or slippery, and not have holes or rocks. There should be no dangerous obstructions such as farm machinery. An enclosed area is safer.

- **Tack and dress.** You will need an all-purpose saddle or a jumping saddle. It should be the correct size, properly fitted, and in good condition. A neck-strap is a good idea. Always wear safe riding clothes and boots, and your ASTM/SEI-approved helmet with harness and chin-strap securely fastened.

- **Jumps.** Poles should be at least 10 feet long and fairly thick (at least 3 inches). You can use jump standards, buckets, or blocks to hold the poles. They should have no sharp points or edges, and no nails sticking out.

- **Instructor.** You will need an experienced jumping instructor to teach you how to ride over jumps safely, how to set safe jumps and obstacles, to help you ride and school your pony for jumping, and to help with any problems that come up. Do not jump without an instructor unless your instructor tells you it is okay to do so. Even experienced jumping riders should never jump alone.

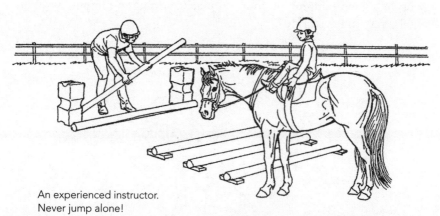

An experienced instructor.
Never jump alone!

Enclosed area with good footing.

Safe dress for riding: ASTM/SEI helmet, boots, etc. (Check your chin-strap before jumping.)

All-purpose or jumping saddle in good condition. (Check your girth before you jump.)

Safe jumping equipment, set up properly.

A quiet, well-trained jumping pony, suitable for the rider.

Pony wears a neck-strap.

Always warm up your pony before jumping!

What you need for safe jumping.

Getting Ready to Jump

Jumping Position

Jumping position is the same as *half-seat* and *2-point position,* which you learned before the posting trot. It is used for jumping, for riding up hills, and as an exercise to help you learn to balance and to get your heels down. This position is important because it keeps you in balance with your pony when he goes over poles or jumps. It makes it easier for him to stretch his neck out to see where he is going, to round his back, and to pick up his feet.

When you practice jumping position, you should balance close to your saddle, not standing up. Your heels must be down and your knees springy, not locked. Your head and eyes must look up and ahead, and your hands should be on the pony's neck or holding a neck-strap. You will need to practice jumping position at a standstill, at a walk, and at a slow trot before you are ready to go over poles. It takes time and practice to develop strong legs and to be able to stay up in a good jumping position, so practice riding in jumping position a little bit every time you ride.

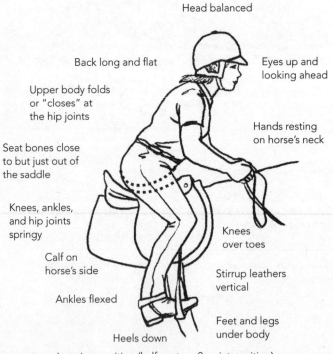

Head balanced

Back long and flat

Eyes up and looking ahead

Upper body folds or "closes" at the hip joints

Hands resting on horse's neck

Seat bones close to but just out of the saddle

Knees, ankles, and hip joints springy

Knees over toes

Calf on horse's side

Stirrup leathers vertical

Ankles flexed

Feet and legs under body

Heels down

Jumping position (half-seat, or 2-point position).

Practice with "Invisible Jumps"

You can practice control and steering over "invisible jumps" before you start riding over ground poles or real jumps. An invisible jump is made by setting up two jump standards as if for a jump (with jump cups removed for safety), but without a jump pole between them. This is a good way to build your confidence and to practice jumping skills safely.

You will need to learn to aim your pony with your head and eyes. Pick out a *target* that is in line with the center of the invisible jump and at your eye level (something like a spot on the wall or a tree branch). As you turn toward the invisible jump and ride straight down the line, keep your eyes on your target. Be careful not to peek down, not even for a second!

At the end of the line, stop your pony while you keep your eyes on your target. If he is a little crooked or off the line, use your leg on his side to make him move over until he is lined up with your target. Then pat him and walk on. Practice aiming at your target with your eyes until you can ride straight over the center of the invisible jump at a walk or a trot without looking down.

Now you are ready to practice in jumping position. Keep your eyes on the target while you walk and then trot over the invisible jump. Keep your hands on your pony's neck or hold the neck-strap over the invisible jump.

Riding over Ground Poles

A ground pole is a pole on the ground, about 4 to 6 inches thick and 10 to 12 feet long. It should be fixed in place so it can't roll under your pony's feet if he should hit it. Ground poles are the lowest and easiest jumps. They help you and your pony get ready for bigger jumps.

Ride over a ground pole just as you have practiced. Steer with your eyes on the target as you walk on in a jumping position so you will feel balanced. As your pony steps over the pole, he should stretch his neck out and look where he is stepping. Your hands must stay firmly on his neck or neck-strap so they don't pull on his mouth. He may want to slow down, so your legs may have to squeeze to keep him walking forward. As he picks up his legs over the pole, his back may feel rounder and he may lift you up a bit. Let your heels sink down while your knees and hips take up the extra bounce. Remember to ride straight, to sit up and stop him at the end of the line, and to give him a pat for doing what you asked him to.

You should be in *jumping position* every time you ride over a pole. This makes it easier for your pony to pick up his feet properly, and if you sit down on his back, you may bump his back and hurt him. Keep your hands on his neck and allow him to stretch his head and neck forward so he can look down at the pole and lift his back as he steps over. You'll need lots of practice walking over ground poles in jumping position before you try trotting over a pole or walking over bigger poles.

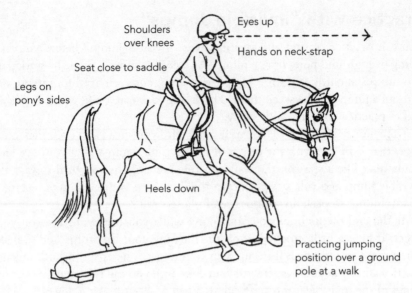

Shoulders
over knees

Eyes up

Hands on neck-strap

Seat close to saddle

Legs on
pony's sides

Heels down

Practicing jumping
position over a ground
pole at a walk

Riding over a ground pole in jumping position.

Beginning Jumping

Here are some common-sense rules for jumping:

- Before you start jumping, you must have good balance and control at the trot. You should be able to walk and trot in jumping position with your heels down. It's a good idea to be able to canter safely before you start jumping.
- Always warm up your pony slowly before you begin to jump. Check your tack (especially your girth) before you jump.
- Don't jump your pony every day—every other day or three times a week is plenty. Too much jumping pounds your pony's feet and legs and can make him sore.
- Don't jump the same jump or course over and over. This can make your pony bored and sour, and he may get stubborn about jumping.
- Never jump alone. Someone should always be on hand in case of an accident.

Jumping Position

Review your jumping position:

- Your stirrups should be at jumping length (just touching the top of your ankle bone). This is usually about one hole shorter than your regular stirrup length.

Good basic jumping position.

- Bend forward from your hips (not from your waist) just enough to let your shoulders come forward over your knees. Your seat should sink backward so that you stay close to the saddle and balanced over your feet.
- Your legs and feet must be under your body, with knees and ankles flexible and heels down. Your stirrup leathers should be vertical (straight up and down). The inside of your legs should touch the saddle and your pony's side, and your toes may turn out a little (but not a lot!).
- Keep your back straight—not round, slumped, or hollow.
- Look ahead and keep your eyes up.

At first when you ride in jumping position, you should hold a neck-strap or the mane, or rest your hands on your pony's neck. As your legs get stronger, you can do it no hands. Never grab the reins to keep your balance—this hurts your pony's mouth.

Jumping Basics

There are five jumping basics that you need every time you jump. They are balance, eyes, sink, release, and finish.

- **Balance.** This means you must be in good balance with your pony. If you are too far forward ("ahead" of your pony) or too far back ("behind" your pony), you are out of balance and cannot stay "with" him when he jumps.
- **Eyes.** This means to look at your target, which keeps your pony straight and keeps you from looking down. Looking down will make you lose your balance.

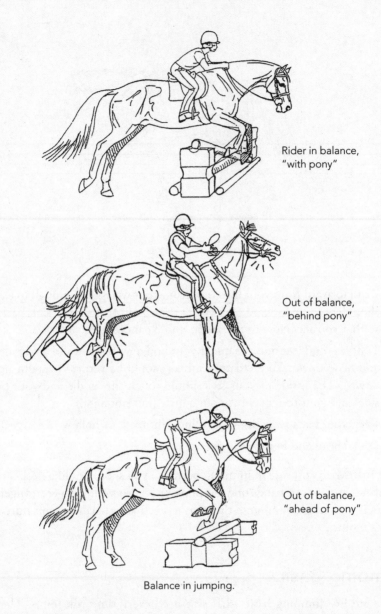

Rider in balance,
"with pony"

Out of balance,
"behind pony"

Out of balance,
"ahead of pony"

Balance in jumping.

- **Sink.** This means to sink your heels down and to let your seat sink back toward the saddle a little. This makes you more secure when you jump. It is the opposite of standing up.

When you jump, the angles at your hips, knees, and ankles close to absorb the thrust (or push) of your pony's jump. If your joints are relaxed and springy, this is easy; but if they are stiff and tight, you may get bounced out

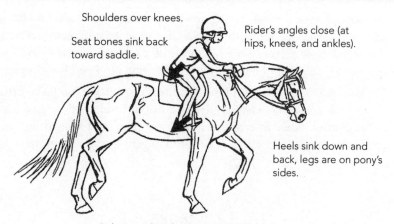

Shoulders over knees.

Seat bones sink back toward saddle.

Rider's angles close (at hips, knees, and ankles).

Heels sink down and back, legs are on pony's sides.

Rider's angles closing in jumping position.

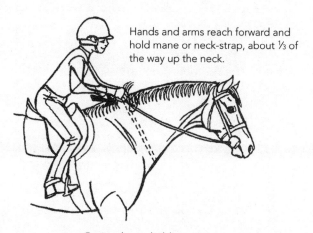

Hands and arms reach forward and hold mane or neck-strap, about ⅓ of the way up the neck.

Basic release, holding mane.

of balance. Your angles should close automatically as your pony jumps. Don't try to guess when he will take off and stand up or lean forward. Instead, just wait for his jump, relax, and let your heels and seat sink.

- **Release.** This means that you must release your pony's mouth to let him stretch his neck and jump safely. To release, reach out and put both hands (holding the reins) on top of your pony's neck about 8 to 12 inches in front of the saddle. Hold the neck-strap or pinch the roots of the mane so your hands can't fly up and jerk his mouth. (This is called a *mane release*. You will learn other releases later in this chapter.)

You should release just as your pony jumps. Keep your hands on his neck until he finishes the jump and lands, then pick them up gently. You must release your pony every time he jumps. If you don't release, he will get a jerk in the mouth, and he will think he is being punished for jumping.

- **Finish.** This means that you must finish your job after a jump. You should sit up, look where you want to go, pick up your hands, and keep your pony under control. Sometimes you finish by stopping on a straight line after a jump, other times the finish may be a turn or getting ready for the next jump.

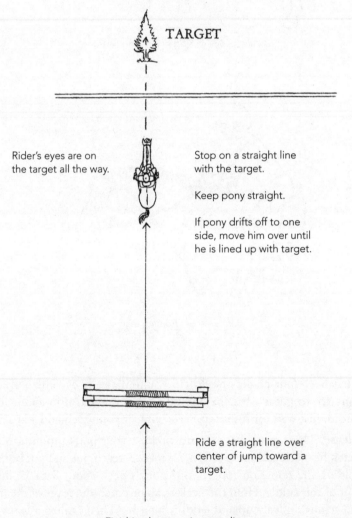

TARGET

Rider's eyes are on the target all the way.

Stop on a straight line with the target.

Keep pony straight.

If pony drifts off to one side, move him over until he is lined up with target.

Ride a straight line over center of jump toward a target.

Finishing by stopping on a line.

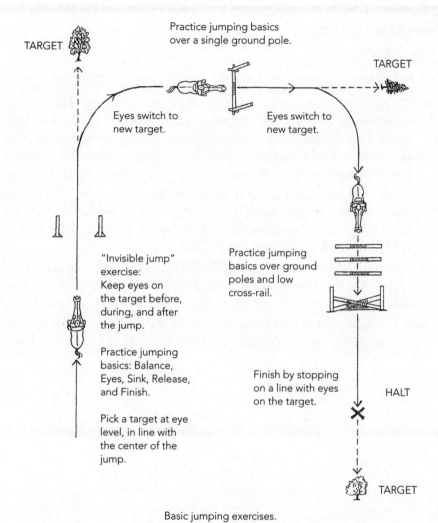

TARGET

Practice jumping basics
over a single ground pole.

TARGET

Eyes switch to
new target.

Eyes switch to
new target.

"Invisible jump"
exercise:
Keep eyes on
the target before,
during, and after
the jump.

Practice jumping
basics over ground
poles and low
cross-rail.

Practice jumping
basics: Balance,
Eyes, Sink, Release,
and Finish.

Finish by stopping
on a line with eyes
on the target.

HALT

Pick a target at eye
level, in line with
the center of the
jump.

TARGET

Basic jumping exercises.

You can practice these basics over an invisible jump, over a ground pole, and then work up to regular jumps. Most people have one or two basics that they have to work harder to remember. As you practice and the basics get easier, they will become habits. Eventually they should be so automatic that you don't have to think about them—you just do them. If you ever have a problem with your jumping, it will help to go back and review your basics.

Simple Jumping

Jumps for Beginners

It is easy to set up good, safe jumps if you follow a few simple rules:

- *Cavaletti* have supports at each end, like a little sawhorse. They can be turned to make low (about 8 inches), medium (about 12 inches), or high (about 18 inches) cavaletti. The kind of cavaletti with X-shaped ends with sharp points should not be used because they can cause injuries. Cavaletti should be made with square or rounded-off ends instead, which are safer.

- *Blocks* can be used with poles in place of cavaletti. They can be turned to make different heights, used as jump standards, or used as "fillers" for larger jumps. These are often plastic. You can also make wooden stands to hold the poles in place at just one height.

- *Poles* must be set so that they will fall if they are hit hard. Use jump cups or pegs, but don't use nails that stick out. Don't wedge poles so that they cannot fall. It is not safe to stack up fixed cavaletti to make a bigger jump.

- A *ground line* is a pole or a part of the jump that lies on the ground at the bottom of a jump. It helps the pony judge how high a jump is and when

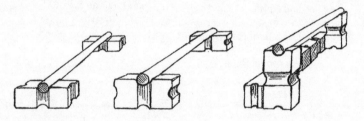

Plastic blocks can be turned or stacked to make jumps different heights. They can also be used as filling material for larger jumps.

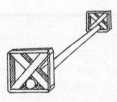

A cavaletto with supports safely enclosed. It can be turned for low, medium, or high heights.

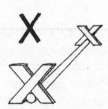

DANGER! This type of cavaletto can cause injury to pony or rider. DO NOT USE!

Blocks and cavaletti.

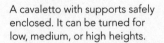

to take off. It may be right under the jump or a little toward the takeoff side. Never jump a fence "backward," with the ground line on the wrong side (the landing side). This is called a *false ground line*. It can fool your pony and cause him to make a mistake. If you want to jump a fence in both directions, put a ground line on both sides.

- *Cross-rails* are made with two crossed rails, lower in the center. They should have a ground line on the takeoff side or on both sides if they are to be jumped from both directions.

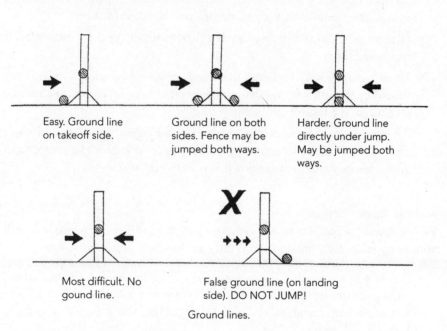

Easy. Ground line on takeoff side.

Ground line on both sides. Fence may be jumped both ways.

Harder. Ground line directly under jump. May be jumped both ways.

Most difficult. No gound line.

False ground line (on landing side). DO NOT JUMP!

Ground lines.

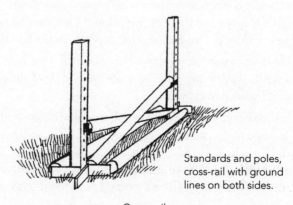

Standards and poles, cross-rail with ground lines on both sides.

Cross-rail.

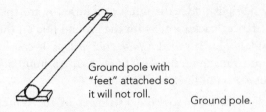

Ground pole with "feet" attached so it will not roll.

Ground pole.

- *Straight rails* (also called *simple verticals*) are made with a rail straight across. They should have a ground line on the takeoff side.
- Ground poles should be fixed so that they won't roll under a pony's feet if he knocks them.
- Small logs (about 10 inches in diameter) are good beginning jumps. They should be smooth with no sharp branches sticking out, and must have safe ground on the takeoff and landing sides.
- All jumps should be set with enough space for a good approach and room afterward to turn easily or to stop. This requires at least 30 feet before and after a jump. More space makes it easier to turn or stop.

Riding Approaches

Riding toward a jump is called the *approach*. A good approach gets you and your pony ready for a good jump. A poor approach can cause mistakes.

- Before you approach a jump, your pony must be moving forward in the right gait (trot or canter), with good rhythm and balance. It's a good idea to make a large circle (at least 60 feet) to get him ready. Be sure you are in balance with him.
- Your pony must come into a jump with enough impulsion, or energy, to jump it. If he is lazy or not paying attention, he will not be ready to jump well and he might stop. Use your legs to keep him awake and ready to jump.
- As you ride toward the jump, plan where you will have to turn to line up with the middle. Pick a target in line with the middle of the jump and aim your eyes and your pony toward it.
- If you cut the corner and turn too soon, you may *undershoot*. This brings you to the jump on a crooked line. Your pony might try to *run out* (go by the jump). If you turn too late, you may *overshoot* and come in crooked. If you forget to look ahead at your target, you may weave or zigzag coming into the jump. Your pony will be confused and might stop or run out.

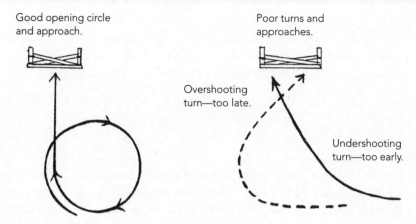

Good opening circle and approach.

Poor turns and approaches.

Overshooting turn—too late.

Undershooting turn—too early.

Turns and approaches.

Single Jumps

Start with a low cross-rail or perhaps a small log only about 8 inches high in the center. When you can keep your balance and all your basics are working well, it can be raised a little. Practice over many small fences before you try bigger ones.

Trotting Grid (Ground Poles) Before a Cross-Rail

The next step is to ride over a trotting grid of three to five ground poles, leading to a cross-rail. This helps your pony take off at the right place. It also helps you get ready for the jump. The ground poles must be spaced so that your pony can step in the middle of the spaces when he is trotting (about 3 feet, 6 inches apart for ponies, and up to 4 feet, 6 inches apart for horses). The distance from the last ground pole to the jump should be twice the distance of the ground poles (7 to 9 feet). When you have done the trotting ground poles well without a jump, you can add the jump at the end and do them together.

Ride over the ground poles in jumping position and release at the first pole. Keep your jumping position (and your eyes on the target) until after the cross-rail.

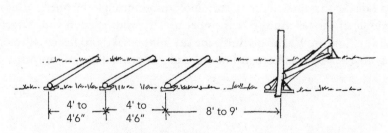

4' to 4'6"   4' to 4'6"   8' to 9'

Distance from last ground pole to cross-rail is twice the distance between ground poles.

Spacing for ground poles and cross-rail.

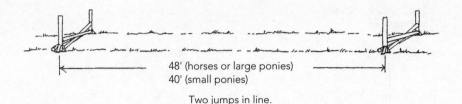

48' (horses or large ponies)
40' (small ponies)

Two jumps in line.

Lines of Fences

When you can jump a single cross-rail well, you can learn to jump two in a line. The second jump should be about 48 feet away in a straight line. This gives you time to finish your first jump, keep your eyes on the target, and ride straight on over the second one. Remember to finish the line by stopping on a straight line or by turning smoothly under control.

It helps to make the second jump a ground pole at first, then build it up to a small cross-rail. This gives you practice in recovering your balance and control after the first jump in time to ride the second jump well.

For now, your jumping should be mostly at a trot while you practice your basics and control. You can ride the approach in a posting trot or a sitting trot, but get into jumping position just as your pony jumps. Don't try to stand up coming into the jumps. If your pony should break into a canter, slow him back down to a trot after the jump. This will help you stay in control.

Jumping a Simple Course

When you put two or more lines of jumps together, it makes a *course*. The idea is to ride a jump course smoothly and with control, thinking ahead. To practice, you can set up a simple course of invisible jumps or poles on the ground. Later, you can raise them to cross-rails or regular jumps.

When you ride into the ring to jump a course, you should have your reins short enough for control, and your pony should be awake and listening to you. Start with a large circle before the first jump. Pick up a posting trot on the correct diagonal, and use the circle to get your pony in good balance and rhythm and lined up with the middle of the first jump. Keep your eyes on your target as you ride the first line of jumps, then look ahead through the turn and aim for the middle of the next jump. Remember to keep your eyes on your target for each line of jumps. When you finish the last jump, make another circle to bring your pony back to a walk smoothly and under control. Thank him with a pat!

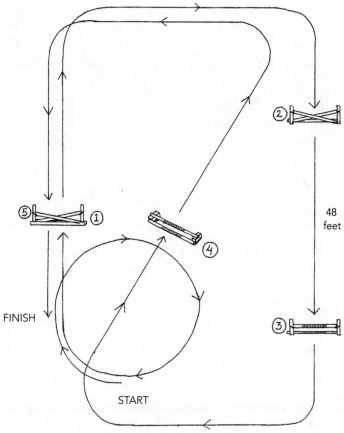

Simple course for basic jumping riders.

Riding over Fences

Here are some important things to know about jumping over fences:

- Jumping is fun for you but hard work for your pony, especially when you are jumping and cantering. Don't jump the same jumps too many times or jump too long. This can make him tired, bored, and sour, and he will not want to jump at all. Don't jump every day because it is hard on your pony's legs. Jumping three times a week, or at most, every other day, is usually enough.

APPROACH   TAKEOFF   FLIGHT

What a rider does during each phase of the jump.
Approach: eyes up, use legs, let pony use his head and neck to see
and judge the jump.
Takeoff: jumping position (shoulders over knees), angles close, hands
release, eyes up, heels down.
Flight: stay in balance, hands maintain release, eyes up, heels down.

How a pony jumps (part 1).

- Always warm up before jumping (15 minutes of walking and trotting, with a short canter or two). Cool your pony out thoroughly afterward and rub his legs down. This helps you notice any small bumps, cuts, or injuries right away.

- Always check your tack before jumping, even if you checked it when you mounted up. Check the girth. Make sure your stirrups are at jumping length, and tighten the chin-strap on your helmet.

- Build safe fences with ground lines on the takeoff side. This is usually a pole on the ground on the takeoff side. Don't jump fences in the wrong direction, with a false ground line. Check the footing. Don't jump when the ground is too slippery or very hard.

- You should have lots of experience over all kinds of low, simple fences before you jump higher ones. This is not only safer for you and your pony, but it helps you build confidence and good jumping habits.

- Always keep a safe jumping distance (at least five or six pony lengths) when you are jumping behind another pony.

- Don't jump a pony whom you can't control, especially cross-country. This is very dangerous for both you and the pony. If you are having trouble with control, or with any part of your jumping, get help from your instructor.

- Never jump alone. Someone should always be on hand in case of an accident.

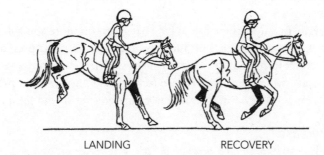

LANDING   RECOVERY

Landing: sink into heels, balance over feet, eyes up, hands maintain release.
Recovery: eyes up, hands following, stay in balance with heels down, use legs
to ride on.

How a pony jumps (part 2).

Types of Releases

Whenever your pony jumps he stretches out his head and neck while in the air, so you must give him a *release*. This means that your hands let him stretch out his head and neck so he can jump. If you don't release him, he will get jerked in the mouth when he tries to jump. This could make him jump badly or even stop jumping.

There are several kinds of releases. Of the four explained here, the first is the most basic and the automatic release is the most advanced. You should try the next release only when you can do the first one very well, and so on.

Basic Release

This release, also called *mane release*, is for riders just beginning to jump. It is also used when things go wrong to keep from pulling the pony's mouth. For a basic release, keep the reins in your hands but open your thumbs and first fingers. Reach forward about 12 inches up the pony's neck, pinch the roots of the mane with both hands, and close your fingers. Hold the mane firmly until your pony has finished jumping. (Instead of the mane, you may use a neck-strap buckled around your pony's neck about 12 inches in front of the saddle.) After the jump, pick your hands up gently and bring them back where they belong for normal control.

Crest Release

This is the next step after the basic release. Reach forward about 12 inches up the pony's neck. Put both hands together on top of the neck and press your knuckles down firmly against his crest. (If you don't press hard enough, your hands might fly up and jerk his mouth.) Keep your hands pressed on his crest until he has finished the jump.

Short Release

This is a crest release that does not reach as far, so it gives you more control. Reach forward toward the bit only about 4 or 5 inches until your knuckles press against the pony's neck closer to the saddle. This release doesn't let your pony stretch his neck as far as the last two releases, so it is used for vertical jumps and jumps where you need quick control afterward. It should not be used over spread jumps.

Automatic Release

This release is also called *following through the air* or *jumping on contact*. For this release, your hands keep contact with your pony's mouth and stay off the neck. As your pony stretches his neck forward, he draws your hands through the air, making your arms stretch just as much as his head and neck stretch out. You have light contact with his mouth during the jump and while he is landing, so this release gives you the most control. (**Caution:** This is an advanced release, to be used only by riders who can do the first three releases perfectly. If you try to jump on contact and don't do it quite right, any mistakes you make will pull on your pony's mouth and may spoil his jumping.)

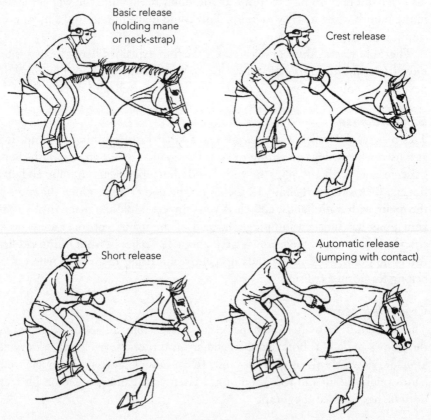

Four kinds of release.

Good jumping form for basic level. This rider is in balance with her pony, with eyes up, heels down, and a good basic release.

Jumping problems. This rider is looking down and is behind the motion, with heels up and knees pinching, and is failing to release the pony's mouth. This can make the rider insecure and the pony uncomfortable when jumping.

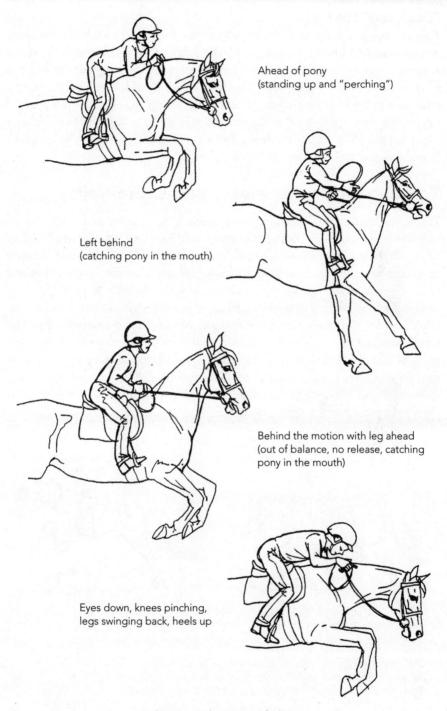

Ahead of pony
(standing up and "perching")

Left behind
(catching pony in the mouth)

Behind the motion with leg ahead
(out of balance, no release, catching
pony in the mouth)

Eyes down, knees pinching,
legs swinging back, heels up

Common rider jumping faults.

"Dropping" the Pony

This is a mistake some riders make when they are trying to release. *Dropping* means suddenly dropping contact with the pony's mouth (loosening the reins) at just the wrong time right before a jump, instead of releasing correctly just as he takes off. Often the rider looks down or leans forward, too. This surprises a pony just as he is getting ready to jump. He might make a bad jump or he might even stop suddenly. If it happens often enough, he will not trust his rider when jumping. To keep from dropping your pony, keep your eyes up and wait to release until you feel him lift for the takeoff.

Trotting Grids, Cavaletti, and Cross-Rails

You have already practiced riding over single ground poles and simple cross-rails. Now you can begin riding over three to five ground poles or low cavaletti (also called a *trotting grid*) with a cross-rail at the end. This helps your balance, suppleness, rhythm, and jumping position. It also teaches your pony to balance himself better, to pick up his feet, and to take off at the right spot.

Cavaletti, or trotting grids, must be set at just the right distances to fit your pony's strides. You must have help from an instructor or an experienced person who can adjust the poles so they are safe and right for your pony. The ground poles or low cavaletti should be set 3 feet, 6 inches (for small ponies) up to 4 feet, 6 inches (for horses) apart. The distance from the last ground pole to the cross-rail is exactly twice the distance between the cavaletti (7 to 9 feet). This gives your pony just the right amount of room to take off.

Small ponies: ground poles 3' 6" apart; 7' from last ground pole cross-rail
Large ponies: ground poles 4' apart; 8' from last ground pole cross-rail
Horses: ground poles 4' 6" apart; 9' from last ground pole cross-rail

Ground poles should be spaced so pony steps in the middle.
Distance to the jump is twice the ground pole distance.
Rider is in jumping position over the ground poles and cross-rail.

Trotting grid with cross-rail.

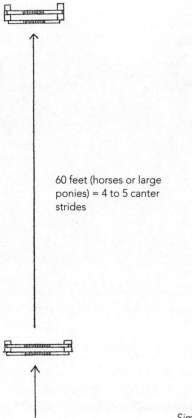

60 feet (horses or large ponies) = 4 to 5 canter strides

Simple line of two fences.

When you ride over cavaletti and cross-rails, approach in a steady posting trot with plenty of energy. At the first pole, take a jumping position (shoulders over knees, heels down, seat close to saddle) and stay in jumping position until your pony has landed after the cross-rail. Let the extra bounce of the cavaletti make your knees and ankles springy so your heels will sink down and your seat stays close to the saddle. Remember to give your pony a release at the jump, and keep your eyes up.

Jumping at the Canter

When you and your pony have plenty of experience jumping at the trot, you can learn to jump at the canter. The easiest way to do this is in stages. You can set up two cross-rails at an appropriate distance for your pony or horse (see the chart that follows for jumping line distances). Trot the first cross-rail, and give an extra leg squeeze and a cluck during the jump. This will encourage your pony to land cantering. When he does, just relax and ride the canter (sitting in

Cantering between jumps. This rider shows good balance and control at the canter, with her eyes up and her heels down

the saddle) straight to the next cross-rail. It may help to count "one, two, three, four," and so on, with his canter strides. Keep your eyes up and heels down, and you will canter on over the second cross-rail.

When you can trot into the first cross-rail and canter the second, you can canter into the first jump. Start with a 20-meter circle at the trot, and pick up your canter (on the correct lead) about halfway around your circle. Canter straight to the jump, keeping your eyes up and counting to keep the rhythm of your pony's strides. (For now, the number of strides doesn't matter as much as staying in rhythm with his canter.) Later, you can canter two fences in a line.

Gymnastic Jumping, or Gridwork

Gymnastic jumping, or *gridwork,* means riding over a series of poles and small jumps set in a *gymnastic jumping line,* or *grid.* This trains a pony to look where he is going, pick up his feet, regulate his strides, jump in rhythm, and use his legs and body well when he jumps. It is also good practice for riders, who can learn balance, maintain rhythm, develop timing, and practice good "springs." All ground poles, grids, and gymnastic jumping exercises must be set at the proper distances for the size of the horses or ponies, their length of stride, and their jumping experience. This must be done by a person with knowledge and experience in jumping and gridwork.

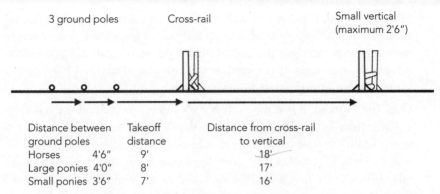

3 ground poles   Cross-rail   Small vertical
                                                      (maximum 2'6")

Distance between ground poles	Takeoff distance	Distance from cross-rail to vertical
Horses 4'6"	9'	18'
Large ponies 4'0"	8'	17'
Small ponies 3'6"	7'	16'

Simple gridwork exercise: three trot poles, cross-rail, one stride to 2'3" vertical.

Gymnastic jumping should be progressive—that is, it should start out easy and simple, gradually adding more ground poles, cavaletti, or jumps as the horse and rider are ready for it. The jumps used should be kept low, especially at first. Gridwork is harder work than ordinary jumping, so it must not be overdone in any jumping session. It takes time and practice.

When you ride a grid, approach the first part of the grid at a straight, steady but lively trot, in a balanced 2-point position. The first time you do it, ride over just the three ground poles at a trot. When that is successful, your instructor will add the cross-rail, and you will trot the first three poles, continue in a trot, and jump the cross-rail. When you are doing well with both the trot poles and cross-rail, the vertical fence can be added, starting small and building the height gradually. Your pony should trot the three ground poles, continue to trot, then jump the cross-rail, take another canter stride, and jump the vertical. You will feel the rhythm and spring as he takes off, lands, strides, and jumps again.

An example of a simple progressive gymnastic jumping exercise is shown above.

Types of Jumps

As you gain experience in jumping, you should learn to jump many different types of low fences before jumping higher or wider ones. The jumps you use should be small, safe, and simple, and they should have a ground line (see pages 104–105). You can use painted jump poles, blocks, cavaletti, and many different kinds of fillers to make different-looking jumps. This helps to teach your pony to jump confidently and easily over any jump you ask him to take. The main kinds of jumps used for this level are:

- **Cross-rail.** Two crossed poles, with a ground pole on one or both sides, used mostly for practice and gymnastic jumping exercises. Cross-rails are easy for ponies and riders, and the low center encourages the pony to jump straight over the center of the jump.

- **Simple vertical.** A jump where all the elements (parts of the jump) line up above each other in a vertical line. A *straight rail* is a vertical with a single horizontal rail and a ground pole. Other types of verticals are gates, pickets, panels, and walls. If the jump is tall, use several poles so it is not too "airy" and hard for the pony to see and judge.

- **Oxer (or "spread").** A jump with two elements, one behind the other, to make a wider jump. The first element should be lower and should have a ground rail; the second element should be slightly higher and should be only one rail. This makes the top of the oxer slant slightly upward from the takeoff to the landing side. It is safer and easier for the pony to see and jump. A *cross-rail oxer* is a cross-rail with a horizontal single rail added just behind the cross-rail to make a low but wider jump. An oxer must never be jumped from the wrong side as this can cause a pony to make a dangerous mistake about where to take off.

Jumping Simple Courses Up to 2 Feet, 3 Inches in Height

When you can canter over two fences in a line, making good approaches and turns before and after the jumps, you can put lines of jumps together to make a course. The jumps should be quite simple (no higher than you are used to, or 2 feet, 3 inches at the maximum), and you should jump each fence by itself, for schooling, before you jump a course. (Later, when you are competing, you will have to jump the course without practicing over it first.)

When you have gained experience riding lines, turns, and simple courses, you can begin to add different types of jumps to your courses, such as verticals and ascending oxers. All jumps should be safe and inviting, with ground lines, and they should not exceed 2 feet, 3 inches.

Suggested Distances for Jumping Lines

	Stride Length	Four Strides	Five Strides	Six Strides
Small pony	10'	50'	60'	70'
Medium pony	10½'	52½'	63'	73½'
Large pony	11'3"	56'3"	67½'	78'9"
Horse	12'	60'	72'	84'

The jumps should be set at good cantering distances (see the previous chart). The actual striding may vary with terrain and the horse or pony's size, pace, and length of stride. Your instructor should help you set jumps and distances so they are safe and suitable for your horse or pony. Some horses or ponies may have a shorter than normal stride; they might take one additional stride.

Be sure that there is room to make a good circle and approach to the first fence, and to turn easily after each line. The fences and distances should be checked by your instructor or an experienced helper to make sure they are safe and right for your pony.

Ride smart: Plan how you will ride your course! Think about where you will make your opening circle, and where you will start your approach to the first fence. Pick out a target to look at to keep you lined up straight over the middle of each line of jumps. Walk through each turn and plan where you should turn

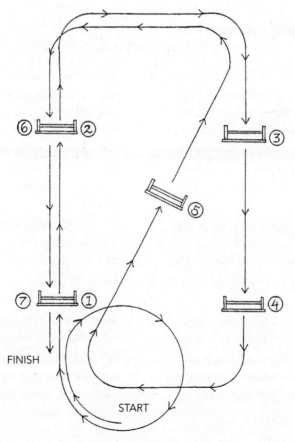

Simple course (maximum height 2'3").

to make a good approach to the next jump. Think about where you will need to use more leg to keep your pony going, and where he might want to go too fast (like going back to the gate!) or cut a corner. When you have made your riding plan, you can mount up and ride the course just the way you have planned it. Afterward, think about how you did. Did your plan work? Was there anything you could do to ride it better the next time?

Pony Jumping Problems

Disobediences (Refusals and Runouts)

When a pony disobeys at a jump, you must do two things: First, handle the refusal or runout properly, and, second, figure out why he stopped or ran out and how to keep him from doing it again. If he refuses more than once, it can get to be a habit.

Why a Pony Might Refuse or Run Out:

What to Do:

1. Rider error: You didn't bring him in straight, didn't use your legs firmly, dropped him, pulled his mouth, or he didn't have enough impulsion (energy) to jump.

1. Ride a better approach: Use your legs, eyes, and release correctly, and make sure your pony is alert and paying attention, with enough energy to jump well.

2. The jump is too big or unfamiliar, or the ground is slippery.

2. Lower the jump, let the pony look at it, and don't jump on bad footing.

3. The pony got off balance or got to such a bad takeoff spot that he didn't think he could jump safely.

3. Try again, riding a better approach (especially straighter and better balanced).

4. The pony is lame or sore.

4. Have the veterinarian check him. Don't jump a lame pony!

5. You are not really sure you want to jump. Ponies can tell!

5. Take time to build up your confidence over easier jumps.

6. The pony is green (inexperienced) or has lost confidence in jumping because of a bad experience.

6. Work slowly over very small jumps to build up the pony's confidence. Good riding is very important.

Handling a Refusal (Stopping)

First, keep your eyes up and keep your balance. Sit up and stay in control. Next, bring your pony right to the center of the jump. Let him have a good look at it; you could even let him sniff the fence if he wants. Don't let him turn away from it and be sure not to allow him to jump it from a standstill. Keep him there while you squeeze your legs and cluck once or twice, to get him to think "Forward!" A lazy or stubborn pony might need a tap of a stick right behind your leg, too. (If you use a stick, use it behind your leg, not on the pony's shoulder, and be careful not to jerk on his mouth when using a stick.) Then turn around, go back and try again, using your legs firmly and adding a cluck to remind him to go forward.

Sometimes it works better to simply go back and ride the fence again with determination, keeping your eyes on your target, steering him straight and using your legs firmly, with a tap of your crop if necessary. But don't just ride in a fast circle back to the jump—you must be in control or your pony may refuse or run out again.

Caution: If your pony is afraid of a jump, you may need to make it lower before you try it again. It may also help to follow another pony over it the first time.

Handling a Runout

When a pony runs out, it is not quite the same as a stop. First, you must get control again, then correct the runout. Sit up deep and tall and stop your pony, then think before you turn him around. You must turn him opposite from the way he ran out (that is, if he ran out to the right, turn him left). This is important to correct his runout. Next, ride him back to the center of the jump and make him look straight over the middle of it. You may need to use your leg and cluck or tap with a stick to make him think "Forward over the middle!" But don't let him jump from a standstill—you must be in control! When you turn around to repeat the jump, turn in the direction that will correct his runout ideas (if he ran out to the right, turn to the left). When you approach the fence again, keep your eyes on your target over the middle of the jump, and use your legs firmly, but don't come in too fast. Be ready to steer sideways if he starts to run out again. Put your crop in the hand on the side he ran out toward; this can help to keep him from running out that way again. (For instance, if he ran out to the left, put your crop in your left hand when you approach the jump again.)

As with a refusal, sometimes it works better to simply go back and ride the fence again with determination, keeping your eyes on your target, steering straight, and using your legs firmly. But don't just circle back to the jump—you must have good control and ride clearly and positively to prevent another runout.

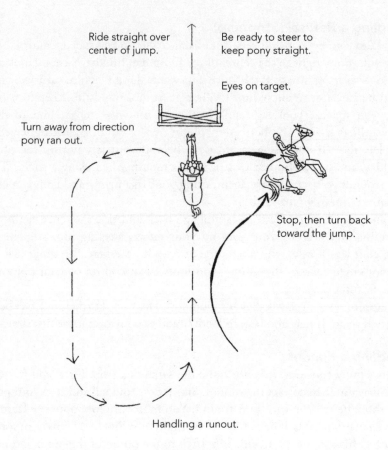

Ride straight over center of jump.

Be ready to steer to keep pony straight.

Eyes on target.

Turn away from direction pony ran out.

Stop, then turn back *toward* the jump.

Handling a runout.

Rushing Jumps

A pony who rushes too fast at his jumps is hard to ride and may not jump safely. It takes an experienced rider to control a rusher and teach him to jump better. This is not the kind of pony for a beginning jumping rider.

Why a Pony May Rush:	**What to Do:**
1. He is too fresh and "full of beans." He may have had too much grain and too little exercise.	1. Longe or exercise him until he settles down. Don't overfeed him.
2. He is nervous about jumping (he may be green or have had bad experiences).	2. Work slowly and calmly over ground poles, cavaletti, and low jumps. A good, patient, and experienced rider is very important.
3. You use too much leg, hang on the pony's mouth, or clash your aids.	3. You need help to improve your riding.

4. You are tense and nervous, and the pony catches your nervousness.

5. The pony is experienced and strong; he takes over when jumping.

4. You must calm down, breathe, and go back to easier jumps to build up confidence.

5. A rushing pony needs an experienced, confident rider. He needs good flat work to make him easier to control. Do one jump at a time; riding in circles or over cavaletti before jumps may help relax him.

Jumping Simple Cross-Country Fences (Maximum 2 Feet, 3 Inches)

Jumping cross-country fences is a lot like jumping in the ring, but there are some differences. Many horses and ponies act more lively and want to move on more freely when they jump outside. This makes for good, bold jumping, but you must have control. Practice stopping and slowing down until your pony comes back obediently to a slower speed when you ask him to. Some ponies may need a stronger bit for jumping outside the ring.

Another difference is that cross-country fences are solid—they do not knock down like ring jumps. This seems scary to some riders, but it actually makes for better jumping. Ponies can see and judge a solid fence (like a log, coop, or brush pile) more easily than a jump made of poles. They usually jump bigger, with more power, and more freely over solid fences. When you jump solid fences, you don't ride differently than you do over other jumps. Just be positive (sure and strong); you don't want to take away your pony's confidence with a halfhearted approach. The way to build your own confidence (and your pony's confidence) about solid fences is to start by jumping very low, easy ones at first. Always check the footing on takeoff and landing first to be sure it is safe to jump.

If your pony is not sure he wants to jump a cross-country fence, give him a chance to stand and take a good look at it. Ride several 20-meter circles in front of the fence at a trot, giving him a look at the jump each time he comes around the circle. When you feel that he is ready to go forward calmly, you can follow another horse or pony over the jump (at a safe distance). This is called *getting a lead over a jump*.

Be careful to look up, keep your heels down, and release properly, so you won't be surprised if he jumps big and catch him in the mouth.

When you follow another rider over a jump, you *must* keep a safe distance. This is *at least* five or six horse lengths back; sometimes more. The rider ahead of you should have landed and recovered before your pony gets to the jump.

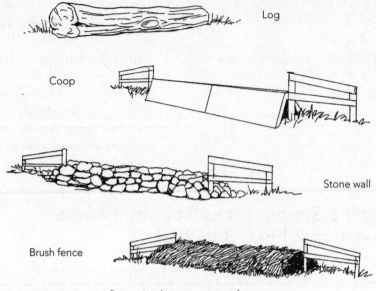

Some simple cross-country fences.

You should be far enough back so that you could stop your pony if the rider ahead has a refusal or a fall. Riding too close is dangerous—for you, your pony, and the rider in front of you.

4

Out and About with Your Pony

As you become a more experienced rider and can ride with good control, you can enjoy the fun of riding with others and riding outside the ring. This can include riding with a group in a ring, trail riding, and exploring new places on your pony. To do this safely, you will need to learn how to handle your pony in a group, in the open, on roads and trails, and when riding over different terrain and common trail obstacles. You'll also need to learn the rules of the road, how to be a safe and courteous rider in a group, and how to help preserve our rights to ride on trails and land.

Riding in a Ring

When you ride by yourself, you have to think only about yourself and your pony (and sometimes your instructor). When people ride together, everyone must follow certain rules in order to be safe and fair to the others. Here are some simple rules for safe and courteous ring riding or riding in an enclosed area:

- If others are riding in a ring when you arrive, ask permission by calling "Door?" before you open the gate and come in. Wait for someone to call back, "Okay!" and make sure it is clear before you enter. If you open the gate suddenly, you could upset someone else's pony.

- Pay attention to your pony and keep him under control. Don't let him wander, get too close to other ponies, or bother them. Don't let him touch noses with another pony—this often makes ponies stamp and squeal.

- Keep a safe distance of at least one pony length from any other pony. Never crowd up close behind any other pony—this could make the other pony kick.

- If you need to stop to fix something, go to the center of the ring. Don't stop on the track, where you would be in the way of other riders.

- If you must pass a slower pony, turn and ride across the ring or circle back to an open space. Never pass close to another pony, or squeeze between another pony and the rail.

- Stay alert and aware of your surroundings, and be polite and considerate of other riders. Don't become so engrossed in your pony and your riding that you accidentally cut off another rider, especially if the rider is jumping. That is dangerous!

- When you are taking a riding lesson, be on time. If you pay attention to the instructor, obey commands promptly, maintain good spacing, and are ready when it is your turn to perform an exercise, you will make it a better lesson for yourself and for others.

- If you are jumping and other people are riding in the ring, call "Heads-up, please!" to warn them before you approach the jump. You may identify the jump by saying "Heads-up for the cross-rail" or "Heads-up for the oxer." However, it is still your responsibility to look out for other people in the ring.

- If several people are riding in a small ring, it is easier if everyone agrees to ride in the same direction and all change direction after a while. In a large and busy ring, people may ride both ways. When you meet another rider, pass like cars on the highway—left shoulder to left shoulder.

- If your pony might kick, you should put a red ribbon in his tail to warn others. However, it is still your responsibility to keep him under control and not let him kick.

- Always be polite to others. If another rider is having trouble, slow down or stop and give her room. Don't interrupt a lesson or someone who is busy training or jumping. Thank anyone who gives you room or helps you, and remember to thank your instructor at the end of a lesson.

Riding outside the Ring

Riding outside can be the most fun of all, but you must be in good control of your pony. Most ponies like to go out, especially with other horses and ponies, and some act livelier outside than they do in a ring. This makes it especially important to keep your pony paying attention to you and under control.

Are You Ready to Ride Outside?

- Be sure you have good control and can stop your pony and slow down easily.

- The first time you ride outside, go with a good, sensible rider (your instructor is best) who has a quiet, well-behaved horse or pony. This sets a good example for your pony and makes it easier for you to have a good ride. Don't ride with people who want to go fast or who cannot control their ponies.

- Always do a safety check of your tack before you ride outside. (See chapter 12, "Tack," for more about taking care of tack.)

- Use fly repellent on your pony and sunscreen or bug repellent on yourself to make your trail ride more comfortable.

- Ride in a safe place, such as a trail or field with good footing. Stay away from highways, traffic, farm machinery, and things that are dangerous or likely to upset your pony. It is best to ride on a calm day, as some ponies may be too lively when it is windy. Don't ride in fields where other horses or ponies are loose—they may bother your pony.

- Your first trail ride should be calm and easy, mostly at a walk, with a little trotting if your pony is easy to control and you have a safe place to trot. Don't go fast when going back toward the barn, and always walk the last 15 minutes of your ride.

- When you ride outside, let someone know where you are going and when you will be back. It is a good idea to carry a cell phone in case of emergency, but don't text or talk on the phone while riding.

What to Do If . . .

- **Your pony eats grass:** Don't let a pony eat grass while you are riding—this can teach him bad manners. Some ponies get their heads down to eat and won't move on. If this happens, sit up deep and tall (don't lean forward), use your legs firmly (even kick if you have to), and pull up and to the side on one rein to get his head up. Some ponies need to wear *grass reins* to prevent them from interrupting the ride to eat grass (see page 50).

- **Your pony acts nervous or sees something that startles him:** Sit deep and tall and remember to breathe. This makes you feel calm and in control, and helps calm your pony. Talk to your pony quietly and squeeze and relax on the reins to slow him down. If you tense up, lean forward, or yell at him, he will get more nervous and be harder to control.

Rules for Safe and Courteous Trail Riding in a Group

It's fun to ride with friends, but it is also important to follow safety rules when you ride together. Ponies in a group copy other ponies. If one shies, they all startle, and if one pony takes off, they all want to go. Some ponies do not like to be bumped or crowded, so you must give them space. This makes it very important for everyone to be considerate of other riders when riding in a group. If one person doesn't think, she can make other people's ponies act up and spoil everyone else's ride.

Here are some rules for safety and courtesy when trail riding in a group:

- Keep a safe distance between your pony and others. Allow at least one pony space between your pony's nose and the next pony's tail. Be firm with your pony about not crowding the pony ahead of him.

- Don't hang back a long way behind the others. Your pony might decide to catch up and go faster than he should.

- When riding on a trail, stay in line. If you ride out to the side, your pony may want to catch up and pass or he may crowd the other riders. It is okay to ride side by side if the trail is wide enough. However, passing other ponies can make them excited and cause trouble, so ask the other rider if it's okay before you pass.

Riding outside in a group is fun, but you must be a safe and courteous trail rider.

- If you want to go faster, ask the others if it is okay with them first. If you start trotting, other ponies will trot too, which can surprise another rider who is not ready.

- If you see something that could be dangerous, like a hole, broken glass, or wire, point to it as you pass it and warn the rider behind you. All warnings should be passed back to the last rider.

- If you ride under a low tree branch, duck your head as you go under it. Never try to hold on to a branch—when you let go, it will snap back and can hit the pony behind you.

- If you need to stop quickly, warn the riders behind you by putting one hand up over your head, like a policeman. This means "Stop." If you see a rider ahead of you put his hand up, put your hand up too, then stop your pony in time to avoid crowding the ponies ahead of you.

- Pay attention to your pony. If he lays his ears back or swings his rump toward another pony, he may be about to kick. Tell him "No!" as you turn his head toward the other pony. This turns his rump away so he can't kick.

- If a rider has trouble, a pony acts up, or anyone has to stop to fix something, all the other riders should stop and wait.

Group Riding in the Open

Many ponies act more lively and want to go forward more when they are outside the ring, especially when they are with a group of ponies. Good control is important for safety, to keep your pony from being a nuisance to others, and so you can enjoy your riding. Some ponies need a stronger bit when they are being ridden outside.

When you ride a pony outside by himself, he may act as if his barn is his herd. He may be slow and stubborn about going away from the stable area, and may want to hurry back home. A pony who will not leave the barn or who acts up and tries to rush back to the barn is called *barn sour*. This can be caused by letting a pony run back to his stable, which quickly becomes a bad habit. If your pony acts barn sour, you will need help from your instructor to teach him to be easier to control. If you always make him walk the last mile back to the stable area, you can keep this behavior from becoming a problem.

Ponies in a group obey their *herd instinct*. This goes back to the time when all horses lived in wild herds. Herd instinct tells ponies that they are safest in the middle of a group, and that they should do whatever the herd does. If one pony startles or takes off, the others will want to, too. If a pony gets left behind the herd, she may get very upset until he can catch up to his friends. Some ponies get stubborn if you try to make them leave the group.

When you ride in a group, you will have to work against herd instinct by making your pony pay attention to you and keep a safe distance from the other ponies (at least one pony length). He may want to crowd closer, but he (or you) could get kicked. No one in a group should take off in a faster gait without asking the others if it is all right with them. If the whole group starts racing, passing each other, or going too fast, some ponies will get excited and become very hard to control. *This is dangerous!*

A group must not ride off and leave one pony and his rider alone, especially if the rider is busy mounting or trying to close a gate. The pony may get upset and try to catch up too fast. When you ride with a group, don't try to hold your pony back and keep him so far behind the group that he gets upset, or he may get very hard to control. Ask the group to slow down and wait for you, or catch up with them and then keep a safe distance.

When you ride outside in a group, you may spot a hazard such as a hidden hole, wire, or a washed-out place in the trail. Each rider should warn the other riders behind them by pointing to the hazard as they pass it, saying "'Ware hole!" or "'Ware wire!" (*'Ware* is a traditional term used in foxhunting; it means *beware.*) You should also pass commands from the ride leader (like "Ready to trot?" or "All halt!") down the line so that all riders hear them.

Trotting and cantering outside in a group requires good control and good sense because ponies may get excited. If one pony takes off, the others will want to go, too.

Here are two ways to help control your pony in a group outside:

- **Pulley rein.** This is a strong rein aid for emergency control. It should only be used when a pony does not pay attention to ordinary aids to stop or slow down, or if he tries to take off or buck. Here's how to use a pulley rein:

    1. Sit up deep and tall, with your heels down. Look up!

    2. With your reins quite short, set one hand firmly on the top of your pony's neck. The rein should be tight.

    3. With the other hand, lift up sharply as you rock your shoulders back. Use a short, sharp lift, not a long pull. If he doesn't behave after one pulley rein, use several, one after the other. Don't use a pulley rein any harder than you need to, but be as strong as you have to in order to get control.

- **Circling.** If you are trotting or cantering in the open and your pony gets "strong" and hard to stop, turn him in a large circle. (Even if he won't stop, he will usually turn quite easily.) Gradually make the circle smaller, and he will have to slow down and then stop. If you have to circle to get control, be careful to do it on good footing and where it is level or slightly uphill. Turning too sharply, going downhill, or turning on slippery footing can make your control problem worse. Your pony could slip and fall.

Pulley rein.

Riding over Natural Terrain and Obstacles
Riding Up and Down Hills

One of the nice things about riding outside is that you ride over different kinds of country, including fields, trails, and hills. Going up and down hills is good for developing balance and strong muscles, in both you and your pony.

Riding Uphill

When your pony climbs a hill, he needs to stretch his neck and his back, so you must lean forward in a half-seat, or a jumping position. If the hill is long or steep, hold the mane so you don't pull on his mouth or sit back on him.

Riding Downhill

When you ride downhill, it's important to stay in balance, with your feet under your center and your heels down. On a gentle slope, you can sit slightly forward. On a steeper hill, you should sit up deep and tall. Don't lean back or brace your feet out ahead of you. This makes it harder for your pony to use his back and his hind legs for balance, and for you to stay in balance with him. Keep your eyes up and look ahead to keep your pony straight.

Always ride your pony straight down a hill or slope, keeping his hind legs in line with his front legs. If he is straight, he can "sit down" a little and use his hind legs to help him balance. If you try to take a slope at an angle or if he gets crooked, he is more likely to slip sideways. Let your pony stretch his neck to look where he is going, but make him slow down and take short steps, especially if the hill is steep.

It is safer for both you and your pony to walk down most hills.

Riding uphill.

Rider in balance, with
feet under body

Riding downhill.

Encountering Natural Obstacles

When you ride outside, you may want to go over small obstacles like logs. These should not be any bigger than the obstacles you are jumping safely and easily in the ring. It's important to check the approach, takeoff, and landing side of all obstacles outside. You wouldn't want to discover a hole or broken glass by accident.

Step-Overs

Some obstacles, like logs or tree roots across a trail or rocky places, are better to step over slowly than to jump. Walk your pony up to the obstacle and halt. Let him stretch his neck out and look at it. Then squeeze or nudge with your legs and ask him to walk on over it. You should be in a jumping position, sitting close to your saddle with your heels down. Hold the mane or a neck-strap so that you won't pull on his mouth.

Low Jumps

You jump low obstacles outside the same way you learned in the ring. Ride your pony straight forward over the middle of the jump, keeping your eyes up and ahead on your target. Use your legs to be sure he comes into the jump with enough energy to jump it, and hold the mane or neck-strap to avoid jerking his mouth.

Riding a step-over obstacle.

If you are riding with a group and you want to jump, someone (your instructor) should check the obstacle first. Everyone should line up beside the obstacle (out of the way) and take their turn, one at a time. After you go over the jump, move out of the way and wait until the last rider is safely over the jump. Then the group may ride on.

Riding through Water

When you are riding outside, you may need to cross a stream. You should start by crossing shallow streams with gently sloping banks. Don't start out trying to cross difficult places like deep water, boggy places, or streams with steep banks.

When you approach a stream, keep your pony moving forward and straight. Use your legs firmly to keep him moving. If he stops, don't let him turn away—make him stand facing the stream until he is ready to go forward. Try following another pony through the water (about one pony length behind him). When he is in the water, you can let him drink, but use your legs firmly to move him forward right away if he starts to paw or bend his knees. (Some ponies like to lie down in water, and they usually paw or bend their knees first.) You may need to use your legs and crop if he does this.

Riding over a shallow ditch.

Crossing Shallow Natural Ditches

When you first start riding over ditches, pick an easy, shallow ditch, one with gently sloping banks. (It should not be a steep ditch or one with *revetted* banks—banks that are straight and faced with wood or stone. Those will come later.)

Keep your pony straight and keep your eyes up. Use your legs firmly to keep him moving forward. The best way to ride over a ditch the first time is to follow an experienced pony at a short but safe distance (about two pony lengths), at a fast walk or a slow trot. Keep your seat in the saddle and your heels down, and be ready to take a jumping position in case your pony jumps. Don't look down or "drop" your pony (by loosening the reins suddenly). This will surprise him and might make him stop.

Riding on the Road

When you are riding outside, it is always best to avoid riding on streets, highways, or near auto traffic if you can help it. Some ponies are frightened by traffic, and even a well-trained pony may spook if something unusual happens. Even if you are careful, not all drivers are safe drivers. Here are some safety rules for riding on public roads:

- If you must ride along a public road, try to stay well off the pavement on the shoulder. (However, this does not mean that you may ride on lawns or sidewalks.) Watch out for trash, especially glass and cans, on the edge of the road and drainage ditches.

- Keep to a walk. Going faster on hard road surfaces is very hard on your pony's feet and legs, and he might slip. In a group, ride in single file, not side by side. The whole group must stay on one side of the road.

- If you see a car coming from the front or the rear, pass a warning down the line to all the riders in front of you or behind you. Pass a warning along if you see a hazard like broken glass, wire, a hole, or a hidden ditch.

- If you must cross a road with a group of riders, everyone should line up at a spot where you can see a long way in both directions. The riders at each end of the line look both ways for traffic. When it is clear, they act as crossing guards while all the riders cross at the same time between them.

Caution: It is *not safe* for one or several riders to cross a road, leaving some riders on the other side. Everyone should stay on the same side of the road and cross at one time when it is safe to do so.

When you ride on public roads, you must obey the traffic laws and any special laws that apply to riders on the roads in your state. These laws are different in each state and in some towns, so you must learn what the traffic laws for riders are in your area. To find out the traffic laws that horseback riders

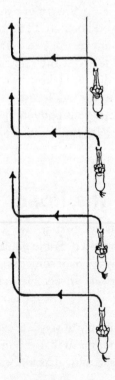

Procedure for crossing a road with a mounted group.

must know, contact your local Department of Motor Vehicles office. The Town Clerk, Police Department, or Sheriff's Department can also tell you if there are any local laws riders must obey.

Remember: *Before you ride on a public road, you must know the traffic laws for your area and obey them.*

Be safe, not sorry—beware of cars and trucks *all the time!* Even if you have the right of way, a driver may not know—or care.

Be a Welcome Trail Rider

Most riders today must ride on public land or on privately owned land if they want to ride on trails. This is only possible if landowners are willing to let riders use their land and trails. Good trail riders are careful and considerate of the land where they ride and polite to landowners. Just one rude or careless rider can cause trouble for everyone. Sometimes public parks or private owners close their land to riders because riders have caused problems. Always remember that riding on someone else's land is a privilege. It's important to be a courteous and responsible trail rider to keep that privilege.

- Always ask permission before riding on someone's land. If you don't know who owns it, don't ride there. Trespassing (especially on horseback) makes landowners angry, and it is against the law.

- Stay off lawns, sidewalks, and gardens, and stay away from picnic areas, where nobody wants hoof prints or manure. If your pony drops manure near somebody's house, borrow a shovel and clean it up.

- When you ride in a field, stay along the edge, especially if the ground is soft. Don't ride through fields that are growing crops or hay. Ponies' hooves cut up the ground and cause damage.

- Leave gates the way you found them. Be careful to close any gate you open. Be very careful not to let livestock get out. If you aren't sure a gate is meant to be left open, close it.

- Leave livestock alone, and be careful not to disturb them. If you take your dog along, be sure she doesn't chase or bother livestock. (It is safer for you and your dog and better for your riding to leave your dog at home.)

- Even if you have permission to ride on somebody's land, don't jump their jumps without special permission.

- Never leave litter behind. If you see litter or trash, take it with you until you can throw it away in a trash can.

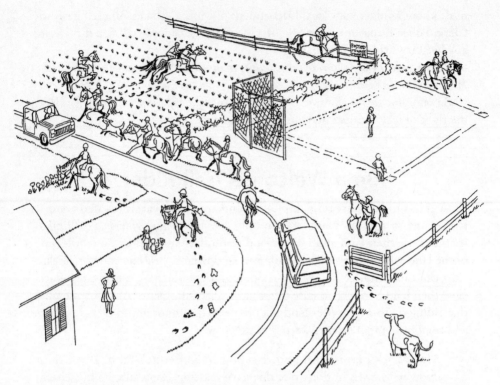

How many things can you find that these riders are doing wrong? Why are they wrong?

- Good trail riders don't hurt the environment. Stay on the trail instead of taking shortcuts in areas where hoof prints may start washouts and erosion. Stay out of especially fragile areas, where horses may cause lasting damage. Don't tie your pony where he can strip the bark from a tree, which may kill it. Don't break off branches unnecessarily or pick wildflowers. Leave nature as beautiful as you found it!

- When you meet anyone else, whether they are on foot, on horseback, biking, or whatever, stop and greet the person politely. It might be the landowner, or his guests or friends. Whenever you meet someone who lets you ride on his land, be sure to thank him!

Land Conservation and Riding Privileges

People ride horses and ponies in a variety of locations across the country. Some places to ride are private land (horse facilities, farms and ranches, arenas, cross-country courses, or fields and forestland owned by individuals, clubs, or corporations), and some are public land (public arenas and show grounds; and beaches, city, county, state, or national parks).

We can have places to ride our horses only through the courtesy of landowners (both private and public). It is very expensive and quite difficult to acquire land to use for horses and to operate a horse facility. In many areas, in order to have a horse facility the owner must apply to the local city council, get permission, be approved, receive a permit, and pay fees, taxes, and insurance.

As horseback riders, we need to be very courteous and grateful to the people who allow us to ride on their land. Without them, we would not have a place to ride. Landowners appreciate polite riders who thank them (in person and with thank-you notes) and greet them with pleasant smiles and waves. Many of them allow Pony Clubs to use their land for free or at a reduced rate because they enjoy watching "a happy child on a happy pony." But if riders are rude or careless, have accidents, cause damage, or become a nuisance, people get annoyed and may stop allowing riders to ride on their property. One rude rider can spoil it for everyone.

It is getting more difficult to keep horse facilities and riding land open as time goes on and cities are spreading into areas where farms and countryside used to be. Public parks (city, county, and national) have more people hiking, biking, and riding motorized vehicles like motorcycles and all-terrain vehicles (ATVs) on their trails. As motorcycles and ATVs become more popular, the rules can change and it becomes more difficult to find trails that are safe for horses. For this reason, it is important for horse people to stay active in the community and help to preserve our rights to ride on public land. A great place to start is your state or county parks department. They can tell you how to volunteer and be active in preserving our ability to ride on public land.

Here are some ideas on how to build a good relationship with a landowner where you ride:

- *Always ask* before riding on anyone's land.
- Treat the land and the landowners with respect. Be polite to hikers, bikers, and other trail users, and especially to landowners.
- Be a safe and responsible rider and follow the rules of the stable or facility.
- Pick up and carry out your trash and any trash you see. Clean up manure after your pony; if you trailer in, clean up around your trailer.
- If you or your pony cause any damage (such as breaking a fence rail), report it immediately, apologize, and offer to fix or replace it.
- Keep your stall, tack, and horse facilities clean and neat (as if a Horse Management judge will be inspecting!).

- Be polite, pleasant, and helpful, and be a good representative of your Pony Club.
- Offer to help! Have a work day at the barn or facility to clean up and get it in good shape to ride. Offer to help build jumps, clear trails, or paint fences.
- Have a party or barbecue for the landowners.
- Send a card or a thank-you note to the landowners for letting you ride there.

Think of some other things your club could do to show appreciation to landowners who allow you to use their property. And if you are lucky enough to be able to keep your horse at home, remember to thank your parents!

PART III

Pony Care and Management

5

Handling, Leading, and Tying Your Pony

When you are in charge of a horse or pony, whether he is your own pony or one you are riding or handling, you must know how to handle him right. Proper handling keeps you, other people, and the pony safe, and prevents accidents. It also makes it easier for the pony to understand what you want him to do and to behave with good ground manners.

Pony Handling

The first thing to know about ponies is that they scare easily. When all horses were wild, they had to be quick to spot anything strange or dangerous in order to run away from it. Ponies still use their eyes, ears, and noses to notice anything new, and if they are surprised or startled, the first thing they want to do is run. If a pony is startled or scared and can't get away, he might kick to defend himself.

A pony's eyes are on the sides of his head, so he can see all around him. However, he has two blind spots—one behind his rump and one right in front of his nose. If you come up to a pony in one of his blind spots without warning (for instance, if you walk up behind his rump or pop up under his nose), he can be startled and might try to get away or kick before he knows who you are.

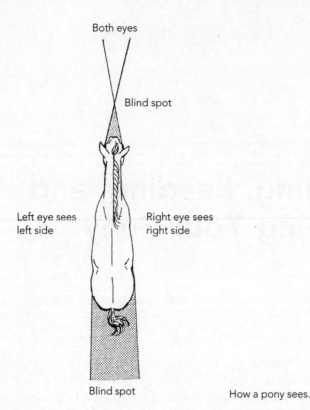

Both eyes

Blind spot

Left eye sees
left side

Right eye sees
right side

Blind spot   How a pony sees.

When you are around ponies, move slowly and speak quietly. Loud noises and sudden movements upset a pony. He can also get excited if he is in a strange place, or if something happens that he isn't used to. If your pony acts nervous, pat him and talk quietly to him to calm him down.

Some Rules for Safe Pony Handling

- Don't run, shout, or make loud noises around ponies. It upsets them and can scare them.
- Remember that some things that seem ordinary to people can scare ponies, especially if sudden movement is involved. Things like balloons, umbrellas, bouncing balls, or even a person on a bicycle can look like monsters to a pony if he isn't used to them.
- Watch out for your pony's feet. He doesn't always look where he steps, and he may step on your feet by accident if you are careless. Anyone working around ponies should wear strong shoes that give some protection—never

sandals, sneakers, or bare feet. (The *USPC Horse Management Handbook* describes approved footwear.)

- Stay away from the rear end of a pony unless you are working on him. He could switch his tail at a fly and whip it across your face, or kick at a fly and hurt you accidentally. It is safer to be near the front than the rear.

- When you are handling a pony around people who are inexperienced with ponies (especially small children), you have to be extra careful, watch out for them, and show them how to behave safely. Be polite, but be firm about safety rules for the safety of everyone.

Approaching a Pony

When you go up to a pony, speak quietly to him so that he knows you are there. Go toward his shoulder instead of straight toward his face or behind him. To make friends, let him sniff your hand; that is how he learns who you are. He will like it better if you stroke his neck or shoulder than if you try to pat his nose or face.

If a pony is tied to a fence or in a tie stall, you may have to approach from the rear. (It is always safer to approach from the front if you can.) Never come right up behind him (in his blind spot) because he might be dozing or not paying attention. Speak to him first, and wait until he turns his head and looks at you, so he knows you are there. Then put your hand on his hip (gently but firmly—don't tickle) and give him a voice command like "Tony, move over." As he moves over, you can walk up to his shoulder.

Approaching a pony safely from the front.

Approaching a pony safely from behind.

Putting on a Halter

When a pony is loose in a stall, he may not be wearing a halter. If he is well trained, he should turn his head toward you when you call him and stand quietly while you put the halter on. (You should have help getting your pony out until you know him well enough to handle him by yourself.)

Make sure the lead rope is snapped to the chin ring (the center ring) of the halter, unless it is necessary to attach it in a special way for extra control. Then follow these steps for putting on a halter:

1. Stand by the pony's left shoulder, facing forward.
2. Put a lead rope around the pony's neck, near the ears (or slightly down the neck). This will keep the pony still while you put on the halter.
3. For safety, make sure the lead rope does not hang below the pony's chest.
4. Hold the halter with the buckle in your left hand and the crownpiece in your right.
5. The pony's nose goes in the middle, between the noseband and chin-strap.
6. Slip the noseband over his muzzle.
7. Reach under the pony's neck with your right hand, pass the crownpiece over his poll, and buckle it behind his ears.

How to put on a halter.

Catching a Pony in a Field

Catching a gentle pony in a field is much like haltering him in a box stall. Here's what to do:

1. Call his name and walk slowly toward his shoulder, not toward his face or his hindquarters.
2. Wait until the pony looks at you so he knows you are there, then walk up and pat your pony quietly on the neck.
3. Put the lead rope around the pony's neck near the ears to hold him still while you put the halter on.
4. Put the halter on, as described in the previous section.

If your pony starts to walk away before you get up to him, do not chase him—instead, stop and wait. When the pony stops, call his name and hold out your hand. If your pony is alone in the field, offer him a treat or a little grain. This may help teach him to come when you call. However, do not give a treat until he has been caught and haltered.

Caution: Do not take treats or a bucket of feed into a pasture where there are other horses and ponies. This is not safe. They may crowd around you and get pushy.

Some ponies become hard to catch because they know that being caught always means they have to work. If you go out and catch your pony sometimes just to give him a treat and a pat and then let him go, he may learn that being caught means nice things, not just work. If your pony is still too hard to catch, ask your instructor for advice.

Leading a Pony

When you lead or hold a pony, *always* use a lead rope or lead shank, unless he is wearing a bridle. Never try to lead a pony, even for a short distance, by holding on to the halter without a lead rope. If he should act up, you might have to let go or you could be dragged. You could get hurt, your pony could get loose, and he could learn a bad habit.

Holding the Lead Rope

There are two ways to hold the lead rope with your leading hand:

1. Hold the lead rope in your fist with your thumb on top, about 6 inches from the halter ring.
2. Hold the lead rope with your thumb facing down, about 6 inches from the halter ring.

Here are some important safety precautions when handling a lead rope, no matter which method you use:

- Be careful not to let your hand and arm hang on the lead rope with a steady pull.
- If you are using a chain-end lead shank, hold the lead rope, not the chain. The chain can cause an injury if it gets pulled through your hand.
- The other hand should hold the rest of the lead rope folded up so it won't drag on the ground.
- NEVER loop a lead rope around your hand. If a pony spooks or takes off, the loops could tighten up around your hand and you could be hurt.
- NEVER let yourself get caught in a lead rope or tie it to yourself in any way—this is very dangerous!

Moving Forward, Turning, and Stopping

It is important that you work with your pony so that he has good manners. You may need help from your instructor or trainer. Your pony needs to stand quietly so that he knows how to wait in line, stand nicely for formal inspection, and stand for vet or farrier care. He needs to know how to back up in case you need to move him out of the way. He needs to know how to trot so that he can be checked for soundness and for other reasons. It is also good to practice leading your pony from both sides.

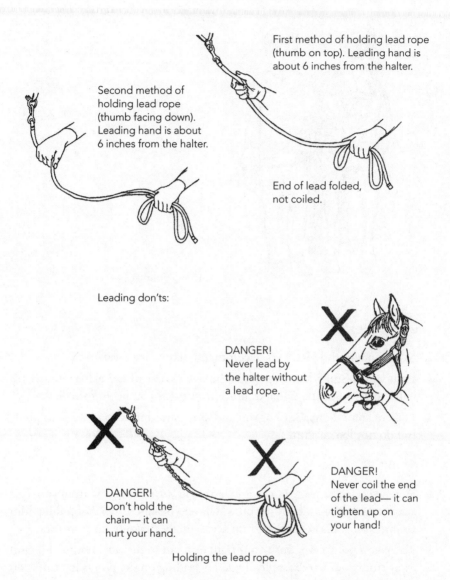

First method of holding lead rope (thumb on top). Leading hand is about 6 inches from the halter.

Second method of holding lead rope (thumb facing down). Leading hand is about 6 inches from the halter.

End of lead folded, not coiled.

Leading don'ts:

DANGER! Never lead by the halter without a lead rope.

DANGER! Don't hold the chain— it can hurt your hand.

DANGER! Never coil the end of the lead— it can tighten up on your hand!

Holding the lead rope.

When you want your pony to move, you must be in a leading position beside his neck, facing the front (forward). If you get out ahead of the pony, you can't see him or control him very well. If you turn around and face him, he may stop and pull back.

Leading position.

To move forward:

1. Say his name and give a voice command, like "Tony, walk on."
2. Push your leading hand forward (the one closest to the halter), under his chin, to give a gentle signal to move forward as you begin to walk.
3. Look at something ahead of you and aim toward it as you lead your pony, but do not look at him.

To turn:

1. When you lead a pony out of a stall or field, turn him away from you. It is safer to turn him away from you whenever you can, instead of pulling him toward you. This keeps him from accidentally stepping on your toes.
2. To make a pony turn, push your right arm out to the side, leading his chin away from you. For example, if you are leading on the pony's left side, you should turn right.

To stop:

1. To stop a pony or make him stand still, give a voice command, like "Tony, whoa," and stop walking.
2. Close your fist on the lead rope and hold your hand still. When he feels the pressure of the halter, he should stop.
3. If he does not stop, give a short tug and release down and backward.

4. If he tries to pull away instead of stand still, use short tugs and releases down and backward or sideways. Long pulls do not work—he will just pull harder against you.

5. When he stops, you should be standing at his side.

You can work on having your pony *stand square*. That means that all four hooves should be flat on the ground and evenly spaced, both front to back and side to side, like a square. He should remain quiet and relaxed.

Jogging Out

When you lead a pony in a straight line at a trot, it is called *jogging out*. This is sometimes done to check for lameness. Here's how to do it:

1. Hold the lead rope with your hand 6 inches from the chin ring.

2. Cluck to the pony or give a quiet voice command, like "Tony, trot."

3. Push your leading hand forward, under his chin and start to jog. (Some ponies can be lazy about trotting, so you may need to carry a whip. Please see the next section, "Training for Better Leading.")

4. Stay beside the pony's neck. If you get out ahead of him and pull, that will usually make him hang back and get stubborn.

Safe way to turn a pony—away from leader.

5. When he begins to trot, aim straight ahead at something and jog beside him in a straight line.

6. When you want to walk, give a quiet voice command like, "Tony, walk," and slow down to a walk yourself.

7. Close your fingers on the reins or lead rope, applying pressure to the halter or bit, then relax the pressure as he comes back to a walk.

Backing Up

There are many times you will need to ask your pony to back up. When asking a pony to back up while leading, turn and face him. Then step forward toward the pony, applying pressure to the reins to guide the pony to back up. Say "Back" as you do this. The pony should back up in a straight line and stop when you do. Be sure to release the pressure as he steps back.

Training for Better Leading

Some ponies need training to move forward properly when they are led. To teach your pony to move out freely at a walk or a trot, you can use a long stiff training whip (about 4 feet long). Here's how to train your pony to move out freely when he is led:

1. Put the pony beside a safe fence or wall so that he will have to go straight.

2. When leading from the left side, hold the lead rope or rein in your right hand, and the end in your left.

3. Carry the whip in your left hand, with the tip trailing on the ground behind you.

4. With your pony walking, give a quiet voice command to trot, and push your lead hand forward as you start to jog.

5. If he does not trot, tap once on his hindquarters by flicking the whip sideways behind you. Tap just hard enough to make him trot, not enough to scare him or make him leap forward. You must tap him within one second of giving the trot command, or he will not understand.

6. When your pony trots, be careful not to pull back on him. Jog with him and praise him right away.

7. Bring the pony back to a walk, and try again. If he trots on command, praise him and don't use the whip. If he is lazy, tap just enough to get him to trot, and then praise him.

You can use this same method to teach a pony to walk out freely from a halt instead of hanging back.

Using a whip to teach a pony to trot on command.

Another way to train a pony to lead is to have a helper follow the pony, giving him a little tap with a whip on the hind leg if he hangs back or does not respond to your command. The helper must be calm and quiet, and must not tap too hard or scare the pony. You want the pony to pay attention to his leader, not to be afraid of your helper. The helper must also be careful not to get within kicking distance.

A well-trained pony can be led from either side. You should practice leading your pony from the right side as well as the left, so that he gets used to seeing you on that side as well.

When leading from the right side, hold the rein or lead rope in your left hand the same as you would with your right. Since most people are more used to handling ponies from the left side, it may take some practice before you can lead as well from the right side as you can from the left. It may take your pony some time to adjust, too.

Tying a Pony

It is very important to tie your pony safely because he could get loose or be hurt if he is tied in the wrong way. A well-trained pony stands quietly when he is tied up. However, if a pony gets frightened when he is tied up, even a well-trained pony may pull back very hard. This can be unsafe for him and for anyone around him, especially if he is not tied properly. If your pony is nervous about being tied up or if he is hard to handle, ask your instructor for help, and don't try to tie him up on your own until he has had more training.

A pony must always be tied up with a halter and tie rope, *never* with a bridle. If he pulls back against his bridle, the bit will hurt his mouth and the bridle or reins may break. Never fasten a tie rope to your pony's bit, or loop his reins over something to tie him up.

Always tie your pony in a safe place. Tie him to a solid object that cannot be pulled loose, broken off, or moved by even the strongest horse. (For example, tie him to a solid fence post, not to a board that could be pulled off the fence.) Be sure there is nothing close by that he could get hurt on or catch his foot in if he should paw, like a wire fence or a nail sticking out of a post. Be sure that there is enough space around him for you to work safely.

Use a good tie rope that will not slip or jam. A cotton, Dacron, or hemp rope is good. Watch out for nylon—nylon ropes can slip loose and flat nylon lead shanks can jam so that they are very hard to untie. Never tie a pony with a chain lead shank—this is only for leading, not for tying. A leather lead shank may break if a pony pulls back, and a pony must *never* be tied with a chain over his nose or under his chin. If he pulls back, he could be injured.

A pony should be tied at about the level of his back. If he is tied lower down, he can injure his neck if he pulls back. He should be tied so that he can turn his head and look around, but not with enough slack to get his foot or his head caught in the rope. About 18 inches from the knot to the snap of the rope is

Tied to solid object, using a safety string
Tied with a halter and tie rope, with quick-release knot
Tied at height of withers, with about 18 inches from knot to halter
Tied in a safe place

Pony tied safely.

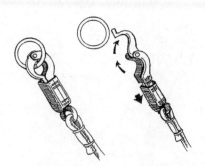

Safety string: a loop of twine that will hold for ordinary tying but will break loose in an emergency.

Panic snap: a special snap that can be released quickly even during a strong pull.

Safety devices for tying.

usually a good safe length for tying. If the snap of the rope reaches to the ground, the rope is too long—the pony could catch his front leg in it.

Sometimes for safety, you may need to use a *safety string* when you tie up a pony. This is a loop, or several loops, of twine. The twine can be made of jute, plastic, or nylon strands. The safety string is tied around the post or ring and you tie the lead rope to it. It is strong enough to hold your pony for ordinary tying, but it will break if he gets scared or pulls back really hard. If this happens, the tie rope could get pulled so tight that you would not be able to untie it. Do not make so many loops that the twine will not break if the pony pulls really hard. It is better to have to catch your pony than to have him get seriously hurt.

A *panic snap*, or *breakaway snap*, is a special snap that can be used on a tie rope or cross-ties. It is made so that you can release a pony even when the rope is being pulled tight. The breakaway snap should be on the tie ring, and the regular snap should be on the end that snaps to the pony's halter.

When you tie a pony, always use a *quick-release knot*. This kind of knot lets you pull on one end and untie a pony quickly if you have to. Other kinds of knots could jam so tight that you would not be able to get them loose, or they may slip and untie by accident.

To tie a quick-release knot, follow these steps:

1. Tie a safety string around the post or through the tie ring.
2. Pass the running end (the end not connected to the chin ring) of the rope through the safety string.
3. Make a circle around the tie rope.
4. Push the doubled end of the rope through the circle and pull it snug. To release the rope, pull on the long end.

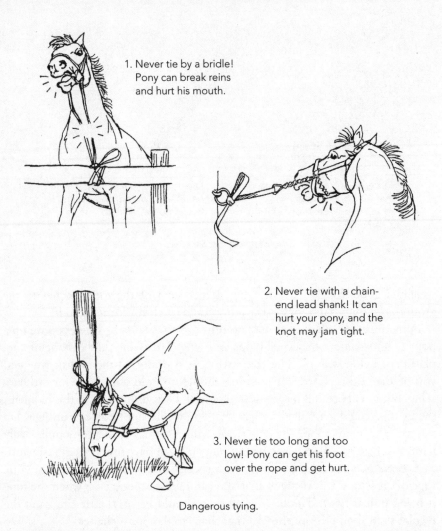

1. Never tie by a bridle! Pony can break reins and hurt his mouth.

2. Never tie with a chain-end lead shank! It can hurt your pony, and the knot may jam tight.

3. Never tie too long and too low! Pony can get his foot over the rope and get hurt.

Dangerous tying.

If your pony might chew on the rope end and release himself, tuck the end of the rope back through the loop.

Another way of tying a pony is to *cross-tie* him with two tie ropes, or *cross-ties*. One runs from each side of his halter to a ring on the wall with a quick-release knot and a breakable safety string or a panic (breakaway) snap. The cross-ties should not be too high (about the height of the pony's back). This is a good way to have a pony stand still while you groom him.

Cross-ties are often used in a stable aisle, where other people may be working. If your pony is cross-tied and someone needs to lead another pony past, unsnap the cross-ties and move him over. Never try to go under cross-ties when you are leading a pony. Don't leave a pony unattended in the cross-ties—if something should happen to make him pull back, he could get into trouble.

Use a safety string (a loop of twine tied through the ring or around the post).

Step 1: Put end of rope through string loop.

Step 2: Wrap end once around rope, making a circle.

Step 3: Slip doubled end through circle.

Step 4: Make knot snug. (To release, pull on rope end.)

To keep pony from untying himself, tuck rope end through loop.

How to tie a quick-release knot.

Pony on safe cross-ties with safety strings.

Getting Ready to Ride

Before you ride, you will need to halter your pony, tie him up safely, groom him clean, pick out his feet, and tack him up (put his saddle and bridle on). It saves time if you go and get your tack, grooming tools, riding helmet, and anything else you need before you get your pony out.

A Pony Club member carrying her tack properly set up.

How to Carry Tack

It is easier to carry tack if you set it up properly first. The stirrups should be run up, and the girth should be unbuckled and laid across the seat of the saddle with the ends tucked through the stirrup irons. The saddle pad should be over the top of the saddle. Your bridle and reins can hang on your shoulder so you have both hands free to pick up and carry your saddle.

A saddle should be set down on a saddle rack, or something like a fence rail. Be careful not to put it on something that will scratch the leather underneath. If you must set it on the ground, set it on the front end, with the cantle leaning against a wall. Put the girth between the cantle and the wall, to keep the cantle from getting scratched. The pad should be on top of the saddle, out of the dirt. The bridle should be hung up by the top (the crownpiece), or carefully laid across the saddle.

Don't let the girth or reins drag on the ground when carrying your tack. They will get dirty, and you or your pony could step on them and trip. Your tack should not be left where your pony could knock it down, step on it, or chew it.

Your Pony Must Be Clean

Before tacking up, make sure your pony is brushed clean, especially his back, girth, elbows, head, and any place the tack will touch him. If there is dirt, dried sweat, or burrs under his tack, he could get a sore. Run your bare hand over

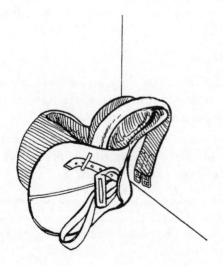

How to set a saddle on the ground.

those places—they should feel soft and smooth. If you feel dirt, dried sweat, or a rough spot, make sure you get it clean and smooth before you tack up. The saddle pad and girth must also be clean, smooth, and dry, or they could make him sore.

Tacking Up

Your pony should be tied up with a halter. A pony must *never* be tied up by his bridle or left with a bridle on even for a minute. He could step on his reins or catch his bridle on something. It makes sense to saddle him first and only bridle him when you are ready to ride. You can leave him tied safely with his saddle on for a few minutes while you get your hat or do something else, but after he is bridled, you can't leave him.

Saddling a Pony

1. The saddle pad goes on first. Put it on a little forward, in front of the withers and slide it back to just over the withers and back, so that the hair is smooth underneath.

   - The front of the saddle pad should be 2 or 3 inches in front of the saddle. If you get the saddle or pad too far back, start over. Don't push the saddle or saddle pad forward as this roughs up the hair underneath and will be uncomfortable for your pony.

   - Some people leave the saddle pad attached to the billets all of the time. This saves time when saddling, but you must be sure the saddle pad is clean and properly attached. After riding, the pad should be taken off to be washed and laid out to dry.

2. Set the saddle gently on the saddle pad.

   - The saddle should sit in the "hollow" behind the pony's withers. If it is too far back, the girth won't reach around him. If it is too far forward, it will tip up in the front and may pinch the pony's shoulders.

   - Pull the front of the pad up into the gullet of the saddle—this makes an air space over the pony's back and keeps the pad from slipping backward. It also keeps it from pressing down on the withers.

3. Go to the pony's right side (*off side*) and fasten the saddle pad so it won't slip out of place while you are riding. The tab should slip over one of the billets, or it may have a Velcro fastener. The buckle guard goes below the saddle pad tab.

4. Still on the right side, buckle the girth to the first and last billets, about halfway up.

   • Remember—bring the girth up through the saddle pad loop.
   • Pull the buckle guard down over the girth buckles.
   • While you are on the right side, check to see that everything is smooth and in the correct place.

5. Go back to the pony's left side (*near side*) and fasten the saddle pad tab or attachment the same way you did on the right.

6. Bring the girth under the pony's belly, taking care to keep it smooth and straight.

7. Buckle the girth to the first and last billets. It should be snug enough to keep the saddle from slipping, but not yet tight.

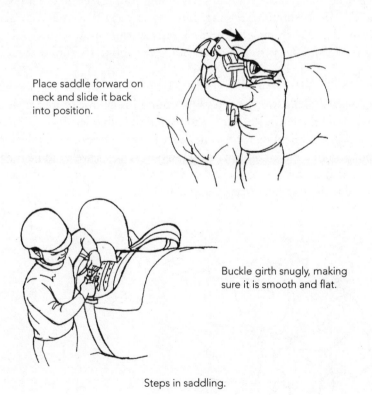

Place saddle forward on neck and slide it back into position.

Buckle girth snugly, making sure it is smooth and flat.

Steps in saddling.

Tightening the Girth

Some ponies *blow up,* meaning they take a big breath while you are tightening the girth, then let it out later, so the girth will be loose. This usually comes from having the girth pulled up very tight and hard, which makes them uncomfortable.

Never hit or kick a pony to make him let out his breath. This can make him hate being saddled, and it might teach him to bite or kick you instead of just blowing up. Instead, take up the girth a little, then untie him and turn him around in a circle. He will forget to hold his breath, and you can tighten the girth a bit more. If you girth him up smoothly and gently, he will learn that you won't hurt him and he may get easier to saddle. Be patient and gentle with your pony when you are tacking up.

For riding, the girth must be snug enough to keep the saddle safely in place, but no tighter than necessary. Very tight girths are uncomfortable and can cause saddle sores. However, a girth that is too loose can cause your saddle to slip, which is dangerous. Check the girth by slipping your fingers under it just below the saddle flap. It should feel snug, but not so tight that you can't get your fingers inside. A girth may loosen as a pony warms up, so you should check your girth again after you have been riding for about 15 minutes and before jumping.

After you have tightened the girth, pick up your pony's front foot and pull his leg forward. This stretches the skin around his elbow, so that it won't get pinched under the girth. Remember to stretch the other leg, too.

If you will not be riding for a while, leave the girth one or two holes loose, so your pony will be more comfortable. However, *never* leave a saddle on a pony with the girth undone or so loose that the saddle could slip off his back. If he moves suddenly, this can cause an accident.

How to check the girth.

Stretching a foreleg.

Running Up Stirrups

For safety's sake, English stirrups *must always be run up whenever the rider is out of the saddle.* This keeps them from catching on things, banging into the pony, or hitting you. If a pony should bite at a fly on his side, he could catch his teeth on a loose-hanging stirrup iron and get hurt.

Here's how to run up your stirrups:

1. Hold the top strap of the stirrup leather.
2. Take the iron and turn it a little, then slide it up the bottom strap (the one next to the saddle) until it touches the stirrup bar.
3. Pull the stirrup leathers down through the iron so that it lies flat. (Do this on both sides of the saddle.)

Always run your stirrups up (on both sides) as soon as you dismount, and any time you see them hanging down on a saddle that is not in use.

Here's how to pull down your stirrups:

1. Put your hand on the bottom of the stirrup iron and turn it a little, so it will slide more easily.
2. Pull it down to the bottom of the stirrup leather.

How to pull stirrup irons down.

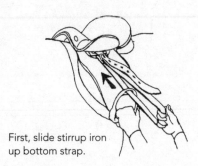

First, slide stirrup iron
up bottom strap.

Then, put all stirrup
leathers down through
stirrup iron.

How to run stirrups up.

Bridling a Pony

Before you put the bridle on, make sure the noseband and throatlatch are
unbuckled and all parts of the bridle are straight. Unbuckle the halter, slip it off
the pony's nose, and re-buckle it around his neck. This keeps him tied up while
you are bridling him. (If your halter has a throat snap, it is not as safe to unsnap
the halter and slide it off over the pony's head. This leaves him loose for a few
seconds, and he could get away from you with nothing on his head.)

Here are the steps for bridling a pony:

1. Unbuckle the crownpiece of the halter, slip the pony's nose out of the halter, and re-buckle the crownpiece on the pony's neck so he will be tied by
   the halter and lead rope while you put on his bridle.

2. Put the reins over the pony's head so they won't drop on the ground where
   you or the pony could step on them.

3. Stand close to your pony's neck on his left side, facing the front. If his head
   is low enough, you can put your right arm over his head and hold the top
   of the bridle (crownpiece) in your right hand.

4. Rest the bit on the fingers of your left hand. Bring the bit up to the pony's mouth and gently squeeze the side of his lip with your thumb.

5. As he opens his mouth, pull on the top of the bridle with your right hand, sliding the bit into the pony's mouth. Your fingers never go into his mouth.

6. Once the bit is in, slip the crownpiece gently over the right ear and then the left. Be careful not to twist his ears or hurt his face with the bridle. Make sure the bit is resting evenly in the pony's mouth before buckling up any bridle parts.

7. Buckle the throatlatch under his throat—not too tight. (You should be able to get four fingers underneath it.)

8. Buckle the noseband (inside the cheekpieces) so that it is snug but not too tight. The noseband should be level, not twisted, and you should be able to slip one or two fingers between the noseband and the pony's face.

9. Run your fingers underneath the browband and crownpiece to be sure the bridle fits comfortably, and pull the forelock out so that it is free of the bridle.

Note: You should be able to slip a finger under all parts of the bridle, and a fist should fit between the throatlatch and the pony's cheek.

If your pony is high-headed or if you are short, you may not be able to get your arm up over his head. Instead, put your right arm around your pony's face with your hand on his nose, as if you were giving him a hug. Hold the sides of the bridle (the cheekpieces) together in your right hand on top of his face, while your left hand offers him the bit and gently squeezes his lip. When he takes the bit, hold the bridle up with your right hand.

You may have to put the crownpiece over his left ear first and then his right. The ears are sensitive, so be careful and gentle so you don't make your pony *head shy,* or hard to handle around the head.

Halter around pony's neck before bridling.

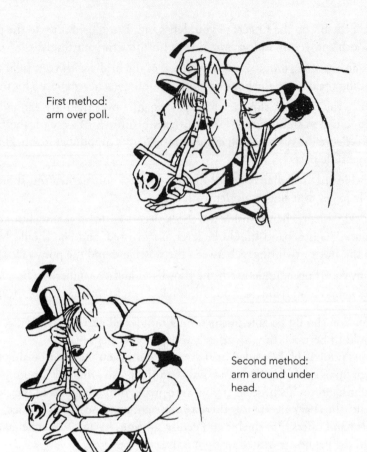

First method:
arm over poll.

Second method:
arm around under
head.

Bridling.

If your pony is hard to bridle, you should have help with bridling until he learns to put his head down and is easy to bridle, or until you get better at it. If you keep having trouble bridling him by yourself, he may learn to hate bridling because it is uncomfortable for him. This can make a pony head shy.

Leading a Pony When Tacked Up

When you lead a pony who is tacked up, handle him with the bridle reins. The stirrups should be run up and the reins should be taken over his head, which gives you more control when leading him. Standing on the left side beside his

Young children need help and supervision when bridling a pony.

neck, hold the reins with your right hand about 6 inches from the bit. Your left hand holds the end of the reins, folded up so they won't drag on the ground.

You lead the pony the same way you do with a lead rope, but remember that the reins are attached to the bit in the pony's mouth, so be gentle. Never let the reins drop on the ground. If a pony steps on a rein, he may give his mouth a bad jerk, and he could break his bridle. Don't let a pony eat grass when he is bridled, or he will soon get into the habit of stopping to eat grass whenever he wants to.

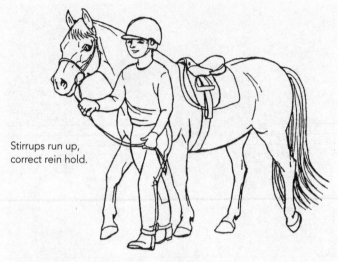

Stirrups run up,
correct rein hold.

Leading a pony while tacked up.

Care after Riding

After a ride, you must untack your pony and put him away cool, clean, and comfortable. You should also take care of your tack and leave the stable area neat and clean. You can always tell good horse people by the way they take care of their animals after riding.

Cooling Out

At the end of a ride, walk your pony around to let him relax and cool out. You can ride him quietly at a walk or get off and lead him.

1. When you dismount, the first thing to do is run your stirrups up (see the earlier section, "Running Up Stirrups").

2. Next, loosen the girth one or two holes so your pony can be comfortable. This should be done as soon as you dismount, before you lead your pony back to his stall, or wherever you untack.

Untacking

Unbridle your pony first, so you can tie him up while you finish untacking and caring for him. Here's how to unbridle:

1. Buckle the crownpiece of the halter around your pony's neck so he will be tied by the halter and lead rope while you remove his bridle.
2. Unbuckle the noseband and throatlatch.
3. If your bridle has a curb chain, unfasten the curb chain on the left side.
4. Slip the crownpiece and reins gently over his ears, and be careful not to let the bit bang his teeth as it comes out.
5. Unbuckle the halter and slip it over his nose in the normal way, then buckle it up again.
6. Hang up your bridle on a peg or a fence post. Don't drop it on the ground.
7. Rinse off the bit as soon as possible.

Then unsaddle your pony. Here's how to unsaddle:

1. Unbuckle the girth on the left side and undo the tabs from the billets, then go around and unbuckle the girth and undo the saddle pad on the right side.
2. Put the girth over the seat of the saddle.
3. Put your hand under the saddle, pad and all, and lift it up and toward you.
4. Hang the wet saddle pad up separately to dry, or put it upside down over the saddle. Do not leave a saddle sitting on a wet saddle pad—the pad will mat down and stay damp.
5. Clean your girth and saddle as soon as possible.

Caring for Your Pony after Riding

After you untack your pony, you should make him comfortable. If your pony has worked hard and is hot and sweaty, he will need special cooling out care. (See pages 177–179 for more about how to cool out a hot pony.) If he has damp or sweaty places, like the "saddle mark" and girth areas, he should be rubbed with a towel and brushed until his coat is smooth. Pick out his feet and check for stones or loose shoes.

If your pony is kept in a stall, he should be put away clean, dry, and comfortable, and he should have a fresh bucket of water. If he is kept outside, he can be turned out in his field. Ponies often like to roll after they have been ridden. This is their natural way of grooming themselves and scratching itchy places.

Turning a Pony Out

To safely let a pony loose in his stall or in a pasture, lead him through the gate and turn him around so that he is facing the gate or stall door. Lead him in straight so he doesn't hit his hip. Close the gate or door behind you before you let him go. Make him stand for a moment, then quietly unbuckle his halter and slip it off.

Never chase a pony or encourage him to take off and run when you let him go. This teaches him bad manners, he could kick at you, and he may learn to pull away before you are ready.

For safety, the halter should be removed whenever a pony is loose in a stall or in a pasture. A pony can catch a halter on a fence, on something that sticks out, or even on his shoe. If his head is caught he will struggle and may be badly hurt if the halter does not break. If you must leave a halter on your pony, it should be a safety halter that has a breakable leather crownpiece or a special safety release that will let go if he should get caught. (Please see the *USPC Horse Management Handbook* for rules about the use of halters at Pony Club rallies.)

Whenever you put on or take off a halter, you should unbuckle it. Don't unsnap the throatlatch and slip it over the pony's ears. This can irritate the pony's ears and make him head shy, and it gives you less control.

How to turn a pony out safely.

Finishing Up

After you have taken care of your pony, you should leave your tack and the stable area neat and clean. The tack should be cleaned after every ride. (See chapter 12, "Tack," for more about how to clean and care for your tack.) If you don't have time to do a thorough cleaning, at least rinse off the bit and dry it with a towel, and wipe the sweat and dirt off the saddle, bridle, and girth with a damp sponge. Hang the damp saddle pad up to dry, and cover the saddle with a towel or dust cover to keep it clean.

Your grooming tools should be cleaned and put away in your grooming kit, and you should sweep or rake the aisle and pick up any manure or trash before you leave. Hang up your pony's halter and rope where it belongs—on his stall or next to the gate of his field.

Note to Parents

Tacking and Untacking

It is important for children to have help and supervision when tacking up and untacking until they are old enough, big enough, and competent to manage on their own. For your child's safety, it is essential that the saddle and bridle be put on correctly every time she rides.

Teach your child to be gentle, deliberate, and patient when tacking up, and avoid all rough methods. Even with kind and gentle horses and ponies, rough or awkward handling during tacking up can upset and annoy the animal. This often leads ponies to develop tricks and defenses that can make them harder to tack up and become unsafe.

6

Taking Care of Your Pony

Because our continent is so large and different regions have different climates, there are different ways of keeping and managing ponies in North America. You might have to handle cold winters in the North, hot and humid weather in the South, dry heat and wind in the Southwest, or other conditions where you live. Keeping a pony on a western ranch, on a horse farm, in a boarding stable, or in your own backyard are all different ways of horse-keeping, but they can be equally good. There is no single "correct" North American method of stable management. However, there are some things that are basic to all good pony care and management, wherever you live.

You will need advice from experts who know about special aspects of pony care and management where you live. Your veterinarian is a good expert to call on. So is your instructor or District Commissioner. Your county Cooperative Extension office has pamphlets (usually free or at low cost) on horse and pony management, feeding, health, pastures, plants, and building stables and fences.

At the Pony Club D Level, you will learn about basic pony care and should begin to do as much daily care as you can. However, you will need to know more about pony care and management before you are ready to take over the care of a pony on your own. An experienced horse person should supervise your pony's care and management, show you how to care for your pony, and help you with any problems.

Stable, Pasture, or Both?

There are three ways to keep a pony: stabled, in a pasture, or a combination (stabled part of the time and in pasture part of the time). Each has good points and drawbacks. Keeping a pony stabled means more daily work, because you will have to do more chores (feeding, stall cleaning, turnout, and so on) and make sure your pony is exercised every day, whether you ride or not. It may also cost more to build or rent a stall and to supply bedding. However, your pony is always there when you want to ride him, and he can be kept cleaner.

A pastured pony lives a more natural life. He can graze and exercise when he wants to, and he is less likely to be too frisky or develop bad habits (*stable vices*) from being closed in and bored. However, he will still need daily visits for feeding, care and pasture maintenance, and he may be hard to catch or covered with mud when you want to ride. Pasturing also requires more land, good fencing, and a shed or shelter, and you will have to provide hay whenever there is not enough good grass. If you have a stable that opens onto a pasture or paddock, you may be able to let your pony go in and out as he pleases. Then you may need to feed and water him inside, clean his stall, and keep him in his stall when you want him inside.

Boarding Your Pony

Many people keep their ponies in a boarding stable because they do not have a good place to keep them at home. In a boarding stable you pay for the rent of the stall, use of the facilities (like riding rings, trails, and tack room), feed, and bedding, and for having your pony fed and watered for you. Some boarding stables offer complete care, including stall cleaning, daily turnout, grooming, and other services. Others charge less if the owner helps with the daily care of the pony. In Pony Club, you may be doing some care, so you should be prepared to go to the stable every day and do some work for your pony, whether you ride that day or not. If you board your pony, your parents and an experienced horse person (like your instructor) should visit the stable with you to see if it offers good care and stable management. It must be a safe and friendly place for you and your pony.

Exercise

All horses and ponies need exercise for their health and happiness. They developed over millions of years as free-roaming creatures. Keeping a pony in a stall without exercise is one of the worst things you can do to him. A pony must be physically fit before you can do hard work without causing injury. If he stands around all week, he will be soft and unfit. It is unfair to him and can hurt him if you work him too hard on the weekend. If you can, try to ride your pony at least a little bit every day, and make sure he has plenty of time turned out in a pasture or paddock or gets some other kind of exercise when you can't ride.

Warming Up

Every time you ride a pony, he needs to be warmed up slowly. Start out by walking for the first 15 minutes. While you are walking, you can practice halts, turns and circles, or other exercises, or you can enjoy a short trail ride. After 15 minutes, your pony can begin trotting and later cantering. This is important to get his heart pumping strongly and his muscles loosened up and ready to work. If you started right out with hard work, he could pull a muscle and go lame.

Exercise or Work?

Your pony's daily work might include ordinary riding, lessons, trail rides, Pony Club rallies, Pony Club mounted meetings, or other activities like competitions or special events. It is best if a pony is ridden five or six days a week (with one day off), but he should be ridden at least three times per week to keep him fit enough for ordinary riding. If your pony is *soft* (not physically fit for ordinary work), you will have to build him up slowly by exercising him a little every day and gradually increasing his exercise, riding him a little longer and working him a little harder each day. To do this, you will need help and advice from your veterinarian and from an experienced horse person who can tell you what your pony needs to get fit and how much work it is safe to do with him. This is important, as your pony can be injured or get sick if you don't condition him properly. (*The United States Pony Club Manual of Horsemanship: Intermediate Horsemanship [C Level]* covers conditioning in more detail.)

There are several ways to exercise a pony when you can't ride him for some reason. If he is turned out in a pasture, he can exercise himself. Turning a pony out for an hour or more before you ride can let him get rid of his extra energy so he will be less frisky when you ride him. Longeing is another way to exercise a pony, but this *must* be done by an experienced horse person who can longe safely and correctly. (Pony Club recommends that longeing be done only by experienced members at the C-3 Level or higher, not by D Level members.) If a pony cannot be ridden or turned out (for instance, if he is lame or if the footing is not usable for riding or turnout), you can lead him in hand for half an hour or so.

Cooling Out a Pony after Work

When a pony works hard he gets hot and sweaty, just as you do when you run and play hard. He *must* be cooled out properly, or he may get chills, develop muscle cramps, or even colic (a painful and serious bellyache). He should always be put away cool, dry, clean, and comfortable after a ride. Cooling out is one of the most important things you can do for your pony.

Basic Cooling Out

Every ride should end by walking your pony for at least 10 to 15 minutes to gradually let his body come back to normal, which helps prevent sore muscles and other injuries. You can ride at a relaxed walk, or dismount and lead him around. (Remember to run up your stirrups and loosen the girth a hole or two when you dismount.) How is his breathing—is he puffing and are his nostrils open wide? Notice how hot and sweaty he feels on his neck and chest, and if the small veins are sticking out under his skin. He is not completely cooled until all of these signs are back to normal, and he should keep walking slowly until he is completely cooled out.

You should lead your pony around to cool him out after hard work.

Water during Cooling Out

When a pony works or sweats (even a little), he loses water and electrolytes and needs to drink enough water to replace them. You may let him drink right away. Walk him some more and offer him another drink. It is important that you don't miss the time when he is thirsty and wants to drink. A good way to do this is to set out a bucket of water and walk your pony in a large circle nearby. Each time you go by the bucket, you can let your pony stop and take a drink, as this won't hurt him. By the time he is completely cooled out and dry, he should have had all the water he wants.

Covering a Pony while Cooling Out

A pony who is very hot should be allowed to cool down to a normal temperature before he is covered (but he should be kept walking while he cools). Covering him too soon keeps him too hot for too long and is not good for him. You will have to check his temperature often as you walk him, so you will notice when he has come back to normal. You can feel his chest. (If you aren't sure whether he is still hot, ask an experienced horse person to check him.) If the weather is cool or windy, she should be covered with a *cooler* (a big square blanket designed for cooling out), so he won't get a chill while his coat is still damp. An *anti-sweat sheet* is a special cover that looks like a fishnet. It helps a pony with a wet coat stay warm while he dries.

Don't cover a hot pony in warm weather. This can make him overheat and keep him from cooling down normally. Don't put a heavy winter blanket on a hot, sweaty pony in cold weather. He may stay too hot under the blanket and

Walking a pony under a cooler.

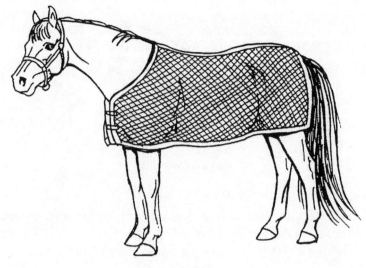

Anti-sweat sheet.

will get the blanket lining wet, which will make it damp and clammy for a long time. If he needs a cover while he is wet, use a cooler or an anti-sweat sheet instead. The blanket should be put on later, after he is dry.

Sponging and Scraping a Wet Pony

If a pony is quite wet and sweaty, you can use a sweat scraper to squeeze most of the water out of his coat. Rubbing the damp places with a towel or with a handful of dry straw will help them start drying. Scrape him quickly, and then get him walking right away. (In cool weather, cover him if he has cooled down to a normal temperature.)

In hot weather, a pony may need to be sponged or hosed off to remove sweat and dirt and to help him cool off. With a big sponge, wash away the sweat and dirt, then scrape the excess water from his neck and body with a sweat scraper. You can rub his head, legs, and other wet places with a towel to get them to start drying. After sponging and scraping, walk the pony until he is dry. You may need to repeat the sponging or hosing and scraping to cool off your pony if he is really hot.

When a pony has wet mud on his legs and belly, it sometimes works best to let it dry and then brush it away. If you brush wet, muddy legs you may scrape mud into his skin and start chapped skin or *mud cracks*. In cool weather, don't use water to clean mud off his legs—this can also cause chapped skin and

Using a sweat scraper.

painful mud cracks. In warm weather, you can wash his legs off with water, but be sure to dry them thoroughly afterward.

The following are signs that a pony is properly cooled out:

- His temperature is normal and his chest feels cool and dry (the same as his normal skin), and he is cool and dry everywhere else.
- His breathing is normal—he is not puffing and his nostrils are not wide open.
- The small veins of his face and neck are back to normal—not sticking out.

A pony should always be left clean, dry, and comfortable after riding. His feet should be picked out, and any sweat marks or mud should be brushed or sponged off. He should have had all the water he wants to replace the water he lost through working, sweating, and during cooling out. If you turn your pony out in a pasture or pen after riding, he may enjoy a roll, which allows him to scratch his itchy places and makes him feel good.

Care after Hard Work

When a pony has done especially hard work (like galloping), he may be very hot and tired. He needs special care and attention right away. As soon as you dismount, run up the stirrups and loosen the girth, but leave the saddle in place while you walk him. (You can lift the back of the saddle and pad for a moment to let air get to his back.) If he is very hot, don't cover him until his temperature has come back to normal.

After your pony has walked for about 10 minutes, stop and check his temperature. If he has cooled down to normal, untack him and quickly scrape his sweaty places. (In warm weather, he can be quickly sponged off and then scraped.) Pick out his feet and check for stones and loose or missing shoes. You should also feel each leg and check for cuts, heat, or swelling. Don't keep the pony standing still for long or let him get chilled while you untack or check his legs. If it is cold or windy, cover him, and get him walking again right away. Later, when he is cool and dry, you can check his legs more thoroughly and go over the rest of him while you are brushing him off.

In very hot and humid weather, a pony may not cool down to a normal temperature quickly enough. He may need to be sponged with water or even have ice applied. An experienced horse person must help you with this, as you could harm your pony if he is not cooled out properly.

A pony who has worked hard should be offered water every few minutes while he walks and cools out. It's important for him to drink all the water he needs to replace the fluids he lost through sweating during hard work. When he is cool and dry, he can be given hay and more water, but he should not be fed grain until he has been back to normal for at least an hour. When you do feed him grain, it should be a small amount (about half as much as usual). He can have the rest of his grain about two hours later. He should be checked over thoroughly for cuts, areas of swelling, or other injuries. All sweat marks should be brushed away before you leave him to rest in his stall or turn him out in his pasture to relax and graze.

After a ride, you should check your pony often for about two hours to see if his temperature has gone up (feel his chest and look at him) or if he is breaking out in a sweat again. If he is damp and sweaty, or if his ears feel cold and clammy, put on an anti-sweat sheet and rub him dry with a towel or several handfuls of dry straw. If the weather is very hot and humid, a pony may break out in a sweat again because it is too hot in his stall. If this should happen, check his temperature carefully and take him outside and walk him until he is cool and dry. If a pony is very hot, appears distressed, or does not cool out easily, you should get help from an experienced horse person (such as your instructor or a Stable Management judge at a rally).

Note to Parents

Warming Up and Cooling Out

It is essential for the pony's health and well-being that he is properly warmed up and cooled out each time he is ridden. Sometimes children neglect this because they are in a hurry to get on with the fun of riding, or because they are pressed for time when ending a ride and taking care of the pony. Children must be supervised by adults until they are sufficiently experienced and responsible, and even then adults should supervise.

The next day, your pony should be led out and jogged to check for lameness or stiffness, and his legs should be checked again for heat, swelling, or injuries.

Grooming Your Pony

There are several reasons to groom your pony:

- To clean him and make him look nice and feel comfortable.
- To check him over carefully for injuries and skin problems.
- To prevent sores from dirt under the tack when you ride him.
- To condition his skin and make his coat shine.
- To promote good circulation of the blood.

Your pony should be groomed or at least checked over every day, whether he is ridden or not. He must be cleaned before he is saddled to prevent dirt from causing saddle and girth sores, and he should be brushed smooth after he has been ridden. The best time to groom a pony thoroughly is after he has been ridden, when his skin is warm. However, for Pony Club mounted meetings, competitive rallies, and other special events, you are expected to have your pony clean and thoroughly groomed for inspection before riding. Your care and grooming of your pony before and after riding are both evaluated in Stable Management inspections.

Grooming Tools

Your grooming tools should be kept together in a grooming kit. The basic grooming kit should include the following tools:

- **Currycomb (rubber or plastic variety).** For loosening caked mud and dirt and rubbing the pony's skin. It should be flexible, not too hard and sharp. (Metal currycombs should be used only for cleaning brushes. They are too sharp to use on a pony's skin.)
- **Dandy brush or stiff brush.** For removing heavy dirt and dried mud. This is good for long coats and pastured ponies.
- **Body brush.** Has short bristles set close together to remove dirt, dust, and *scurf* (dried sweat and dandruff) from the coat and skin. This is the best tool to get a pony really clean!
- **Soft brush or finishing brush.** Has long, soft bristles to remove dust and for brushing sensitive parts such as the head and legs.
- **Hoof pick.** For picking out the feet.

- **Hoof brush.** Small, stiff brush for cleaning the feet (an ordinary scrub brush works well). Some hoof picks have a hoof brush at one end.
- **Sponges.** Use two smaller sponges for cleaning eyes, nose, lips, and dock. Use different colors or shapes or mark them "face" and "dock" so they won't get mixed up. Or use disposable (non-alcohol) baby wipes or wet wipes, which are more sanitary. Start by wiping the eyes, then the nostrils, then the lips with the baby wipe, then use it to wipe off the pony's dock. A larger sponge is used for washing the pony.
- **Mane comb or hairbrush.** For untangling the mane and tail (after picking out tangles with your fingers). Metal mane pulling combs are used only to pull or shorten the mane, because they break off too many hairs if used as a mane comb.
- **Stable rubber or towel.** Used to remove stains or for a final polish after grooming. This is also good for rubbing out sweat marks.
- **Water brush.** For wetting down the mane and tail and scrubbing away stains. (This can be a plastic scrub brush from the grocery store, or a special brush made for this purpose.)

There are some other things you may want to keep in your grooming kit, like a Styrofoam scraper block for removing botfly eggs, hoof dressing and a brush to paint it on with, a *cactus cloth* (a special grooming cloth for removing stains and sweat marks), and fly repellent.

Contents of grooming kit.

How to Groom a Pony

Before you start to groom your pony, he should be tied up correctly in a safe place. (See chapter 5, "Handling, Leading, and Tying Your Pony," for instructions on safe tying.) Don't try to groom a pony when he is loose in a stall or not wearing a halter. If he tries to move around or get away, you will have no control and you could get hurt.

After your pony is safely tied, follow these steps for grooming him:

1. Pick out his feet with the hoof pick. (For instructions on picking up the feet safely, see pages 216–219.) Use the hoof pick from heel to toe, so you won't accidentally dig it into the *frog* (the softer center part of the hoof) or jab yourself. Clean the cleft of the frog (the groove down the middle), and the spaces on each side of the frog. Use a hoof brush to brush the foot clean so you can check it thoroughly. Check that each shoe is tight and the *clinches* (the bent-over ends of the nails) are smooth.

2. Use the rubber or plastic currycomb to rub the skin in circles or from side to side, starting at the top of the neck and working back and down. Go easy on sensitive places. This tool breaks up caked mud, loosens scurf, and rubs and stimulates the skin, but it can be too harsh for some ponies. Don't use a currycomb on the head, lower legs, or anyplace that is especially sensitive.

3. Starting at the top of the neck, brush the coat with the dandy brush (or stiff brush) in the direction the hair grows. Use short, snappy strokes to get down to the skin and flick the dirt out. The dandy brush takes away the larger bits of dirt loosened by the currycomb. You can use this brush on the body, neck, and legs, and on the head if your pony doesn't mind. If your pony is very sensitive or if he has been clipped, use a softer brush.

4. The body brush is used to clean away dirt, dust, and scurf from the skin. Use short, firm strokes going the way the hair grows, with firm pressure to get between the hairs, right down to the skin. After every few strokes, clean the body brush by scraping it across the teeth of a metal currycomb, or use the dandy brush to clean it. This way, the dirt goes into the brush and then out into the air, not back on the pony. You can use the body brush all over your pony's body, head, and legs. It is the best brush for getting the coat really clean and shiny. Because it is soft, it can be used on clipped ponies and those with sensitive skin.

5. A soft brush or finishing brush, with long, soft bristles, may be used to remove dust. It is good for sensitive places like the face and legs, and for ponies whose coats have been clipped. It is not as efficient as a body brush at getting the skin and coat clean. Use it with long, smooth strokes.

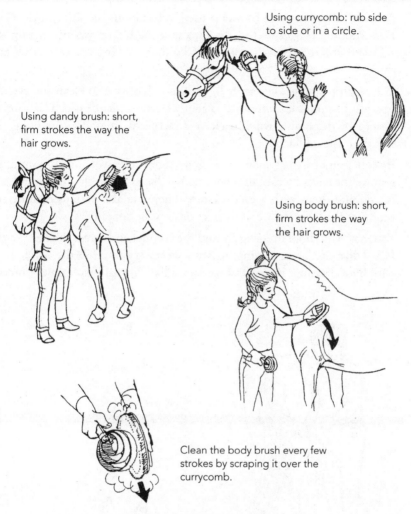

Using currycomb: rub side to side or in a circle.

Using dandy brush: short, firm strokes the way the hair grows.

Using body brush: short, firm strokes the way the hair grows.

Clean the body brush every few strokes by scraping it over the currycomb.

Steps in grooming a pony.

6. The mane and tail should be carefully picked free of tangles, taking just a few hairs at a time so you don't break off or pull out hairs. Part the hair and use the body brush to clean the skin and the roots of the hair one section at a time. You may use a hairbrush or a smooth plastic comb to brush the mane and tail hair, starting at the end of the hairs and working carefully up the tail. To be safe when you work on the tail, stand to one side, not right behind the pony.

7. A stable rubber or folded towel is used to bring out the shine of the coat. Firm rubbing (across and in the direction the hair grows) warms up the skin and spreads the skin oils over the hair, making the coat sleek and shiny.

8. Use a damp sponge, cotton ball, or disposable wipe to clean the eyelids, nostrils, and muzzle. You can also gently clean inside the ears. Use another sponge or disposable wipe to clean underneath the tail and around the sheath or the udder.

9. If your pony still has manure or grass stains after you finish grooming, remove the spots by rubbing them with a damp towel, shampooing them, or rubbing them with a cactus cloth. There are also various commercial products available (follow the directions on the container).

10. You may paint hoof dressing around the coronet and across the heels of the feet. For everyday grooming, it is not necessary to cover the whole hoof with hoof dressing. For special occasions like Formal Inspections, you can

Stand to one side while working on the pony's tail.

Wipe eyelids, lips, and muzzle with damp sponge. Use another sponge to clean the dock.

More grooming.

paint hoof oil over the whole hoof wall and coronet band. Be sure to wipe away any excess dressing with a paper towel so there is no sticky extra dressing left on the hoof or the heels.

11. For a final touch, wet your water brush and dampen the roots of the mane, and brush it neatly over to the right side of the neck. You can also dampen and brush down the hairs at the top of the dock.

Grooming a Pastured Pony

A pony who lives outdoors usually has healthy skin and hair and does not need to be groomed daily, except to get him clean for riding and for special occasions. He should be checked over and have his feet picked out every day, whether he is ridden or not, and his eyes, nose, and dock should be cleaned. In some parts of the country, a pony must be checked for ticks, especially in his mane and tail. Besides that, he will need only currying and brushing with the dandy brush to make his coat smooth. The body brush will not do much good on a pony who rolls every day, and you do not want to remove the natural grease and scurf from his coat, as it protects him from getting wet and cold. After riding, sweat marks should be brushed out or rubbed out with a towel or cactus cloth.

Controlling Flies

When horseflies, mosquitoes, or other biting insects are a problem, you may need to use a fly repellent to keep your pony comfortable. Fly repellents (fly sprays, wipes, roll-ons, and fly strips) have strong chemicals, so always use them according to the manufacturer's directions. Don't use them near your pony's eyes or get fly spray in his feed or water. Always wash your hands after using fly spray.

Other things you can do to keep biting flies away from your pony include using an ear net or ear bonnet, which covers his ears and forehead, or a fly mask (made of fine mesh that he can see through), which keeps flies out of his eyes (and sometimes covers his ears). If the flies are very bad, it may help to let him stay in his stall or in the shade during the day and turn him out at night. In some parts of the country, it may work better to keep him in at night and turn him out during the daytime. This depends on what kinds of flies, gnats, or mosquitoes are troublesome in your area.

Brush the coat with the dandy brush in the direction the hair grows. (You may need help with grooming.)

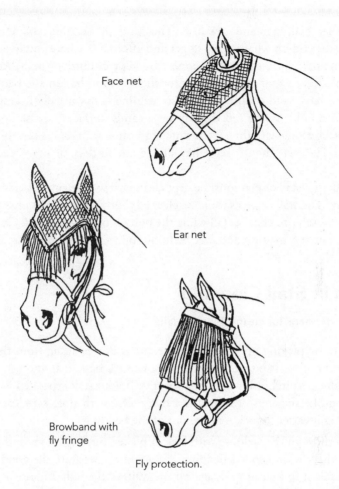

Face net

Ear net

Browband with
fly fringe

Fly protection.

Keeping your pony's stall as clean as possible at all times, keeping small paddocks free of manure, keeping manure piles or manure in muck buckets away from the stable, and not allowing food or sugary snacks or drinks out in the open will help control flies, too.

Stall Cleaning and Bedding

If your pony is kept in a stall, you will have to use some kind of bedding to keep his stall clean and dry and to give him a cushion to stand and lie down on. It is very hard on a pony's legs to stand on a hard surface like boards or concrete without enough bedding, and he can get sores on his legs if he lies down on a hard surface. There are many kinds of bedding, including straw, wood shavings, wood pellet bedding, and sawdust. The kind of bedding you choose will probably depend on what is easy to get and affordable where you live.

In some parts of the country, ponies are kept in outdoor pens. An outside pen should have a roof over part of it for shelter from the sun and bad weather. Most pens have sand or dirt footing, so bedding is not usually necessary. Hay and grain should not be fed directly on a sandy surface because ponies may swallow sand along with their feed, which can cause *sand colic*, a serious stomach problem. The pen should have hay and grain feeders to keep feed off the ground.

Your pony's stall or pen must be kept clean or it will become wet, smelly, and unhealthy. The stall or pen should be cleaned thoroughly at least once a day. (It is easier and safer to clean a stall while the pony is out.) When you clean a stall, you take out the manure and wet bedding, but any good bedding should be saved.

Steps in Stall Cleaning

Here are the steps for cleaning out a stall:

1. Begin by picking up all the manure and soiled bedding from the surface and throwing it into a wheelbarrow or muck basket. If you use straw for bedding, a pitchfork works best for this. If your stall is bedded with something like shavings or sawdust, a *stall picker* with tines set close together makes it easier to pick manure out of the bedding.

2. Sort through the bedding with fork or picker, turning it over and throwing out the wet and soiled bedding and manure. Separate the good bedding and pile it in a clean spot, against the walls of the stall. Be sure to find and clean out the wet spots.

3. If the pony will be out for several hours, you can dust the wet spots with lime and leave the floor bare. This lets the floor dry out and air. Lime helps to neutralize the ammonia found in urine and reduce the smell.

4. Before you put the pony back in his stall, you should "re-bed" it. Add just enough fresh bedding to replace what you took out, and mix it with the bedding you saved. Don't waste bedding, but use enough to give your pony a dry, comfortable cushion to stand and lie on. Spread it evenly over the floor, and bank it up higher against the stall walls and in the corners. This helps keep your pony from getting cast (stuck) if she rolls in her stall.

5. Some stalls have rubber stall mats. Since the stall mat provides some cushion for your pony's legs, you do not need to use as much bedding as you would in a regular stall. However, it is important to use enough bedding to soak up the urine and give the pony a clean, dry, and comfortable place to

lie down. Stall mats can also be used under hay feeders in outdoor pens on sandy ground, to keep ponies from eating hay from the ground and picking up sand, which can cause sand colic.

6. It keeps the stall and the aisle neater if you sweep the bedding back away from the doorway and from underneath the water bucket. Sweep or rake the stable aisle after you have finished cleaning and bedding the stall.

7. When you are cleaning a stall, notice anything that needs repairs or could hurt your pony (like splinters or nails sticking out) and take care of it right away. The feed tub should be cleaned, and the water bucket dumped, scrubbed, rinsed out, and filled with fresh water.

8. *Picking out* a stall means doing a quick pickup of manure instead of a thorough cleaning. If you pick out your pony's stall later in the day (besides cleaning it thoroughly), it will stay cleaner and save you work. It also saves bedding.

Stable Cleanliness and Manure Disposal

A neat and clean stable area is safer and healthier, has fewer flies, and is nicer for you, your pony, and your neighbors. Flies breed in manure, wet and rotting hay and bedding, and spilled grain. Besides keeping your pony's stall clean, remember to sweep or rake tack and feed rooms, barn aisles, and the area around

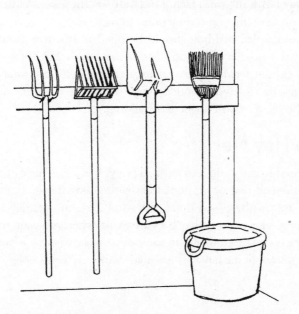

Stall cleaning tools. Left to right: pitchfork, stall picker, scoop shovel, broom, and muck basket. Always hang tools with points turned toward the wall.

Cleaning a stall. Bedding is banked around the edges to help keep the pony from getting cast if he rolls in his stall.

your stable every day. Muck baskets, forks, and rakes should be hung up safely out of the way (with the tines facing the wall), so the aisle is clear and safe. Put trash in a trash container, and remember to recycle!

Manure and soiled bedding should be piled neatly at a distance from the stable, so you will not have flies and odors around the stable. It can be composted and used as garden fertilizer, or you may arrange with a farmer or a manure removal company to have it hauled away. A manure pile generates heat, so it should not be piled against a wooden building.

Using a Hay Net

A *hay net* is used to carry and feed hay to a pony. It is a bag made of rope or plastic twine with one end that opens and closes with a drawstring. There are also hay bags, which are usually closed on all sides and have an opening on one side to allow for eating. Hay nets and hay bags are useful when you want to give hay to a pony when he is tied to a trailer or in some other place where it is not good to feed hay on the ground. Some hay nets are made with very small holes in the netting,

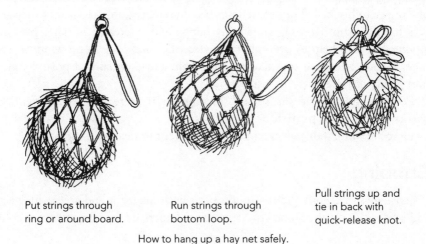

Put strings through
ring or around board.

Run strings through
bottom loop.

Pull strings up and
tie in back with
quick-release knot.

How to hang up a hay net safely.

which makes a pony take longer to eat his hay. This kind of hay net may be helpful for overweight ponies or those who eat up their hay too quickly.

To fill a hay net, open it up wide and stack several flakes of hay in it, then pull it up over the hay and close it by pulling the drawstrings.

Hay nets must be tied safely or they can cause accidents. The hay net hangs lower when it is empty, so remember to tie it a bit higher when it is full. If it's too low your pony could get his foot caught in it and be hurt. Don't tie a hay net to the same ring a pony is tied to. If he should pull back and pull the ring loose, the hay net would be attached to his halter rope and could scare him.

To tie a hay net safely, hang it at a height so that when it is full, the middle of the hay net is about eye level. When it is empty, the bottom of the hay net should be no lower than the point of the pony's shoulder, so the pony can't get a hoof caught in it. Pass the rope through a ring or over a board and run it back through one of the hay net sections at the bottom. Tie it with a quick-release knot so you can get it loose easily when it is empty. (See page 159 to learn how to tie a quick-release knot.)

Stable Vices

Stable vices are bad habits some ponies learn, usually out of nervousness or boredom. Ponies who are kept in stalls or pens most of the time often have them. They are not good for the pony and sometimes can cause health problems or damage to his stall. They sometimes become such strong habits that they are very hard to stop. Keeping your pony happy and interested in what goes on around him can help to prevent stable vices. Let him look out a window, see other horses, have stall toys like a rubber ball, and especially, if possible, give him plenty of time in the pasture.

Ponies with stable vices are usually showing that they are unhappy. Prevention works better than punishment.

Here are some stable vices and ways to prevent or deal with them.

Cribbing

When *cribbing,* a pony grabs a solid object with his teeth and arches his neck while he swallows air. Some cribbers suck so much air that they may get colic

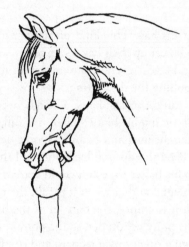

A cribber.

Cribbing strap (padded with fleece) worn to prevent cribbing.

or become thin and run down. A *cribbing strap* buckled tightly around the throat can be used to stop a pony from cribbing, but it does not cure the habit.

When a pony wears a cribbing strap, it must be taken off for an hour or two every day to let the skin underneath dry out and to keep sores from forming under the strap.

Wood Chewing

The pony chews on wood but does not suck in air. He can damage his stall, fences, or anything made of wood. A pony who chews wood may have a vitamin or mineral deficiency or may lack salt. He may also chew wood if he is hungry or is not getting enough hay, or if he is bored because he is kept in a stall or pen all the time. If your pony gets plenty of hay, vitamins, minerals, and salt, and is getting turned out enough but still chews wood, you can paint the wood with a bad-tasting coating that is made to discourage wood chewing. (Be sure that anything you paint on his stall is safe for ponies.)

Stall Kicking

Some ponies kick the walls of their stall when they are anxious to be fed, jealous of their neighbors, or upset. Some just seem to like to make noise. Hanging a rubber stall mat over the kicking area sometimes helps, as it cuts down on the noise and may prevent the pony from injuring himself.

Pawing

Some ponies paw, digging holes in their stall floors, when they are excited or waiting to be fed. Some do it for attention. Putting down a rubber stall mat may keep the pony from digging holes, even if he still paws.

Weaving

A *weaving* pony sways from side to side, swinging his head and shifting from one foot to the other. This habit is usually seen in nervous ponies. A stall screen with a U-shaped cutout lets the pony look out, but makes it hard for him to weave.

U-shaped stall screen to prevent weaving.

Stall Cards

Stall cards are important to have at home and anytime you take your pony anywhere. They provide quick access to information about your pony that may be important in an emergency situation, especially if you are not there or when your pony is stabled away from home. Anyone who notices that a pony is showing signs of discomfort or is in any kind of trouble can quickly notify the pony's rider, owner, or veterinarian by using the contact information on the stall card.

The *baseline vital signs*, which include temperature, pulse, and respiration (TPR), listed on the stall card tells what is normal for this pony. This information could save time, avoid confusion, and help a veterinarian evaluate the pony's condition and determine if treatment is needed.

Making a Stall Card

You may copy and use the following sample stall card or design your own. There is no single way to design a stall card, but it must have all the required information and be neat and organized so it can be easily read.

You can print up a stall card and put it in a plastic cover or have it laminated. Fasten it securely to your pony's stall door where he cannot reach it and damage it.

Information for Stall Card

Pony's name: _____
(Must be the same as on Coggins test, Equine release, health papers, and insurance)

Rider's name: _____
Rider's emergency contact information:
Phone number (area code) _____ Number _____
Work number (area code) _____ Number _____
Cell phone (area code) _____ Number _____
Staying at _____
Other contact information _____

Pony's information:
Age _____   Sex _____   Height _____
Baseline vital signs (taken at rest):
Temperature _____ degrees F   Pulse _____ beats/minute   Respiration _____ breaths/minute
Known allergies _____
Stable vices or handling notes _____
Photo of pony (without tack) or physical description _____
_____

Color _____   Breed _____
Markings _____

Emergency contact information:
Name of owner/agent of pony (must be of legal age): _____
Phone number (area code) _____ Number _____
Cell phone (area code) _____ Number _____
Staying at _____
Other contact information _____
Pony's regular veterinarian _____
Phone number (area code) _____ Number _____
Pony's regular farrier _____
Phone number (area code) _____ Number _____

Insurance information:
Is this pony insured? _____ (if yes, list insurance info in Notes section)
Name of insurance company _____
Phone number (area code) _____ Number _____
Policy number _____
Name of policyholder _____
Is pre-authorization required prior to treatment? _____

Notes

7

Nutrition and Condition

Your pony must be fed and watered properly every day in order to be comfortable and stay in good condition. This is one of the most important responsibilities for anyone who owns or takes care of a pony. As a Pony Club member, you should learn how to feed and water your pony safely, and know what your pony is fed, his feeding schedule, and some basic rules for feeding ponies. You also need to know what is considered good condition and notice if your pony is getting too fat or too thin. However, the complete care and feeding of a pony take more knowledge and experience than you can get from this book. If you own a pony, you must have help from your instructor or another experienced horse person with learning how to feed and take care of your pony.

Feeding and Watering

There are three ways to keep a pony: *stabled, in pasture,* or *stabled part of the time and in pasture part of the time.* A stabled pony is given all his feed and water in his stall. A pony living in pasture may get most or part of his feed from eating grass, but this depends on the kind of pasture he lives in, the climate, and the level of work expected of him. If the pasture does not have enough good grass (for instance, if it is too bare, weedy, or covered with snow), the pony will need extra feed.

Your Pony's Digestion

Horses and ponies have developed over thousands of years as grazing animals. Their stomachs are small, so their digestion works best when they eat small amounts often. (In nature, wild horses and ponies graze and move almost constantly.) They cannot handle a lot of food all at once, especially on an empty stomach. They need natural roughage (bulky food like grass or hay), and plenty of water at all times for good digestion.

A pony's digestion can easily get upset if he is not fed properly, and this can be serious. He can get *colic* (a bellyache), or *founder* (a condition that can cripple his feet). This is why it is so important to follow proper feeding practices.

Feeding Schedule

A pony should be fed on a regular schedule—at the same times every day. Ponies get used to regular feeding times. If they are not fed on time, they get upset, can become ill, or may damage the stall or injure themselves by kicking, banging on the stall, or chewing on wood.

Ponies need to eat small meals several times a day; never one big meal all at once. A stabled pony must be fed at least twice a day (three times a day is better). Some pastured ponies are fed only grain or extra hay once a day (depending on how much extra food they need and how they are managed), but they can graze as much as they need to.

Write down and post your pony's feeding schedule—what times he is fed and how much he gets for each feeding.

My Pony's Daily Feeding Schedule

Pony's name: _____

My pony is fed _____ lbs. hay (grass, alfalfa, etc.) _____ times /day

My pony is fed _____ lbs. grain _____ times /day

Supplements: _____

What Ponies Need to Eat

Ponies need five basic kinds of nutrition: *roughage, concentrates, succulents, water,* and *salt.*

Roughage

Roughage means bulky food, like grass, hay, and some special feeds like beet pulp and range cubes. A pony must have plenty of roughage for good digestion. Some kinds of roughage are:

- **Grass.** The most natural food for ponies. Different kinds of grasses grow in different parts of the country.
- **Hay.** The most common source of roughage. There are many kinds, including timothy, clover, Bermuda, oat hay, and alfalfa. Alfalfa is the richest kind of hay.
- **Other roughage.** These include range cubes, hay pellets, and sugar beet pulp.

Concentrates

Concentrates are foods that have more food value concentrated in a smaller amount. For ponies, concentrates include grain, mixed feeds and pellets, and supplements. Ponies need concentrates when they require more nutrition than they can get from the hay or pasture grass they eat. Ponies might need concentrates if they are young and still growing, old, nursing a foal, doing hard work, getting fit, or need to put on weight. However, if none of these conditions exist, then a pony may need very little grain or no grain at all, especially if he has plenty of good grass or hay. It is important not to overfeed grain as it can make a pony sick, lame, or overweight; cause colic, or make a pony too frisky or hard to handle.

Some kinds of concentrates are:

- **Grain.** Oats, corn, barley, and bran are the most common.
- **Mixed feed and feed pellets.** These are made by mixing different grains. Some are ground up and pressed into grain pellets.
- **Supplements.** Vitamin and mineral supplements (usually powders or pellets) are sometimes added to the feed in small amounts when a pony needs extra nutrition to improve joint health, coat quality, or for other special needs.

Succulents

Succulents are juicy foods like fresh grass or carrots. **Caution:** *Never* feed grass clippings to a pony. They wilt quickly and can cause serious colic, which can result in death. Even fresh, unwilted grass clippings may contain lawn-care chemicals that can poison a pony.

Water

As with all animals, a pony must have plenty of fresh, clean water at all times. It keeps him healthy and helps him to digest his food.

Salt

Ponies need salt to keep the proper chemical balance in their bodies. They lose salt when they sweat, especially in hot weather, but they need salt at all times because they usually cannot get enough salt from their natural food. It can be given loose or in a salt block. There are special salt and mineral blocks made and balanced especially for horses.

Pony owners may not always use the same kinds of feed because different kinds of feed are grown in different parts of the country. You will have to find out which kinds of roughage and concentrates are available where you live, and which feed is the best feed for your pony. Ask for advice from an experienced horse person like your instructor, veterinarian, local feed stores and hay dealers, or your Cooperative Extension office.

Giving Treats and Tidbits

Ponies love treats like carrots and apples. It is nice to give your pony a tidbit when he has done well or after you ride him, but he must have good manners. Some ponies get so greedy for treats that they nip or get pushy. These ponies should not be given treats by hand. Instead, you can put treats in their feed bucket. Treats must be good for ponies to eat (not candy or junk food!) and it is better not to feed sugar to ponies because it often makes them nippy. Carrots or apples are better, but they should be sliced up so they can't get stuck in a pony's throat.

To give a pony a tidbit safely, you should put the treat in the middle of your flat hand with your fingers together and your thumb tucked in. Hold your hand firm as he may push hard against it to get the treat he enjoys. Don't hold a treat with your fingers—the pony might get your fingers with the treat by mistake. If you offer a treat and then jerk your hand away, he might think you are teasing him and try to grab it.

How to give a pony a tidbit safely.

Feeding Water, Hay, Grain, and Salt

Water, hay, grain, and salt are the basics of a pony's diet. Water is the most important, hay or pasture grass is the most common way of providing roughage, and ponies may or may not need grain for extra energy and other nutrients. Salt must be provided because ponies need it but do not get enough salt from hay, grain, or grass.

Water

Water comes first. A pony should have water available all the time so he can drink whenever he needs to. A pony needs 8 to 12 gallons of water a day, or even more. It is especially important to make sure he drinks plenty of water in cold weather. Ponies can easily get *dehydrated* (lacking enough water for good health) during cold weather, when they may not drink enough, especially if the water is extremely cold. This can lead to *impaction colic* (a kind of colic caused by food blocking the intestines).

Ponies like to drink only fresh, clean water. If the water is dirty, a pony may not drink enough. This can make him thin and run down, or even sick. To keep your pony's water clean, empty his bucket, scrub it with a brush, and rinse it out each day before you fill it with fresh water. Baking soda or salt can be used

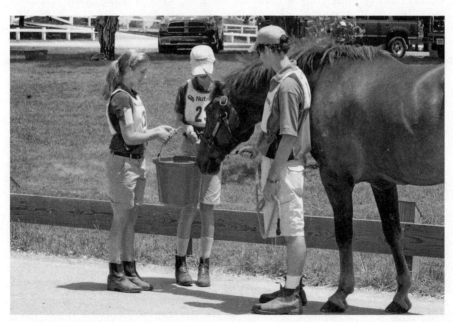

Pony Clubbers water their ponies during a rally. (Make sure your pony always has plenty of fresh, clean water.)

to help scrub your buckets clean. Be sure to rinse them thoroughly. Water tanks in pastures must be kept clean, too. They should be scrubbed out when they are dirty, or at least once a week.

In cold weather, you must be sure that your pony's water is not frozen over so that he cannot drink. You may have to break the ice in the water tank or dump the ice out of his bucket before you refill it, at least twice a day. Sometimes a special water bucket heater or stock tank heater can help.

Remember to water your pony often when you are at a show, rally, or any Pony Club event.

Hay

Hay comes in *bales*, which can weigh from 40 pounds to over 75 pounds. When you open a bale, immediately fold up the strings or wire and put them in a trash bin or a bag for recycling. If they are left lying around, they can get tangled in equipment, injure the pony, or cause people to get caught in the strings and fall. A hay bale comes apart in sections, or *flakes,* about 3 to 4 inches thick. Depending on his size and the kind of hay, a pony might get one or two flakes of hay at a feeding. Your adviser (an experienced horse person, instructor, or veterinarian) should show you how much hay to feed your pony. Weigh an average-size flake of hay (use a feed scale or baby scale), so you know how many pounds of hay your pony gets for each feeding and each day. One flake can weigh from 1 to 5 pounds.

Write down the amount of hay for each feeding on your pony's feed chart.

Always check each flake of hay for dust, mold, or trash. Good hay smells sweet, like newly cut grass. Moldy hay smells musty and may have white or gray patches. Moldy or dusty hay can give your pony a cough or make him sick, so if you find any, put it aside and do not feed it to your pony.

If your pony wastes a lot of hay, cut down on the amount, but check the leftover hay to be sure it is good hay that he is leaving. Some people like to shake out the hay into a loose pile, which makes it easier to check for mold and for the pony to eat. This is fine for some kinds of hay (like grass hays) but not a good idea for hay like alfalfa, as many of the leaves and small pieces will be lost.

Hay can be fed in a hay feeder or manger, in a hay net, or on the ground. A hay feeder should not be so high that dust and seeds can fall into the pony's eyes and nose as he eats. A low trough makes a good hay feeder for pens and pastures, as it keeps hay off the ground and cuts down on wasted hay. If you use a hay net, it must be tied safely and hung high enough so that a pony cannot get his leg caught in it. (See pages 192–193 for more about hay nets and how to hang them safely.) Feeding hay on the ground is the easiest and the most natural way for a pony to eat, but some hay will be wasted, and the pony may pick up internal parasites or worms because the hay gets manure in it. If you feed hay on the ground, put it in a corner of the stall or a dry place in the pen or pasture. Hay must not be fed on sandy ground because ponies swallow sand along with the hay, which causes a stomach problem called *sand colic*.

When you feed hay to a pastured pony, it should be fed in a dry open area, away from fences, gates, corners, or anything a pony could get hurt on. If there is more than one pony, put out extra piles of hay and space them at least three or four pony lengths apart (about 30 to 40 feet). This gives each pony a chance to get some hay, even if he gets chased away from one pile.

Grain

Grain is a concentrated feed. It can make a pony sick if he gets too much all at once. Ponies love grain and will eat as much as they can get. It is very important to keep grain safely locked up in a grain bin, so your pony can't get into it if he should get loose from his stall or pasture. If he does get into the grain bin, he may eat until he gets colic or founder, and he could even die. Always remember to close up the feed room securely before you leave.

Your adviser will have to help you decide how much grain your pony needs, and whether he needs any vitamins or other supplements. You can measure out his grain in a feed scoop or a coffee can, then weigh it on a feed scale or baby scale. Feed is best measured in pounds. Write down on your feed chart how many pounds and what kind of grain your pony gets for each feeding. Also write down any special supplements and how much he gets, if you use them.

Grain should be fed after your pony has had water and been given his hay, and after he has been completely cooled out if he has been ridden. Use a feed tub or bucket that is smooth, with no sharp edges. The feed tub can be placed on the ground, but your pony may waste a lot of grain this way. It is better to hang the tub at about the height of his shoulders.

The grain should be measured into a container or bucket with any vitamins or supplements mixed in, and then dumped into the feed tub. Never mix old, stale, leftover feed with fresh feed. Feed tubs and buckets should be kept clean, especially in hot weather, when sticky feed tubs attract flies.

When you feed grain to a pastured pony, he should have a feed tub or grain feeder to eat from. If there is more than one pony, it is better to put the ponies in their own stalls to eat their grain (if you have stalls), or tie them up until all are finished. If you feed grain to a group of loose ponies, they will fight over it and some ponies may not get their share or get hurt.

Insist on good manners from your pony when you feed him. Teach him to step back and wait while you put his grain in his feed tub. However, don't tease him or make him upset by making him wait longer than necessary. If you give him his hay first, he will not be so hungry and is apt to behave better.

Salt

Salt is important for a pony's good health and condition, especially in hot weather. Salt comes in blocks, which may be plain salt (white), or with iodine or trace minerals added (red). A pony should have a salt block in his stall, either attached to the wall in a salt block holder or kept in his feed tub, or you could feed loose salt in a small tub instead. He should also have a larger salt block in the pasture, placed on a salt holder to keep it off the ground. A pony should be free to lick as much salt as he needs, whenever he wants to. It is best to use mineral salt blocks that are made especially for horses. There are also brown ones with molasses in them, and some ponies tend to eat them right up!

Pasture Grass

Grass is the most natural food for ponies. However, not all grass is equally good to eat. If a pasture does not have enough good grass (if it is bare and overgrazed, weedy, or covered with snow), a pony cannot get enough good feed and will need extra feed (like hay and perhaps grain) to stay in good condition. A pony will get thin and can starve on a poor pasture.

In the spring, the new grass grows fast and has a lot of water in it. This can upset a pony's digestion and can cause laminitis, or founder, a painful condition that can cripple a pony's feet. Very rich pastures are not good for ponies (especially small ponies). A pony can become overweight on a rich pasture and may suffer from founder. In the spring, or if your pasture is too rich for your pony, you may have to limit his time in the pasture each day or use a *grazing muzzle*, which attaches to the halter and allows a pony to eat only a limited amount of grass. (If you use a grazing muzzle, the halter must have a safety breakaway feature.) If your pony is not used to the new or rich pasture, you will have to slowly let him get used to it by starting with 20 minutes a day and gradually increasing his daily pasture time over two or three weeks.

Some horses and ponies suffer from a metabolic condition that makes them prone to laminitis, especially if they eat too much rich grass. They need careful management and may have to be restricted from the pasture. Your veterinarian can advise you about how to manage such ponies.

Different kinds of grass (such as bluegrass, clover, orchard grass, and Bermuda grass) grow in different areas. You will need to find out which grasses grow in your pasture, and whether it has enough good grass for proper nutrition. There are also some poisonous plants to watch out for. Your adviser, veterinarian, or the Cooperative Extension office can teach you about pasture grasses and plants in your area that are poisonous to ponies.

Remember, never feed your pony grass clippings! They can make him very ill and even cause death.

Some Rules for Good Feeding

- Feed small amounts often, not one big meal all at once. Ponies have small stomachs, and this helps them digest their food more easily.

- Feed plenty of roughage (hay, beet pulp, hay cubes, or grass, but never grass clippings). This is necessary for good digestion.

- Feed according to a pony's size, condition, age, breed, temperament, and the work he does. If a pony works hard, he will need more feed (especially grain). If he works less, his grain should be cut back. If he has a day off or stops working, his grain should be reduced or cut out entirely. If you cut back on his grain, give him some extra hay to make up the difference. Some ponies don't get any grain and just get roughage.

- All changes in feed should be made gradually over ten days to two weeks. It takes that long for a pony's digestion to change over to handle a new kind of food. You can cut grain back quickly, but it should be added more slowly.

- Feed on a regular schedule every day. Don't be late! Your pony may get upset, and so may his digestive system.

- Feed only clean, good-quality hay and grain. Dusty, spoiled, or poor feed and food with bugs or trash in it won't give your pony good nutrition and can make him sick.

- Keep feed tubs, hay feeders, and water buckets clean.

- Clean, fresh water must be available at all times. Water tanks and buckets must be kept clear of ice in the winter.

- Salt should be available at all times, in a salt block or loose. It is usually best to use the kind of salt that has minerals added and is made for horses.

- Do not ride your pony when his stomach is full—it may give him indigestion. He should have an hour to digest his grain before working hard. A pony must be completely cooled out after work before being fed grain or he may colic.

- Learn how your pony normally eats. If he isn't eating the way he usually does (for instance, if he doesn't want to eat, eats very slowly, spills grain out of his mouth, or slobbers), he might be sick.

- If ponies are kept together in a pasture, be sure that each is getting enough to eat and that no one is chased away from his feed by other ponies.

- Give water first, then the hay (so the pony is not so hungry), and last, the grain.

Things to Do to Learn About Feeding and Nutrition

1. Visit a feed store with your Pony Club (call ahead and ask if it's okay). The staff can show you different kinds of feed and how they are processed and mixed. You could ask for a small sample (baby food jar) of each kind of grain to learn what it looks like. Ask: How can you tell good grain from bad? What is the most economical feed to buy?

2. Ask a horse nutrition expert (from your county agriculture extension service or from a feed company) to come and talk to your Pony Club about feeds and nutrition.

3. Visit a farm that grows hay. Ask the farmer to show you different kinds of hay and the difference between good and poor hay. He can tell you about the kinds of plants that make good hay; when they should be cut and baled; what makes hay get dusty, moldy, or weather damaged; and how to store your hay properly. Collect samples of different kinds and grades of hay.

4. Organize your feed room. Get large trash bins to hold grain and label them (they should close tightly to keep mice out). Put up shelves to hold such items as buckets, scoops, and supplements. Sweep the feed room clean. Put a horse-proof latch on the feed room door so your pony can't get in, and always be careful to close the door! It is easier to do chores in a neat stable, and you will be proud of the way your feed room looks.

Weight and Condition

Condition means the state of a pony's health and fitness. A healthy pony looks healthy, not sick. A *fit* pony is a healthy pony whose muscles, heart, and lungs have been built up or conditioned for work. A pony could be healthy but *soft*, or *unfit*, and therefore not ready to do hard work. It is unkind to work a pony too hard for his level of fitness, as this can hurt him or make him sick.

There is a range of condition, from very thin to very fat. A healthy pony is somewhere in the middle. Some horses and ponies may have a metabolic condition that makes them prone to becoming overweight. This requires careful management, because it can lead to serious health and soundness problems. It is important to know your pony's condition and to notice if he is putting on weight or losing weight. Ask your veterinarian about your pony's condition and how to improve it.

Note to Parents

Nutrition, Feeding, and Watering

Feeding a pony properly is one of the most important responsibilities of an owner. A pony is completely dependent on his owners for his feed, well-being, and even his life. You must know about the pony's basic condition and feeding requirements and be sure that your child is doing a good job of feeding and watering him regularly. You must also be responsible for providing a regular and consistent source of feed. Working with your child on planning the pony's ration, buying and storing feed, and supervising daily feeding chores is a good way to teach your child about the responsibility that comes with owning an animal.

If your pony is boarded out and somebody else takes over the feeding chores, it is still important for you and your child to know how the pony is fed, to be sure that he is being properly fed and to help with the process as much as possible. This makes it easier to make sensible decisions about your pony's feeding, care, and work, and to avoid the problems caused by improper feeding.

This book does not go into enough detail about feeding and pony care to teach a child or a novice pony owner enough to take full charge of feeding and caring for a pony. You will need an experienced horse person as an adviser—preferably your veterinarian along with your child's instructor. It is best to consult your veterinarian about the nutritional needs of your child's pony, especially if the pony appears ill or not in the best condition, or if you are dealing with a young, growing pony, a mare with a foal, or an older pony.

Kinds of Condition

A pony's condition can be judged using the *body condition score* from 1 to 9 to evaluate fat and condition. A score of 1 would be a starving horse with bones noticeably sticking out and no fat left. A score of 5 would be the ideal condition, neither too fat nor too thin. A score of 9 is an obese horse with fat filled in everywhere, covering the ribs, neck, hindquarters, and a crease down the back.

Here are examples of condition and body condition scores:

- **Very poor condition (body score 1 or 2).** The pony is terribly thin and appears to be starving. His ribs show, his backbone sticks up, and his muscles are wasted. He may be sick or starved and is probably infested with worms. He is weak and depressed and cannot be ridden until he is in better condition, which may take many weeks.
- **Thin condition (body score 3).** The pony is thin, with little fat between the muscles and skin. His ribs show and can be felt easily. His muscles look thin, with hollows in his flanks and hindquarters. His withers are thin and sharp, and he can get saddle sores easily. He is likely to be depressed and dull, and

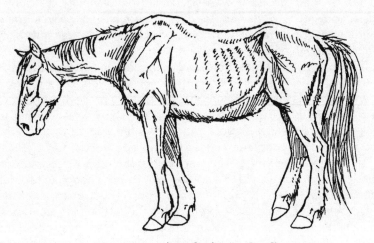

Very poor condition (body score 1 or 2).

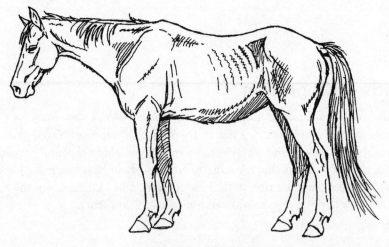

Thin condition (body score 3).

he is probably infested with worms. In the winter, ponies may be thin under their long coats, but you might not notice it unless you feel their ribs.

- **Good condition (body score 5).** The pony is neither thin nor fat. His muscles are well developed and his skin is loose and flexible. His coat is shiny and he looks and feels good. Some fit horses (like racehorses) are light in flesh, with a tucked-up belly and a rib or two showing. Show horses may be slightly fat, showing dapples and a *bloom,* or special shine, on their coats.

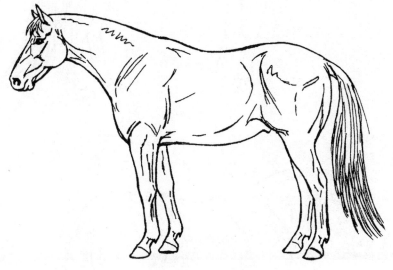

Good condition (body score 5).

Note to Parents

Weight and Condition

Children need the help of a knowledgeable adult in evaluating a pony's fitness and condition and correcting any problems. This is essential for the health, well-being, and humane treatment of the pony. Your veterinarian, your child's instructor, or the District Commissioner can give you an honest appraisal of your pony's condition and suggest feeding, exercise, and other measures to get him fit for Pony Club riding. A child who comes to a mounted meeting or rally or any Pony Club event with a very thin, severely overweight, or unfit pony may not be allowed to ride. The child will need help in understanding what her pony needs and why she must limit her riding.

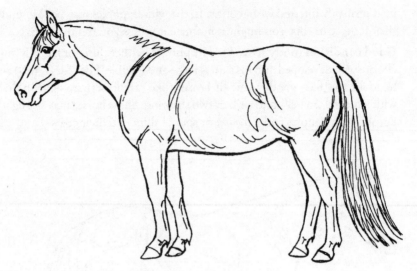

Fat condition (body score 7).

Very fat or obese condition (body score 9).

- **Fat condition (body score 7).** The pony is round and fat over his back, the top of his neck, and his hindquarters and rump. His ribs are covered with a layer of fat and there is a crease down his back. His belly is large and his hindquarters look round instead of muscled. He sweats easily and cannot work hard without puffing. He needs to go on a diet and get fit before he can do hard work, and he may be in danger of foundering.

- **Very fat or obese condition (body score 9).** The pony has heavy fat deposits on his neck, shoulders, back, ribs, and hindquarters. His withers may be hidden in fat, his belly is large, and his muscles may feel soft and jiggly. He sweats and tires easily and cannot do even slow work without puffing. He is in danger of foundering and urgently needs to lose weight before he can do even ordinary work safely.

8

Your Pony's Feet and Shoeing

Nothing is more important to your pony than good, sound feet. If his feet are not properly cared for, he will be uncomfortable and he may go lame or stumble, and you will not be able to ride him. Good hoof care includes picking out and checking your pony's feet every day, conditioning the feet, and having a *farrier* (a horseshoer) trim or shoe his feet on a regular schedule.

Cleaning and Checking the Feet

Your pony's feet should be picked out every day, whether you ride him or not. A pony may pick up a stone in his hoof or step on a nail, which can get stuck in his foot. If you didn't pick out his feet and missed it, his foot could be hurt and he could go lame.

Always pick out your pony's feet before and after you ride.

Puncture wounds, which are caused by stepping on something sharp, can be quite serious. If your pony goes lame or if you should find a nail or a wound in your pony's foot, don't try to remove it yourself but call your veterinarian right away.

Another reason for picking out your pony's feet is cleanliness. If his feet are left packed full of dirt and manure for too long, or if he stands in a wet, dirty stall or pen that is not cleaned often enough, he can get a foot infection called *thrush.* This is caused by a fungus or bacteria that live in wet, dirty feet. Thrush attacks the *frog* (the soft center part of the foot) and makes it rot; it looks like black ooze and has a very bad odor. Picking out your pony's feet daily and keeping his stall clean is the best way to prevent thrush.

Picking out the feet also lets you check your pony's shoes (if he wears shoes) and the condition of his feet. You should notice a loose shoe or a bent nail, or if his feet are growing too long or starting to crack. This means he needs attention from the farrier.

Good hoof care includes picking out and checking your pony's feet every day.

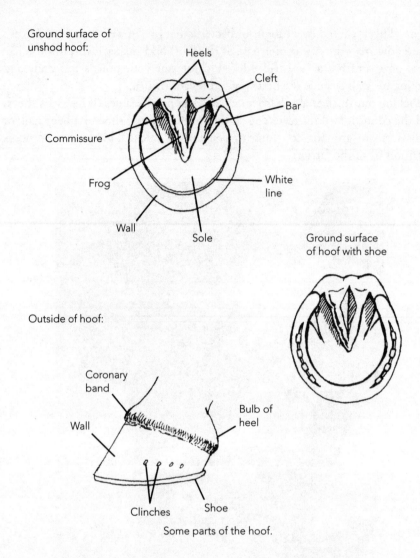

Some parts of the hoof.

How to Pick Up a Pony's Foot

Your pony should be trained to pick up his feet when you ask him to. (If he is difficult about picking up his feet, an experienced horse person must help you handle his feet safely and train him to pick them up easily.) You must handle his feet properly to be safe, and to make it easy for him to do as you ask. At first, you should have help with handling and cleaning your pony's feet.

To pick up a front foot safely, follow these steps:

1. Stand beside the pony's front leg, facing the tail.
2. Run your hand down his leg to the back tendons below the knee. Squeeze with your fingers and say "Pick up." Sometimes it helps to lean into him a little too.
3. When he lifts the foot, hold it by the hoof (not by the pastern).
4. When you are finished, set the foot down gently.

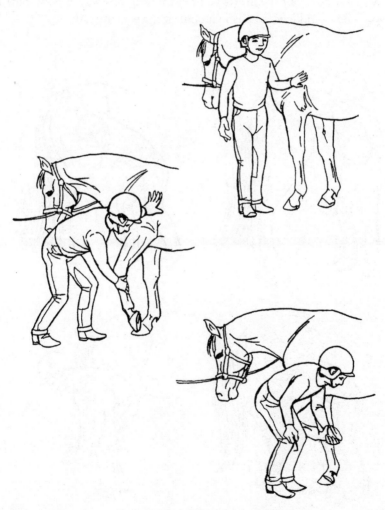

How to pick up a front foot safely.

To pick up a hind foot safely, follow these steps:

1. Stand beside the pony's hindquarters, facing backward.

2. Put your hand on the hindquarters and slide it down the outside of the hind leg to the back tendons below the hock. Squeeze and pull forward gently and say "Pick up."

3. When he lifts his foot, it comes forward first. Use your hand to guide the leg back until it is a little behind him.

4. Bend your knees and slide your thigh behind the pony's hind foot. Hold the hoof, not the pastern. (If you hold the leg this way, a pony can't kick you—he would have to push you out of the way instead.)

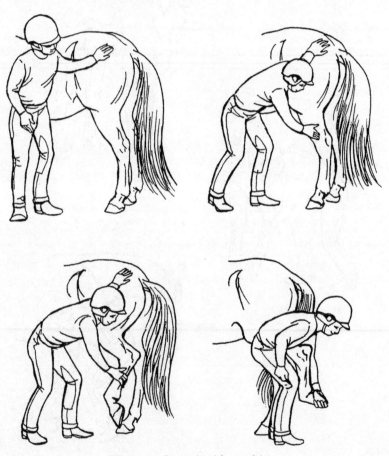

How to pick up a hind foot safely.

There are other ways to pick up a pony's feet, but this is the method recommended for D Level Pony Clubbers because it is simple and safe.

Your pony will pick up his feet more easily if you always use the same signal to ask him to lift his foot and pick them out in the same order. When you are finished with his foot, set it down gently—don't drop it. If he puts his foot down before you are finished, make him pick it up again right away. Be careful where you put your own feet—your pony will not look out for them when he sets his foot down!

For safety, don't put your arm around the inside of the hind leg from the front. If the pony should snatch his hind leg up quickly, he could catch your arm. Don't pull his hind leg out to the side or hold it up too high. This hurts his leg and makes it hard for him to balance. It will make him want to take his leg away from you.

How to Clean the Feet

You will need a hoof pick and a stiff brush. (The kind of hoof pick with a brush on the end is a help.) Pick up your pony's foot and hold it by the hoof, not the pastern. Dig the point of the hoof pick into the dirt at the back of the foot, beside the frog. If you can get the pick under the packed dirt, it will come out quicker and easier than if you scrape a little at a time. Always pick from the heel toward the toe. If you pick from toe to heel, you could poke the hoof pick into the frog by accident or jab yourself.

Clean all the dirt from the sole of the foot, the spaces beside the frog and the *cleft* (the groove in the center of the frog). Use the brush to clean away loose dirt and to brush mud and dirt from the outside of each hoof, so you can see the condition of all the parts of the hoof.

Never kneel or sit when you are working on your pony's hooves—you can bend down or squat, but always stay on your own feet for safety. Remember to sweep up the dirt you pick out of your pony's feet when you are finished.

How to pick out a hoof.

Hoof Condition

The condition of your pony's feet can change, depending on his health and the conditions he lives in. If he lives in a dry, dusty place, his feet may become dry and hard and sometimes crack. You can help by applying hoof dressing around the coronet and across the heels. (It is not necessary or helpful to paint the whole foot.) It may also help to let him spend more time in damp grass, so his feet will absorb moisture naturally. If your pony lives in wet, swampy conditions all the time, though, his feet may become too soft. The hooves may break off easily, and his shoes may not stay on. You will need to keep him in drier conditions to help his feet get tougher.

Hoof Growth, Trimming, and Shoeing

A pony's hoofs grow all the time, like your fingernails—about ¼ inch each month. Some ponies' hooves wear down faster than they grow, because of the work they do and the hard or sandy ground over which they are ridden. They need shoes to protect their feet and keep them from becoming sore. Other ponies' feet grow faster than they wear down. They get long feet, which puts strain on their legs and can make them stumble. These ponies need to have their feet trimmed to keep them at a normal length. Some ponies' feet grow unevenly so that their feet are out of balance, which makes it hard for them to move well. It is unkind and unsafe to let a pony's feet get too long, cracked, sore, or badly out of balance, and he cannot be ridden that way. Even if he is not being ridden, he cannot move comfortably in the pasture if his feet are neglected or in poor condition.

Ponies who are shod usually need to have their shoes *reset* every six to eight weeks. This means removing the shoes and trimming away the extra hoof, then replacing them. When shoes get old and worn out, new shoes are needed.

Your pony should have his feet checked by a farrier every six to eight weeks, whether he is ridden or not, to see if he needs his feet trimmed or his shoes reset. (Some ponies with special foot problems need to be checked every four or five weeks.) A farrier is an expert on trimming, shoeing, and balancing ponies' feet. He should check your pony's feet regularly, even if there is not much hoof growth. He can tell if your pony's feet are in good condition, and if they are balanced correctly so that your pony can move without strain on his legs. If you aren't sure whether your pony needs shoes, ask your farrier.

You should get to know the normal shape of your pony's hooves and notice any cracks or changes that appear in his feet. Talk to your farrier about any changes you see in your pony's feet, or any problems or changes in the way he moves (especially tripping or stumbling). A pony's frog may shed or peel twice a year. You may see some ragged pieces hanging from the frog. While some shedding is normal, if you think there is a problem with your pony's feet, ask your farrier.

Signs That a Pony Needs Shoeing or Trimming

The first sign that a pony needs shoeing or trimming is long feet. Often the toes grow longer than the heels. This can make a pony trip and stumble, and it puts extra strain on her tendons. If your pony wears shoes, there are some other signs to look for. As the hoof grows longer, the shoe seems to sit farther down the foot, away from the heels. This can cause the end of the shoe to press on the space between the bars and the wall, making a painful bruise called a *corn*. The wall of the foot may start to grow over the edge of the shoe, and the *clinches* (the ends of the nails) will stand up from the wall of the foot instead of lying down smooth and tight. Some nails may loosen up or even fall out. Finally, the shoe may become loose. You can hear it click as the pony walks on a hard surface, and you may be able to move the shoe with your fingers. If you do not have the pony reshod, he may lose the shoe. It is best to make an appointment with your farrier several weeks ahead. You can even make the next appointment while he is currently doing your pony.

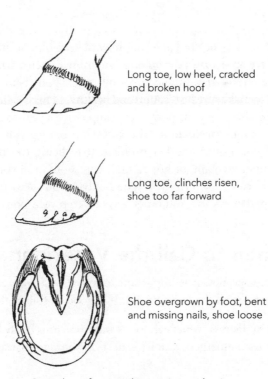

Long toe, low heel, cracked and broken hoof

Long toe, clinches risen, shoe too far forward

Shoe overgrown by foot, bent and missing nails, shoe loose

Signs that a foot needs trimming or shoeing.

9

Health Care and Veterinary Knowledge

When you own or ride a pony, you need to know when he is feeling well and when he is sick or lame, and how to keep him healthy. Every pony owner should have an *equine veterinarian* (an animal doctor who treats horses and ponies). The veterinarian should check out a new pony before you and your parents buy him to make sure he is sound and healthy. (This is called a *prepurchase exam*.) He should also give your pony a checkup twice a year to make sure he is healthy and to give him vaccinations (shots). If your pony gets hurt or sick, if he goes lame, or if you notice another problem (like being too thin or too fat, having a skin rash or a cough, or not eating), you should call your veterinarian. The veterinarian can also give you good advice on deworming, feeding, vaccinations, dental checkups, and other ways to keep your pony healthy.

When to Call the Veterinarian

As you learn about ponies, it is important to know what you can take care of yourself and when to call the veterinarian. It is good to follow these rules:

- If a pony is in distress (won't eat, looks very sick, or is badly hurt), or if you think there is an emergency, don't wait. Call the veterinarian right away.

- If you know there is a problem, but you don't know what it is or how to help your pony, your veterinarian is the best person to call.

- If you don't think there is an emergency, and you aren't sure whether you should call a veterinarian, call your instructor for advice. Don't just wait to see if the problem will get worse!

Signs of a Healthy Pony

A healthy pony who feels well is alert and content. His eyes are clear and bright, he breathes normally, and he is interested in what is going on. His coat is shiny and his skin is loose and supple. He may lie down and stretch out for a while, but he will get up easily. He stands normally on all four legs; he may rest a hind foot, but he doesn't rest a front foot. He likes to eat, and he drinks normally. He passes manure about eight times a day in normal manure balls (soft manure is normal for ponies on pasture), and his urine is clear or light yellow. His vital signs (pulse, respiration, and temperature) are in a normal range for that pony. (See the following section.)

A healthy pony.

Vital Signs

It is a good idea to know your pony's normal vital signs. There is a normal range for horses and ponies, but normal for an individual pony may be a little higher or lower. Take your pony's vital signs when he is feeling well and write them down so if he appears to be ill, the veterinarian can compare his vital signs with what is normal for him.

An older Pony Club member, an experienced adult (your instructor), or the veterinarian can help you take and record your pony's vital signs. These are:

- **Pulse,** which measures your pony's heartbeat—usually between thirty and forty-five beats per minute.

- **Respiration,** or breathing rate—usually between eight and sixteen breaths per minute.

- **Temperature**—between 95.5 and 101.5 degrees, taken with a rectal veterinary thermometer. When taking a pony's temperature, a glass veterinary thermometer may be more accurate than a digital one, but either is acceptable.

Your pony's normal vital signs should be recorded in his health record, and should be listed on his stall card (see page 197) when you stable him at a Pony Club rally, competition, or at home.

Signs of Sickness

Here are some important signs of sickness that should make you get help for your pony from your veterinarian:

- **Colic (belly pain).** The pony may stop eating, break out in a sweat, look at or nip his belly, paw the ground, and stretch out as if to urinate. He may lie down and get up again, or roll from side to side, or even sit on his hind-quarters, like a dog. All of these are signs of colic, which can be quite serious and even fatal. Call your veterinarian immediately, and while you are waiting for him, walk your pony slowly and don't let him roll.

- **Coughing** (especially a wet cough with mucus in his throat), **runny eyes and nose** (especially if mucus is white, yellow, or green).

- **Coughing with great distress (choking).** He may even be coughing green stuff out his nose. He keeps walking, pacing, or looking around. This is an emergency and your veterinarian should be called immediately.

- **Diarrhea** (loose, runny manure), or dry, hard manure balls.

- **Pony is depressed.** He does not want to move, eat, or take an interest in what is going on. He may stand stiffly or hunched up. If lying down, he does not want to get up. He may act dull, cranky, and irritable, especially if you ride him.

- **Fever.** A fever of more than 1 degree above his normal (102 degrees or higher). Fever in the feet (the feet will feel hot to your touch) can be serious, especially if the pony stands with his front legs out ahead of him, moves stiffly, or lies down and does not want to get up. (This could mean laminitis, or founder, which is an emergency. Call your veterinarian immediately.)

- **Not wanting to eat or not eating normally.** Pony refuses to eat, drools, or drops food out of his mouth.

- **Losing weight, has a dull coat, or a change in his usual eating habits or behavior.**

- **Injuries.** Cuts, swelling, heat, or tenderness in a leg or elsewhere; a closed or swollen eye; lameness, bleeding.

If you need to call your veterinarian, first write down all your pony's symptoms. If possible, get an experienced horse person to take your pony's vital signs (his pulse, respiration, and temperature). It is easier for the veterinarian to decide how serious your pony's problem might be if you give him all the information in a clear and organized way.

Recognizing Lameness

To tell if a pony is lame, lead him at a jog. Keep the lead line loose so he can move his head up or down freely. Jog him in a straight line on hard, level ground, like a driveway. Sometimes you can hear that his hoof beats are uneven; one may sound louder and one much quieter, like "CLIP, clop."

When a pony is lame, he favors his sore leg. He may stand with his weight on the good leg and rest the sore one. When he moves, he tries not to step hard on his sore leg. If it is a front leg, he throws his head up when he steps on the sore leg and down when he steps on the good leg. The sore leg usually takes a shorter step. If it is a hind leg, he carries his hip higher on the sore side and throws his head down as the sore hind foot touches the ground. He will usually take a shorter step with the sore leg.

Colic signs: stretching out, pawing, biting or kicking at belly, sweating

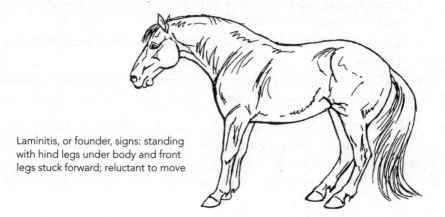

Laminitis, or founder, signs: standing with hind legs under body and front legs stuck forward; reluctant to move

Depressed pony, not eating normally

Signs of sickness.

Lame in front leg:

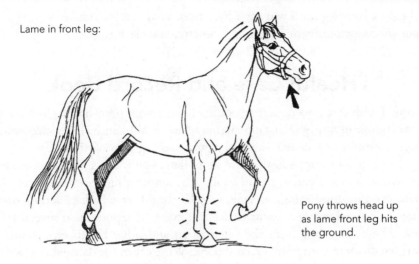

Pony throws head up
as lame front leg hits
the ground.

Lame in hind leg:

Pony's head goes
down as lame hind
leg hits the ground.

How to tell when a pony is lame.

If your pony goes lame, clean out his feet and check for stones, a twisted or loose shoe, or something like a nail stuck in his foot. Feel his legs to see if you find a place that is tender (he flinches or shows he's uncomfortable when you touch or squeeze it), or that feels hot or puffy. It helps to compare the lame leg with the other leg.

Call your veterinarian or ask your instructor for advice, and don't ride your pony until you find out what the problem is and treat it. Some lameness can be made worse if you work the pony. (If you are out on a ride and your pony goes lame, it is okay to walk him back home slowly.) Don't put liniment or anything else on a lame leg until you get advice from your veterinarian. It is all right to put antibiotic ointment on a minor cut after you clean it.

Health Care and Record Book

Good health care on a regular schedule will keep your pony healthy and prevent small problems from growing into big ones. Basic health care includes vaccinations, regular deworming, dental care, and regular shoeing or hoof trimming.

To keep your pony's health care up to date, you will need a record-keeping system such as a calendar, record book, or a computer file. Note the dates when vaccinations, deworming, shoeing, or other health care is due. Write down a note to call the veterinarian or farrier and make an appointment several weeks ahead of time. Visits from the veterinarian and other health care should be written down in your pony's record book. Write down the date, what was done for your pony, and any notes or instructions. Shoeing and foot trimming should also be recorded in your book.

Worms and Deworming

Ponies are exposed to several kinds of *internal parasites* (worms) all the time. They can damage a pony's intestines, heart, and lungs, make him thin and unhealthy, and they can even kill him. Every pony owner should have his pony treated for worms regularly.

A deworming program should be worked out with your veterinarian after he examines a sample of your pony's manure for parasites. There are many different kinds of *dewormers* (medications that remove worms, usually a medicated paste). Your pony will probably need to be dewormed two to six times a year, depending on how many parasites he has. Parasites can build up a resistance to dewormers, so you should not use dewormers more often than you have to, and your veterinarian may recommend that you use different types of dewormers from time to time. This ensures that you will reduce all types of parasites and helps to reduce resistance to dewormers.

Your veterinarian will advise you on how often your pony should be dewormed and what kind of dewormer is best to use.

Vaccinations

Every pony needs vaccinations to protect him against certain diseases. These should be given at least once a year. In most parts of the country, certain shots are necessary every six months or even every three months. Your veterinarian can tell you which shots are most important for your pony and in your part of the country. It is much better (and costs less) to prevent your pony from getting a serious disease than to have to treat one.

The most common diseases your pony should be vaccinated against are:

- **Tetanus.** This is a fatal disease caused by bacteria that enters through a wound. The vaccination is given once a year. A tetanus booster shot may be necessary if a pony gets a deep cut or a puncture wound.

- **Equine encephalomyelitis (sleeping sickness).** There are three types in North America: Eastern, Western, and Venezuelan. This disease is transmitted by mosquitoes from birds to mammals. The vaccination is given once each spring.

- **Influenza (flu).** If your pony goes to shows and events where he meets other ponies, this shot is especially important. Influenza is a very contagious virus that is spread by aerosol droplets (especially coughing). The vaccination requires two shots or it can be given intranasally (in the nose), and the protection usually lasts six months.

- **Rabies.** Ponies can get this rare but fatal disease from the bite of an infected animal. If there is rabies among the wildlife in your area (especially foxes, skunks, and raccoons), your pony must have a rabies shot. This vaccination is given once a year.

- **Equine herpes virus (rhinopneumonitis).** This is a virus that can cause a respiratory disease or other problems such as abortion. Talk to your vet about whether your pony should be vaccinated for this disease.

- **Potomac horse fever.** This disease causes severe gastrointestinal problems such as enteritis (inflammation of the intestines) and diarrhea, along with lack of appetite and laminitis. It is caused by *Neorickettsia risticii* and is found in a parasite that lives in freshwater snails and aquatic insects, which the pony may accidentally ingest. This disease is a problem in the warm summer months. Ponies are vaccinated every six to twelve months, or more often if they are in a high-risk area.

- **West Nile virus.** This virus is transmitted by mosquitoes from birds to mammals. Its effect on horses can vary from no symptoms to severe central nervous system problems. Ponies are vaccinated every spring and again in the fall in warmer climates,

- **Anthrax.** This disease is caused by bacterial spores that may be within dead animal carcasses. These carcasses can be baled with hay, especially in round bales, and your pony can accidentally eat the bacterial spores. There is a vaccine that can be given in areas where this disease is common.

- **Botulism.** This disease can be fatal and is caused by bacterial spores that may be within fermented hay or hay contaminated with dead animal carcasses. There is a vaccine that can be given in areas where this disease is common.

- **Equine viral arteritis.** This disease is caused by a virus that is transmitted by aerosol droplets or during breeding. There is a vaccine available, but it is highly regulated by veterinarians.

- **Strangles.** This disease is caused by bacteria that is easily spread through the air or by objects around the horse (such as buckets or even human hands). There are different types of vaccines available, but none is completely effective. Ponies can be vaccinated if they are at risk of being exposed to strangles. Young horses and ponies, and those who are exposed to many strange horses during shipping or at sales, shows, and competitions, are most at risk.

There are other diseases you may need to vaccinate your pony against, depending on where you live, or certain shots may be required by your club or barn. Ask your veterinarian and your Pony Club District Commissioner for information.

Treating Minor Cuts

Sometimes your pony may get a cut. If it is deep, bleeding a lot, gaping open, or on the pony's eye, you need to call the veterinarian. If you think a cut may need stitches, call the veterinarian, because if you wait too long the cut may not be able to be stitched.

You can usually take care of minor cuts yourself, with some help from an older Pony Clubber or your instructor. Remember the acronym *ACT*: *assess* the cut, *clean* it, and *treat* it. Here are the steps for handling a minor cut:

1. **Assess** the cut. Look carefully at the cut, how deep it is, how much it is bleeding, and where it is located. Decide whether it's a minor cut that you can handle yourself, or if you need help. (It never hurts to ask someone to check it for you.)

2. **Clean** the cut. This can be done by gently running hose water over it for 10 minutes, and then cleaning it with saline solution or an antibacterial soap. Sometimes the hair has to be trimmed away from the cut so that it stays out of the cut.

3. **Pat it dry** with a clean gauze pad.

4. **Treat** the cut. Apply a little antibiotic ointment. This may need to be repeated daily. Do not use harsh medications, which may injure the healing tissues.

If a wound needs to be bandaged, ask an older Pony Club member or your instructor for help.

Bandaging Legs

There are several kinds of bandages you might need to use on a pony:

- **Shipping bandages.** For protection against bumps and scrapes when traveling.
- **Stable bandages.** For protection and warmth in the stall and to prevent the legs from swelling after hard work or an injury.
- **Polo bandages.** For light protection of the legs during work or turnout.
- **Treatment bandages.** For protection and treatment of injuries.

Caution: All bandages must be put on correctly or they can damage your pony's legs. Do not try to put on a leg bandage without hands-on help from someone who is experienced in bandaging legs correctly.

Bandages are made up of *leg wraps* (usually knitted, flannel, or special elastic material about 9 feet long), *leg pads* (made of sheet cotton, polyester, cotton quilts, or special leg pads), and *fasteners* (Velcro, pins, or masking tape). *Polo bandages* are made of fleece, so the padding is incorporated into the bandage.

Polo Bandages

Polo bandages, or *polo wraps*, are made of fleecy material; they are soft and fuzzy on both sides and come in many colors. They are stretchy and are usually 9 feet long and 5 inches wide, though pony-size polo wraps may be shorter. Polo bandages are used for warmth and to give some protection to a horse's legs during riding, longeing, and sometimes turnout. However, polo bandages do not work well when they get wet, and they can pick up burrs and twigs, so they are not a good choice for cross-country schooling. If you choose to use polo bandages, you should have hands-on help from someone who is experienced at putting them on properly, and your instructor should check them before you ride.

When putting on a polo bandage, start by holding the end of the bandage on the outside of the leg, at the middle of your pony's cannon bone. Wrap the bandage counterclockwise on the left legs and clockwise on the right legs. Pull the bandage firmly against the front of the leg, not the back, so you are pulling on the front of the cannon bone instead of against the tendons. Keep the bandage smooth and the pressure even to reduce the risk of causing a pressure injury to the tendon.

As you wrap, spiral downward, overlapping each wrap about one-half the width of the bandage. Wrap downward until you have covered the fetlock joint, and pass the edge of the bandage under the ergot at the back of the fetlock joint. Then wrap upward around the cannon bone to just below the knee or hock. Secure the bandage with the Velcro fastener and add tape if needed (be sure the tape is applied in a spiral so the pressure is not tight). It is important that polo wraps are securely fastened because if a bandage comes loose, a horse can step on the end and trip.

When using bandages, always wrap either both front legs or both hind legs, not just one leg. It is important to wrap evenly and smoothly with just the right amount of tension, as uneven wraps can slip, come undone, bind the leg, or cause pressure injuries to the tendons. All the bandages should be done by the same

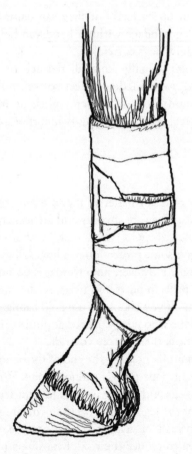

Polo bandage.

person so the pressure is the same on all legs. Never leave bandages on longer than you need to; polo wraps should be removed when you untack after riding. Polo bandages must be washed and kept clean so there is nothing to irritate your pony's legs, and his legs should always be clean and dry before you wrap them.

Remember to be safe when bandaging. Someone more experienced (your instructor or a more experienced Pony Club member) should help you with bandaging. Your horse should be tied up or held by someone while you work. It is wise to wear a helmet, especially during fly season, as a pony could kick at a fly and hit you by accident. Never kneel or sit on the ground while bandaging, as you cannot get up in a hurry; bend down or squat instead.

Shipping Boots and Bandages

Ponies sometimes can slip or scramble in a trailer, or they may step on their own feet or another pony's feet if they should lose their balance. It's a good idea to use shipping boots or bandages on your pony whenever he travels.

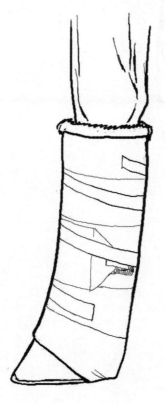

Shipping bandage.

Shipping boots or bandages should protect the legs from the hoof to the knees and hocks. They should cover the heels and the coronet, the pastern and fetlock joint, and the tendons up to the bottom of the knee or hock. A shipping bandage should be firm, snug, and well padded to protect against bumps and scrapes.

Because shipping boots are quick and easy to put on, they are sometimes used instead of bandages. They are a good choice for pony owners who do not know how to put on shipping bandages properly. Shipping boots must cover the coronet and heels as well as the tendons. Some shipping boots are tall enough to protect the knees and hocks as well as the lower legs.

Shipping boot.

Learning More about Horse Health Care

It is important to learn all you can about your pony's health and veterinary care, and especially to recognize signs of illness or other problems. If you get to know your pony well as you care for him, you will notice any little problems before they have a chance to become serious problems. Here are some other ways to learn about keeping your pony healthy:

- Be sure to read the books and pamphlets on your USPC reading list.

- You can get excellent information on such things as health care, deworming, and diseases from the Cooperative Extension (part of the U.S. Department of Agriculture), your county agent, the 4-H Horse Club program, some horse health care companies, and horse books and magazines. Much of the information is free or inexpensive. You may want to start a file of magazine articles, pamphlets, and other horse health care information for yourself and your Pony Club.

- Ask a veterinarian to come and speak to your Pony Club about such topics as first aid for ponies, which diseases to vaccinate against, deworming and parasite control, and pony health problems.

Note to Parents

Health Care

Good health care is essential for the well-being of a pony. This requires visits from the veterinarian and some expense. Try to find an equine veterinarian, and develop a good working relationship with her. If you use the same veterinarian, she will get to know your pony and can give you the best advice on health and pony management problems. Be sure to treat your veterinarian in a professional manner: Schedule appointments well in advance, give her all pertinent information in a clear and organized way, have the pony in the barn, be on hand to help when she is due to visit, and above all pay the bill on time!

10

Safe Traveling and Trailering

In Pony Club, you may often want to haul your pony in a trailer to a lesson, a rally, or some other Pony Club activity. If your pony is well trained for trailering and you are careful and sensible, it is quite simple. However, if a pony has a bad experience with a trailer, he can become very hard to load or haul in a trailer, and it may even become dangerous for him and for you. It is very important to get help and advice from an expert when you are learning to load and haul your pony, especially if he is not used to loading and traveling in a trailer.

Preparing for Travel in a Trailer

Shipping a pony safely in a horse trailer requires some knowledge and planning. Before traveling, you will need to be prepared in the following ways:

- The trailer and tow vehicle must be safe, serviced, and properly hitched; have the correct insurance and licensing paperwork; and the driver must be experienced in hauling horses. You will also need someone who is experienced in loading ponies safely and quietly to help you.

- The pony must be trained to load and unload easily and ride quietly in a trailer. This takes experience and practice.

- The pony must have the right traveling gear for protection.
- You should take along the equipment you will need to keep the pony safe and comfortable while traveling and after he arrives.

Equipment for Travel

To travel safely, your pony should wear the right equipment. He must never be saddled and bridled when traveling because the tack could catch on the trailer when he is loading or unloading. This could hurt the pony and damage your tack. He should have the following:

- A strong, properly fitted halter made of leather or a synthetic material with a breakaway feature, and a strong tie rope.
- Shipping boots or bandages on all four legs to protect against bumps or scrapes during loading and traveling.
- A tail bandage or tail guard to protect his tail in the trailer (optional).
- A sheet, blanket, or fly sheet if the weather requires it. (A sheet can also be used to keep dust off the pony when traveling on dirt roads.)
- A head protector (used on ponies who throw their heads up and could bump themselves).

Some of this equipment (like bandages) should be put on by someone who has experience with bandaging. The person who helps you trailer your pony may be able to help you bandage his legs and tail, or you can use shipping boots, which are easier to put on. Shipping boots usually cover a portion of the knees and hocks. See page 233–234 for more on shipping boots.

What to Take Along

When your pony travels, you should take along the equipment you will need to take care of him. This includes the following:

- Hay net filled with hay (to keep the pony content in the trailer).
- Water bucket and your own water. Five-gallon containers with lids/caps can be purchased at stores.
- Equine first aid kit to let you take care of a cut or minor injury. (The basic items that you should carry are shown below and described in detail in the *USPC Horse Management Handbook*. Ask your veterinarian or an experienced horse person for advice, too.)

Pony prepared for shipping.

A simple equine first aid kit, which should always be carried when trailering a pony.

- Halter, extra tie rope, and chain-end lead shank (for control if you need it).
- Muck basket, rake, and broom for cleaning up.
- Utility kit to let you fix broken items or in case of an emergency. (The basic items you should carry are described in detail in the *USPC Horse Management Handbook*.)
- Your tack and grooming kit.

Loading and Unloading

Before loading your pony, have everything else loaded and checked. The trailer should be on level ground, with the back step as low as possible, or the ramp steady. The front exit door should be open so that the trailer is lighter inside and the pony can see through, and so you can get out that way. The trailer floor can be covered with shavings to give your pony better footing. (Most trailers have rubber floor mats and this may make the footing more slippery depending on the type of mats. Mixing the shavings with sand will help.)

If your pony is traveling alone in a double trailer, he should ride on the left (driver's side), so that his weight does not make the trailer drift toward the shoulder of the road. You can move the partition over to give him more room. Have a tidbit ready for him.

Loading a Pony

Lead the pony straight forward into the trailer. If your trailer has breast bars, you may walk in ahead of him and slip under the breast bar as he follows you in. If your trailer is the kind with a solid front, your pony should be trained to step into the trailer as you stand beside the door. It is not safe to walk into a closed trailer stall with a pony.

When your pony goes in, give him a tidbit and *wait until someone has fastened the tail bar or back door behind him before you tie him up.* **Caution:** *Never* tie a pony's head when the tail bar or back door is open behind him. This can cause him to pull back and panic. He could even flip over backward.

Your pony should be tied with a quick-release knot or a special trailer tie with a quick-release snap. The tie rope should be long enough so he can reach his hay net, but not so long that he can turn his head around or nip at his neighbor.

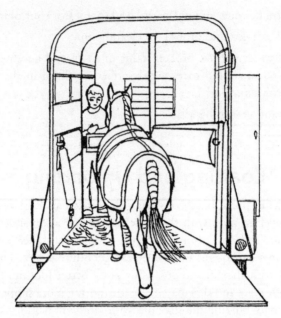

Loading in a ramp type trailer with breast bars: You can lead the pony into the trailer and go out the door in front.

Loading safely in a step-up type trailer closed in front: Pony should be trained to go freely into the trailer on command. You should not go into the stall in front of him.

Safe trailer loading.

Unloading a Pony

Before unloading, the trailer should be parked on level ground. Avoid unloading on a highway, on slippery ground, or too close to anything a pony could bump into.

Caution: Always untie your pony's head before you lower the ramp, open the back door, or unfasten the tail bar.

A pony must never be tied up in a trailer when the tail bar is undone. If you forget to untie his head and he begins to back off while he is still tied, he can get frightened, pull back, and fall over backward.

When you are ready to unload, your helper should unfasten the tail bar. Back your pony out slowly in a straight line. A helper should stand beside the ramp to keep him straight so he doesn't step off the side of the ramp by mistake.

Safe unloading.

Note to Parents

Trailering

Trailering is one area in which children must have expert adult help. Unless you are experienced in loading and hauling horses, you should seek help from an expert before you try to trailer a pony yourself, even for a short distance. Asking a horse or pony to enter an enclosed box on wheels and stand quietly while traveling down a highway goes against the animal's natural instincts. If a pony is nervous or inexperienced, or if you make a mistake when loading or hauling, he may get upset and cause problems that are very difficult to handle, if not dangerous. It is necessary to practice loading a pony before you must take him on a trip—never try to load a pony, especially for the first time, when you are late or in a hurry. A calm, confident, and quiet attitude is everything in handling the pony during loading and unloading.

Hauling a horse trailer with live weight is not as simple as towing other kinds of trailers. Driving too fast, making abrupt turns, braking, or changing your speed can upset the pony's balance and cause him to become frightened, slip or scramble, or even fall down. When hauling a horse trailer, you must drive especially smoothly, slowing down to 5 mph or less for sharp turns and avoiding abrupt braking or acceleration. Remember that the extra weight and length of a horse trailer requires more time and more distance when stopping, accelerating, or pulling out into traffic. Allow extra distance between your vehicle and the vehicle ahead, and do not change lanes unnecessarily or tailgate.

If you ride along with a horse person who is experienced and sensible about loading, hauling, and unloading, you'll learn how to do it correctly and will be safer and more confident when you are ready to take over the job of trailering your child's pony yourself.

PART IV

Pony Knowledge, Tack, and Turnout

11

Pony Talk: Pony Parts, Colors, and Conformation

When you talk about ponies, you will want to know the right names for everything.

In order to describe a pony, you should know his size, gender, color, and markings. This can help you pick a particular pony out of a group of ponies. The next sections tell about pony colors, markings, size, age, and more.

Pony Colors

A pony's *color* means the color of his body, head, tail, and mane. What color is your pony?

There are many colors, shades, and variations of colors for horses and ponies, and many words that describe variations of color. It is helpful to have a list of colors like the one below to start with, but you may wish to search on the Internet or in books for names, pictures, and examples of all the variations of horse and pony colors. You will have fun looking at the rainbow of colors.

There are a few things to remember when describing color. The *base color* means the basic color of the horse's body. *Points* (such as black points) means the color of the ears, mane, tail, and lower leg. Some horses have markings over the base color, such as dapples, a dark stripe down the back, or dark spots. White markings on the face or the legs do not change the color of the pony.

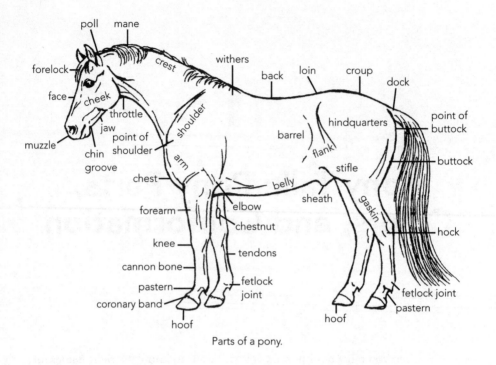

Parts of a pony.

Here are the most common colors of horses and ponies:

- **Black.** All black with black points and no brown highlights.
- **Brown.** Dark brown or nearly black with brown highlights.
- **Bay.** Brown or reddish brown body with black points (mane, tail, and legs).
- **Chestnut (also called *sorrel*).** Reddish brown with the same color or lighter tail, mane, and legs. A chestnut does not have black points. Chestnuts may be dark chestnut, red chestnut, or light chestnut; the mane and tail may be red, brown, or blond.
- **Grey.** Grey or white with dark skin, eyes, and muzzle. Greys are born dark colored and grow lighter as they age until they are nearly white. (True white ponies are born white with pink skin.) Variations of grey include:

     Iron grey. Dark grey, nearly black, with some white hairs. Many grey ponies are iron grey when they are young and become lighter with age.

     Dapple grey. Mottled grey with dapples or circles of white color all over the body.

     Rose grey. A chestnut horse who has turned grey. These horses have a purple, red, or brown tinge to their coats throughout the greying process. They can have dapples. Their manes are darker than the coat color.

Flea-bitten grey. Speckled grey with tiny black, brown, or red spots. This color got its name because it looks like the horse was bitten by fleas.

White grey. These horses may look white, but they are not. Their skin is dark, especially around their eyes, ears, and nose. They are born another color and grow lighter with age.

- **Dun.** Duns come in many colors, such as *red dun* (dun with chestnut), *grullo* (dun with black or faded grey color), *bay dun* (dun with bay), and *mouse dun* (dun with brown). Duns have a *face mask* (dark face), *dorsal stripe* (a dark stripe down the back), *leg barring* (zebra stripes on the legs), dark points, and a dark mane and tail.

- **Buckskin.** A tan color, ranging from dark gold to yellow or cream, with black points and a black mane and tail. They do not have leg barring or a dorsal stripe like a dun. Some buckskins are dappled.

- **Cremello.** Cremellos have blue eyes and hair the color of cream.

- **Palomino.** Golden coat with white mane and tail.

- **Pinto.** Large colored patches of any color and white. A *piebald* is black and white. A *skewbald* is any other color with white.

- **Roan.** Roans are a solid color with white flecking throughout the coat. They come in several colors:

    Strawberry roan. Chestnut with white flecking, making it seem pink.

    Blue roan. Black with white flecks, giving it a blue tinge.

    Red roan. Bay with white flecks, giving it a red look.

Roans' manes and tails can be flaxen for strawberry roans, and other roans may have *frosting* (where the top hairs of the mane or tail are very light in color).

- **Appaloosa.** Has small round spots or speckles. May be dark with light spots, white with dark spots, roan with patches of spots, or dark with a white "blanket" and spots over the hindquarters. No Appaloosa has the same patterning of spots. Appaloosas come in a wide variety of colors, but the basic patterns include leopard, blanket, snowflake, roan. Appaloosas have a white *sclera* (edge of the pupil of the eye), striped hooves, and spots on the muzzle and under the tail.

Pony Markings

Markings are white areas on a pony's face or legs. White markings make a pony unique and can help you identify him.

Face markings. Left to right: star, snip, blaze, strip, and bald face.

Face Markings

Face markings are white areas on a pony's face and head. A pony may have more than one face marking or two markings, such as a star and a strip, may be combined.

Leg Markings

Leg markings are usually described by where they reach on the leg (for instance, white coronet, white half-pastern, and white half-cannon).

Other Marks

Other markings include the following:

- **Brand.** A design burned into the skin to identify an animal.
- **Freeze brand.** A brand made by freezing instead of heating. The hair grows in white. Usually letters or numbers are used.
- **Scar.** A permanent mark left by an injury that has healed.

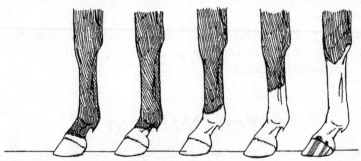

Leg markings. Left to right: coronet, half-pastern, sock (white to top of fetlock joint), half-cannon, and stocking.

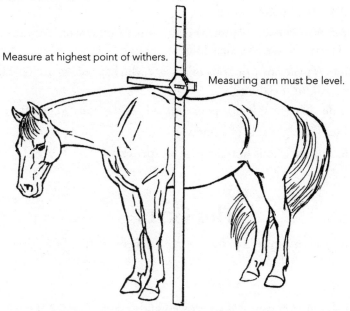

Measure at highest point of withers.

Measuring arm must be level.

How to measure a pony's height.

Measuring Height

The size of a pony is measured in *hands* from the ground to the withers. One hand equals 4 inches. A horse measuring stick is used for measuring.

In this country, a horse measures over 14 hands and 2 inches (written as "14.2 hands"). A pony measures less than 14 hands and 2 inches when it is mature (fully grown). There are small ponies (up to 12.2 hands), medium ponies (from 12.2 to 13.2 hands), and large ponies (from 13.2 to 14.2 hands). A pony is not a baby horse.

Pony Terms

The following common horsemanship terms include those that are used to describe a pony by age and gender:

- **Mare.** A mature (fully grown) female horse or pony who is 4 years old or older.
- **Filly.** A young female horse or pony under 4 years old.
- **Colt.** A young male horse or pony under 4 years old.
- **Foal.** A baby horse or pony of either sex under 1 year old.
- **Yearling.** A horse or pony who is 1 year old.
- **Dam.** A horse or pony's mother.

- **Sire.** A horse or pony's father.
- **Stallion.** A mature (fully grown) male horse or pony who is 4 years old or older. He can be used for breeding.
- **Gelding.** A male horse or pony of any age who has been neutered. He cannot be used for breeding.
- **Near side.** The left side of a pony (the side of the pony we mount).
- **Off side.** The right side of a pony.
- **Green.** A pony who is untrained or inexperienced.

The Gaits

Gaits are the ways in which a pony can move. There are four basic gaits.

Walk

The *walk* is a four-beat gait. It is the slowest and easiest to ride. A pony walks at about 4 miles per hour.

Trot

The *trot* is a two-beat gait. It has *suspension* (bounce) because the pony goes up in the air between beats. A pony trots at about 6 miles per hour.

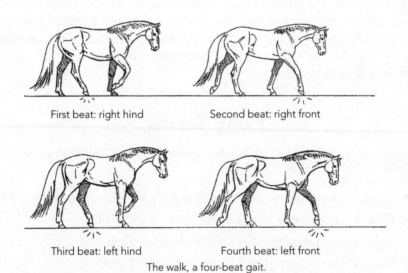

First beat: right hind   Second beat: right front

Third beat: left hind   Fourth beat: left front

The walk, a four-beat gait.

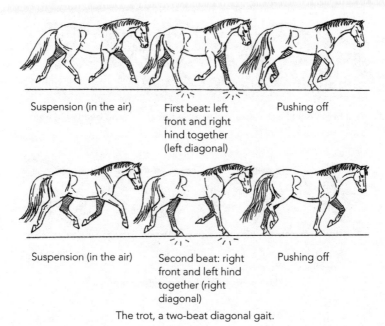

Suspension (in the air)

First beat: left front and right hind together (left diagonal)

Pushing off

Suspension (in the air)

Second beat: right front and left hind together (right diagonal)

Pushing off

The trot, a two-beat diagonal gait.

Canter

The *canter* is a three-beat gait. It has suspension because the pony goes up in the air between strides. A pony canters at about 8 miles per hour.

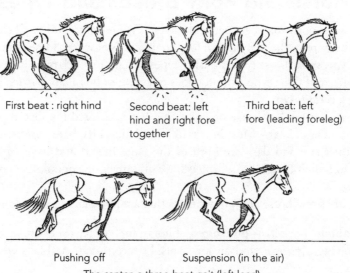

First beat : right hind

Second beat: left hind and right fore together

Third beat: left fore (leading foreleg)

Pushing off

Suspension (in the air)

The canter, a three-beat gait (left lead).

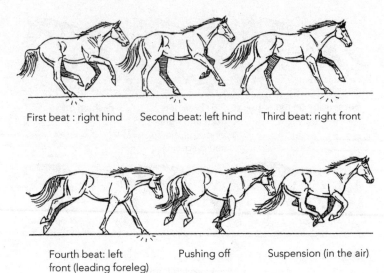

First beat : right hind   Second beat: left hind   Third beat: right front

Fourth beat: left   Pushing off   Suspension (in the air)
front (leading foreleg)

The gallop, a four-beat gait (left lead).

Gallop

The *gallop* is the pony's fastest gait. It is a four-beat gait with suspension because the pony goes up in the air between strides. A pony gallops at about 15 miles per hour or faster.

Horse and Pony Breeds and Types

Any horse or pony may be a particular type. *Type* refers to build and characteristics, which make the pony useful for certain kinds of work. Some examples are hunter type, sport-horse type, pleasure type, western or stock type, gaited saddle horse type, and draft type. A pony does not have to be of any particular breed to be of a certain type.

A *breed* is a kind of horse or pony who has been bred for special purposes over a number of years. Most horses of a particular breed are *purebreds* (which means their sire and dam are both of the same breed) and have registration papers from their breed club. *A grade* horse or pony is one of unknown or mixed breeding.

Here are some horse and pony breeds that are popular in North America:

- **Arabian.** The oldest pure breed of horse, used today for endurance riding, showing, dressage, and all kinds of pleasure riding. Arabians are usually small, high spirited, and intelligent, with a dished (slightly curved) face, fine skin and coat, short back, and a high tail carriage.

- **Thoroughbred.** First bred hundreds of years ago in England just for racing, but now also used as hunters and jumpers and for eventing and dressage. Many have been on Olympic teams. They are tall, lean, and rangy, with long legs, necks, and bodies. Thoroughbreds are fast, sensitive, and powerful, have good endurance, and move with long, low strides.

- **Quarter Horse.** Originated in colonial America and bred for short-distance racing and cow ponies. Most Quarter Horses have some Thoroughbred

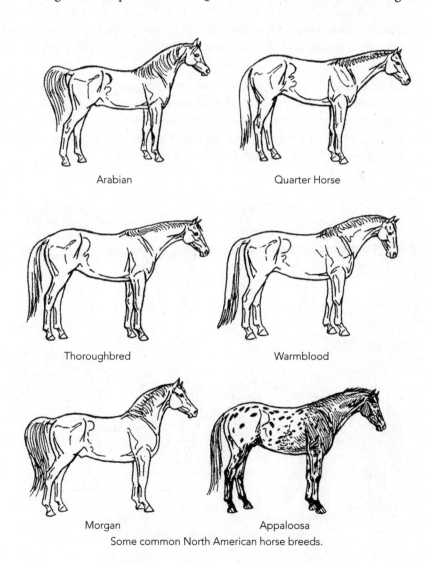

Arabian Quarter Horse

Thoroughbred Warmblood

Morgan Appaloosa

Some common North American horse breeds.

blood. Today they are used for every kind of riding from ranch work to showing, jumping, pleasure riding, and racing. They have strong, muscular hindquarters and sturdy conformation, and are usually calm and intelligent.

- **Morgan.** Originated in the United States and descended from one small stallion, Justin Morgan. Morgans are compact, powerful, and intelligent. They are used for driving as well as for all kinds of riding. Morgans are known for their endurance.

- **Appaloosa.** Originally came from the northwestern part of the United States. Appaloosas are a spotted breed with some Thoroughbred and Quarter Horse blood. Once bred as Indian ponies, they are now used for all kinds of riding, including western, English, jumping, trail, and pleasure riding.

- **Warmbloods.** Not a single breed, but rather a group of breeds that cross hot-blooded Thoroughbreds and Arabians with cold-blooded draft horses. Many are imported from Europe. Warmbloods are usually tall, strong, and athletic. They are bred for jumping and dressage, and some are used for driving. Many Olympic team horses are Warmbloods.

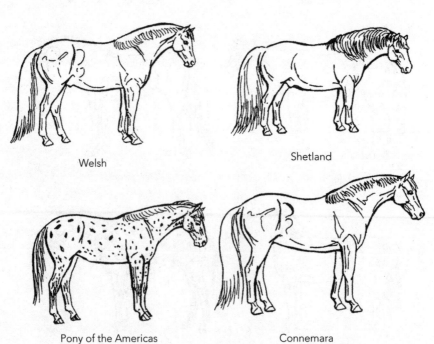

Welsh

Shetland

Pony of the Americas

Connemara

Some common North American pony breeds.

- **Welsh.** Originally came from the mountains of Wales in Great Britain. Welsh ponies have some Arabian blood. They are medium-sized with beautiful heads, compact bodies, and a "floating" trot. They are used for pleasure riding, jumping, and driving.
- **Shetland.** Originally came from the Shetland Islands off the coast of Scotland. They are very small (under 12.2 hands) but sturdy, strong, and smart, and they are used as children's ponies for riding and also for driving.
- **Connemara.** Originally came from Ireland. Some are medium to large ponies and some are small horses. They are tough, strong, and hardy, with pretty heads, strong bones, and good sense. Most are used for pleasure riding, hunting, jumping, eventing, and driving.
- **Pony of the Americas (POA).** A breed of pony that is the size of a Welsh pony and has the color of an Appaloosa. POAs are used for children's ponies and are ridden English and western. They also jump and drive.

Conformation

Conformation means the way a pony is built. Good conformation makes a pony a pleasure to look at, but it is more important than traits like a pretty color or a long tail. Having good conformation also means the pony can move and perform better, may have smoother gaits, and is likely to be stronger and less likely to break down than a pony with poor conformation.

Here are some basic conformation points to look for in a pony.

Overall

A pony should look well balanced, and all of his parts should fit together well. (No part should look too big or too small for the rest of him, like a head that is too big, legs that are too short, or a back that is too long.)

Head

A pony should have a well-shaped, attractive head that is not too large and is well set on his neck. It should be wide at the jaws, with large nostrils; large, kind eyes; and a pleasant expression. A well-balanced head with wide jaws makes it easier for a pony to respond to the bit and to balance himself. Large nostrils can take in more air, and large eyes with a kind expression usually mean a good disposition.

Faults: A coarse, heavy head, a head that is poorly set on the neck, narrow jaws, small "pig eyes," small nostrils, and an unpleasant expression—all are undesirable.

Neck

A good neck is medium long and slightly arched, blending smoothly into withers of medium height. It is *clean* (not thick and puffy) at the throat, and neither too thick nor too thin. A good neck makes it easier for the pony to use his head and neck for balance, and to flex (or bend) his neck correctly when he responds to the bit.

Faults: A short, thick neck (*bull neck*) goes with short, choppy gaits and makes it harder to balance. A neck that dips on the top and bulges on the bottom is called a *ewe neck.* It makes it hard for the pony to flex his neck properly, and he may carry his head too high.

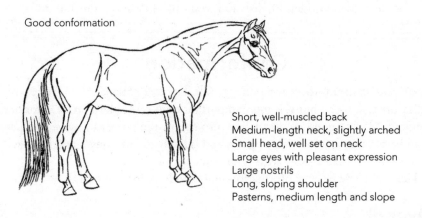

Good conformation

Short, well-muscled back
Medium-length neck, slightly arched
Small head, well set on neck
Large eyes with pleasant expression
Large nostrils
Long, sloping shoulder
Pasterns, medium length and slope

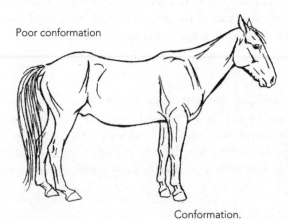

Poor conformation

Long, hollow back
Short neck
Ewe neck (dips on top,
    bulges underneath)
Large coarse head, set
    on neck at awkward
    angle
Pig eyes, unpleasant
    expression
Small nostrils
Short, upright shoulders
Short, upright pasterns
Long, flat hind pasterns,
    too much slope

Conformation.

Back

A good back is short and well muscled, blending smoothly into a wide, well-muscled loin and medium-height withers. This makes the pony's back stronger and able to carry weight better, and good withers help keep the saddle in place.

Faults: A long back is weaker and hard to fit with a saddle, especially if it is also hollow. High withers are harder to fit with a saddle. Low withers (especially when covered with fat) do not hold the saddle in place well.

Shoulder

A good shoulder is long (from the top of the shoulder blade to the point of the shoulder) and sloping. This gives a longer stride and smoother gaits, and helps a pony jump well.

Faults: A short, upright shoulder (nearly straight up and down) causes rough gaits and a shorter stride. It also makes it harder for a pony to fold his front legs well when he jumps.

Pasterns

The pasterns act like shock absorbers, so they must be strong and springy, with medium length and slope.

Faults: Short, upright (almost straight up and down) pasterns cause rough gaits, which pound a pony's feet and legs and make him less comfortable to ride. Pasterns that are too long or that slope too much (almost flat) give smoother gaits, but they are weak and are easily injured.

Describing a Pony

There are many reasons you might have to describe a pony clearly—to tell someone what he looks like, or to pick a particular pony out of a group of ponies. A complete description should give the pony's size, age, sex, color, markings, breed or type, and any obvious conformation characteristics. (For instance, a good description would be the following: Dancer is a 7-year-old Welsh gelding, 13.2 hands, dark bay with a star, and with a right hind leg that is white to mid-pastern. He has a long back, a Roman nose, and a scar on his left shoulder.)

12

Tack

Your pony's saddle, bridle (including the bit), and other equipment are called *tack*. When you saddle or bridle a pony, you *tack her up*. *Untacking* is taking her tack off. A store that sells tack is called a *tack shop*. When you are talking about tack, you need to know the proper names for the different parts.

There are many kinds of tack, including English, western, and special tack for certain kinds of riding, like racing. In Pony Club, *English tack* is used because it is best for a balanced seat when riding and jumping. It's important to choose the right kind of tack for the kind of riding you do, and tack that fits both you and your pony. It's a good idea to get advice from your instructor when buying tack to be sure that you get the right kind.

Knowing about tack and equipment is important for your safety and control. You should know what kind of bit you use on your pony and how it works on her mouth. You must learn how to adjust your tack so it fits your pony properly and to check it each time you ride. It's also important to learn how to clean and care for your tack and how to keep it in safe condition and good repair. Good tack can be expensive, but if you take good care of it, it will last for many years. At Pony Club mounted events, every rider's tack must be checked for safety and proper fit before he is allowed to ride.

Names and Parts of Tack

Your pony will need a halter, a lead rope, and maybe a lead shank:

- A *halter* is used to handle, lead, and tie a pony. It has no bit, so it can be safely used for tying a pony. All ponies should have a clean, properly fitted safety halter. It can be made of leather or a synthetic material with a break-away feature.
- A *lead rope* is used to lead and to tie up a pony. It may be made of cotton, hemp, or a soft, braided synthetic material.
- A *lead shank* (flat leather, web, or nylon) may be used to lead a pony but must not be used to tie him as these materials do not make good tie knots and may jam tight or break. If you plan to tie your pony, use a lead rope.
- A *chain-end lead shank* or lead rope may be used for extra control when leading a pony. It must never be used to tie a pony.

Parts of a Saddle

An *all-purpose balanced seat saddle* is the best type of saddle for Pony Club riders.

Here are the parts of an English saddle:

- **Saddle tree.** The frame, usually made of wood, fiberglass, or plastic, that makes up the shape of the saddle. It is covered in leather or synthetic material. The tree determines the size, length, and width of your saddle.
- **Seat, or dip.** The lowest and widest part of the saddle where the rider's seat bones rest.

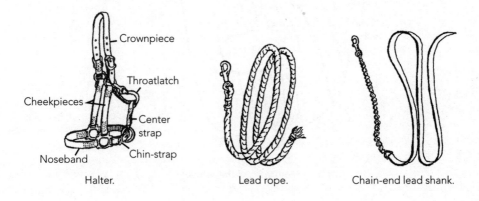

Halter.   Lead rope.   Chain-end lead shank.

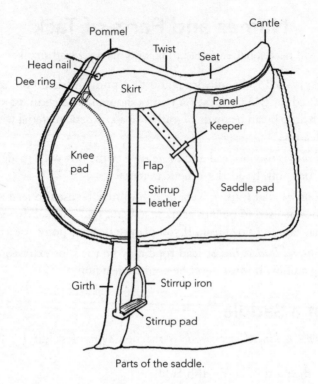

Parts of the saddle.

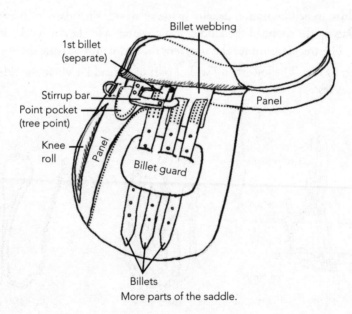

More parts of the saddle.

- **Pommel.** The front part of the saddle. It is higher than the seat to provide security for the rider. It should always allow room for the withers.

- **Cantle.** The back of the saddle that is raised higher than the seat to give security.

- **Skirt.** The small flap of leather that covers the stirrup bar to help prevent the rider's leg from rubbing on the buckle of the stirrup leather. It also helps to keep the buckle of the stirrup leather from unbuckling and sliding down.

- **Panels.** The padded and shaped underside parts of the saddle that run from under the cantle to the front of the saddle. The panels provide cushioning between the horse's back and the saddle.

- **Gullet.** The arched area under the pommel, and the channel that runs the length of the saddle on the underside between the panels of the saddle. It must be wide enough to provide clearance for the horse's spine and withers.

- **Saddle flap.** The large piece of leather on the outside of a saddle that goes under the rider's legs. It helps prevent the rider's knees from being rubbed by the girth buckles and the horse's side from being pinched by the stirrup leather. Some saddle flaps also have knee pads.

- **Sweat flap.** The large piece of leather on the underside of the saddle that goes between the billets and the horse. It helps to protect the rest of the saddle from the sweat of the horse.

- **Billets, or girth straps.** Straps (leather or synthetic) attached to the saddle tree; the girth is buckled to these straps. They have several holes used to adjust the tightness of the girth. There are usually three billets, with the front billets usually attached to the tree and the rear two usually attached to webbing that goes over the tree. Some saddles such as dressage saddles have long billets to buckle the girth below the saddle flap.

- **Buckle guard.** This piece of leather protects the saddle flap from getting worn by the buckles of the girth. Saddles with long billets do not need buckle guards.

- **Knee roll.** Padding under the saddle flap that is right under the rider's knee or in front of the thigh to give the rider more support. Some saddles have very thick, very thin (pencil roll), or long (banana roll) knee or thigh rolls, or no rolls at all.

- **Dee rings.** Metal D-shaped rings attached to the flaps on the front of a saddle, to which certain pieces of equipment such as a breastplate can be attached.

- **Head nail.** The metal nail head placed at the front of a saddle below the welt that separates the pommel from the skirt.
- **Stirrup bar.** The part of the saddle tree that allows stirrups to be attached. It is made of strong metal riveted to the tree. The stirrup bar is usually kept in the *open* position so if the rider should fall and start to be dragged, the stirrup leather can release from the saddle, freeing the rider. There are some stirrup bar designs that cannot be closed.
- **Stirrup iron.** The metal part of a stirrup in which the foot of the rider rests; it provides support and leverage.
- **Stirrup pads.** Rubber inserts that fit inside the bottom of the stirrup iron where the rider's foot rests, designed to provide traction.
- **Stirrup leathers.** Leather (or synthetic) straps that attach the stirrup iron to the stirrup bar. They have many holes so they can be adjusted to change the length of the stirrups.
- **Stirrup leather keeper.** Loops sewn onto the saddle flap to secure the end of the stirrup leather and keep the strap out of the way so it doesn't get under the rider's leg. Some saddles have a slot cut into the saddle flap through which the leather is passed.
- **Girth.** The wide strap that goes under the horse's belly and buckles to the billets to hold the saddle in place. Girths are made of leather, cotton, nylon, or other synthetic materials.

Additional tack used with the saddle include the following:

- **Girth extender.** An H-shaped piece of tack with buckles on one end and straps with holes on the other. It is designed to lengthen a girth that is too short.
- **Crupper.** An adjustable leather strap used to keep the saddle from slipping forward. It has a padded loop that passes around the pony's tail, and a strap that attaches to a T-shaped fastener, which is attached to the back of the saddle.
- **Saddle pad.** The purpose of a saddle pad is to protect the pony's back and to protect your saddle from the pony's sweat. It can also help, temporarily, to minimize the effects of an ill-fitting saddle. Saddle pads come in various shapes and materials. Some (also called *numnahs*) are shaped like the saddle, while others, like dressage pads, have more of a square shape. They can be made of cotton, sheepskin, or synthetic material.
- **Grab or safety strap.** A small leather strap with buckles that attaches to the Dee rings of a saddle to give the rider a handhold.

Girth extender

Grab strap or safety strap

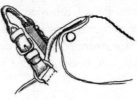

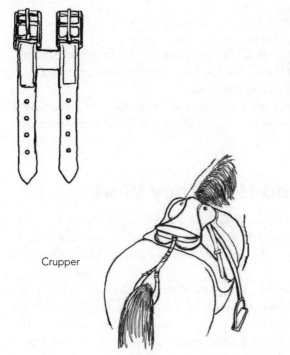

Crupper

Additional tack used with the saddle.

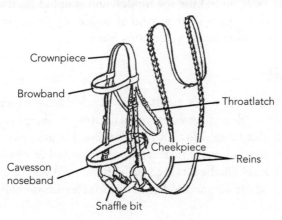

Crownpiece

Browband

Throatlatch

Cheekpiece

Cavesson
noseband

Reins

Snaffle bit

Parts of the snaffle bridle.

Parts of a Bridle

A *snaffle bridle* is the simplest type of bridle and is the type most commonly used in Pony Club riding. There are other kinds of bits and bridles, such as Kimberwickes and pelhams, which are described in the following section. D Level Pony Club members should not use bits or bridles that are severe or that are designed for advanced training purposes.

Caution: Never tie a pony by a bridle or snap a cross-tie into the bit ring. He may pull back and hurt her mouth badly, and he may break the reins or the bridle.

Bits and How They Work

The *bit* (made of metal, rubber, nylon, or plastic) in your pony's mouth is important because it lets you tell him what to do when you ride him. You should know how your pony's bit works so you can control him without hurting his mouth.

Bits should work by pressure, not pain. Ponies are trained to listen to bit pressure and changes in pressure (stronger, lighter, left, and right), and to obey by stopping, turning, slowing down, changing their balance, and so on. If the bit hurts his mouth, a pony will be unhappy and confused, and he may get scared or angry. He then will not do what you want him to do, or he will not be able to do it well.

A Pony Club rider should use the mildest and simplest bit that will control his pony safely. This is usually some kind of *snaffle bit*. Some ponies may need a *Kimberwicke* or *pelham* bit, or some other kind.

Snaffle Bit

A *snaffle bit* has two rings and a mouthpiece, which is usually jointed and made of smooth metal, nylon, plastic, or rubber. (Rough, sharp, or twisted wire mouthpieces are discouraged for Pony Club riding.) Snaffle bits work by *direct pressure*. This means 1 ounce of pressure on the reins makes 1 ounce of pressure on the pony's mouth. Snaffle bits are usually fairly mild bits. They are used for training ponies and for advanced riding, as well as for pleasure riding and beginning riders.

Kimberwicke Bit

A *Kimberwicke bit* is a mild curb bit, with a metal, nylon, plastic, or hard rubber mouthpiece. Because it has a *curb chain* and *shanks*, it works by *leverage* and

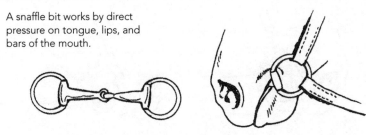

A snaffle bit works by direct pressure on tongue, lips, and bars of the mouth.

Jointed snaffle bit.

multiplies the pressure. For example, 1 ounce of rein pressure might cause 2 or more ounces of pressure on the pony's mouth. It is stronger than most snaffle bits, so riders should be careful when using it. However, a Kimberwicke is quite mild compared to other curb bits. It is useful for ponies who don't pay attention to a snaffle bit, but whose riders cannot handle double reins.

The *Uxeter Kimberwicke* bit is a particular kind of Kimberwicke bit with two slots in which the reins can be fastened. The upper slot is the mildest and the lower slot makes the bit stronger. Putting the rein around the ring so it can slide freely makes the bit more like a snaffle, with very little leverage.

Pelham Bit

A *pelham bit* is a double-rein bit. The top rein goes to the *snaffle ring*. When you use that rein, it acts like a bar snaffle bit with direct pressure. The bottom rein goes to the *curb ring*. When you use that rein, it acts like a curb bit, with leverage. A pelham bit is always used with a *curb chain*, which lies under the pony's chin in the curb groove. It has *shanks*, which makes it a leverage bit. Long shanks (more than 5 inches) make a pelham bit more severe and are discouraged for most Pony Club riding. Pelham bits may have metal, nylon, plastic, or rubber mouthpieces.

A pelham bit is stronger than most snaffle bits. Some ponies need the extra control of a pelham bit, but the rider must be able to handle double reins.

A *bit converter*, or *rounding*, is sometimes used to change a pelham into a single-rein bit. This is a pair of round leather straps that buckle to the snaffle

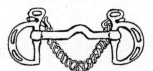

A Kimberwicke bit acts like a mild curb bit, squeezing the mouth between the bit and the curb chain.

Uxeter Kimberwicke bit with rein slots.

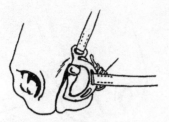

Rein in upper slot, mild curb effect

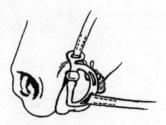

Rein in lower slot, stronger curb effect

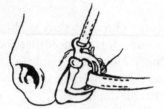

Rein around ring, mildest effect (almost like snaffle bit)

Kimberwicke with different rein placements.

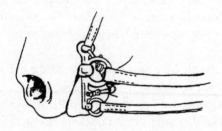

Curb hook

Snaffle ring

Lip strap ring

Shank   Curb chain   Curb ring

A pelham is a double-action bit. The top rein acts as a snaffle and the bottom rein acts as a curb bit.

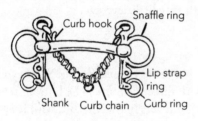

Pelham bit with double reins.

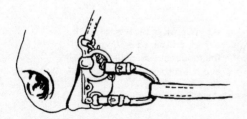

Pelham bit with bit converter (for use with single rein).

and curb rings on each side of the bit. The single rein is attached to the loop of the bit converter. This makes a pelham bit act like a Kimberwicke bit with only one rein. It is usually used with beginning riders.

Types of Protective Boots

Sometimes ponies need protective boots on their legs when they are ridden so they don't get hurt. There are different kinds of boots that protect different parts of the legs. Some types of these boots are *galloping boots*, *brushing boots*, *tendon boots*, *splint boots*, *ankle boots*, and *fetlock boots*. *Sports medicine boots* are designed to support the tendons, ligaments, and other structures of the legs during exercise. *Brushing boots*, *splint boots*, and *ankle boots* protect against accidental blows, especially in ponies who tend to strike one leg with another as they move.

If your pony needs boots, it is very important that they are put on correctly or they could do more harm than good. If boots are put on incorrectly, they can come loose and trip your pony. Your pony's legs must be brushed and clean, and the boots must be clean and in good repair before you put them on to prevent sores and rubs. Your instructor should show you how to put the boots on your pony and should check them for you.

Splint boots are used to protect the splint bones and lower legs. These boots should be worn high on the cannon bone with the fasteners to the outside and the tails of the buckles to the back. If there are only two straps, fasten the top one first. If there are more than two straps, adjust the middle strap first, then the top, and work down the leg. Then slide the boot down the leg so it fits over the fetlock joint and allows the hair on the leg to lie straight. Do not leave splint boots on longer than necessary on hot days because they cause extra heat and sweat underneath the boots.

Bell boots are used to protect the bulbs of the heels from being stepped on by the hind feet. If the bell boot has fasteners, wrap the bell boot around the hoof, fastening it on the outside or front, depending on the kind of fastener. If there are no fasteners it helps to warm the bell boot first before stretching it over the hoof.

Shipping boots are used when trailering ponies (see chapter 10, "Safe Traveling and Trailering"). Shipping boots or bandages must cover the heels, coronary band, pastern, fetlock joint, and tendons to the base of the knees or hocks. Some types of shipping boots protect part of the hock and knee, depending on how high they go. They must cover these areas in case a pony steps on his own feet or strikes his leg against the trailer.

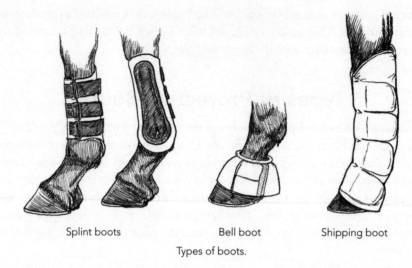

Splint boots   Bell boot   Shipping boot

Types of boots.

Taking Care of Your Tack

Good tack is expensive, but it can last for many years if you take good care of it. However, even the best tack can be ruined quickly if it is not cared for properly. There are four words to remember when taking care of your tack: *clean, condition, place,* and *repair.* Here's a closer look at what each step entails:

- **Clean.** Each time you use your tack, it gets sweaty, dirty, and dusty. This makes the leather harsh and dry and rough on the pony's skin and on your hands. It also makes the leather dry out and crack faster if it is not cleaned. It is unkind to ask a pony to take a rough, rusty, or dirty bit in his mouth. Saddles, bridles, and other tack should be cleaned each time they are used, and stripped down for a thorough cleaning each week. Washable saddle pads and girths or girth covers should be laundered each week.

- **Condition.** Leather is animal skin that has been treated, or *tanned,* which seals the smooth side and leaves the underside able to absorb water, fat, or oil. The natural fat and oil that leather contains help keep it strong and supple. However, leather loses its natural fat when it gets wet and dries out; when it is exposed to heat, sweat, salt, and dirt; and when it is not cleaned or conditioned regularly. *Conditioning* means replacing the lost fat in the leather by working in fat or oil, usually neatsfoot oil or a vegetable oil (such as olive oil). This should be done after the leather is clean. After the leather has been cleaned and conditioned, apply glycerine saddle soap to seal the pores of the leather and protect it.

- **Place.** Your tack must be kept where it is clean and dry and where it won't be dropped, scratched, knocked over, or chewed by animals. It should not

Every time you clean your tack, check it for loose stitching or other problems.

be kept in a damp place like a cellar, or it will mildew. It must be kept away from heat (like a radiator) or it will dry out and crack. The saddle should be covered and put on a saddle rack. Equipment like bridles, halters, and martingales should hang on bridle racks. Saddle pads should be hung on a clothesline or rack to dry, not left underneath the saddle. A sawhorse makes a good saddle rack, especially if you tack a strip of carpet over it to protect the bottom of your saddle. Pet food cans or small coffee cans can be nailed up to make inexpensive bridle racks.

- **Repair.** All tack must be checked for damage and wear every time you use it or clean it. You should give everything a careful check before any special

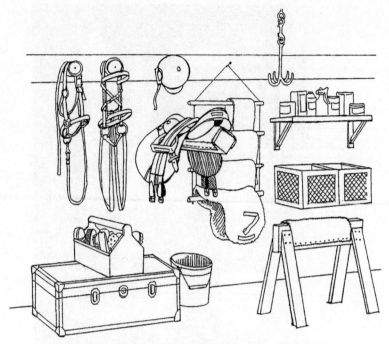

Tack hung up neatly in a well-organized tack room.

event like a Pony Club rally. Small problems like loose stitching can be easily fixed if you notice them early. If you let repairs go, your tack can be ruined and can become dangerous for you and your pony.

To clean your tack, you will need the following:

- Small sponges (two or three) and clean rags
- Small bucket with warm (not hot) water
- Leather cleaner (like castile soap or Murphy Oil Soap)
- Leather conditioner (pure neatsfoot oil, vegetable oil like olive oil, or Lexol Leather Conditioner)
- Leather protector (glycerine saddle soap)
- Leather wipes (may be used for an occasional quick wipe-over, but not as a substitute for a thorough cleaning)
- Saddle rack or sawhorse and a tack-cleaning hook to hold tack

Some other items that may be helpful are an old toothbrush or a plastic mesh dish scrubber (for removing heavy dirt from the rough side of the leather), toothpicks (for cleaning stitching and holes in straps), steel wool (to remove rust from metal items), and paper towels (for cleanup).

Cleaning tack is broken down into four steps: preparing, cleaning, conditioning, and protecting the leather.

Preparing

For a thorough cleaning, strip the saddle by removing the girth, stirrup leathers and irons, and the saddle pad. Rubber stirrup pads should be taken out of the irons. The bridle should be taken apart. The bit and stirrup irons should be placed in a bucket of warm water to soak while you clean the leather.

When you must do a quick wipe-over instead of a thorough cleaning, take off the girth and saddle pad but leave the stirrup leathers and irons on. (This way you can clean the bridle and leathers, but remember where the buckles should go.) Unbuckle the leathers and run the irons down to the buckle ends. On the bridle, unfasten the reins and cheekpieces from the bit and undo all keepers and runners, but leave the bridle buckles in place. You can use a sponge slightly dampened with glycerine soap or a leather wipe to quickly wipe over the saddle, stirrup leathers, girth, bridle, and reins while the bit soaks clean. This quick cleaning can be done daily if you are short of time, but you should do a thorough cleaning every week to keep your tack in good condition.

Cleaning

Fill a small pail with warm (not hot) water. Dip a clean rag (or sponge) in the water and wring it out nearly dry. Rub it over the leather to remove dust, dirt, and sweat. (If any water stays on the surface of the saddle, the sponge is too wet.) Don't forget to clean both the outside and the underside of the leather. Remove all the "jockeys"—dark, greasy dots or patches of dirt that stick to the leather. These are often found on the underside of the leather where it touches your pony. You may have to use a plastic mesh dish scrubber or an old toothbrush to remove them, but be careful not to scratch the leather. Use lots of elbow grease but not too much water to get the leather clean. Use a rag to wipe away any excess water.

If the tack is really dirty, you may need a stronger cleaner. Use a damp sponge and a leather cleaner like castile soap or Murphy Oil Soap. Don't use enough water to make the soap lather. If you do, the leather will get soaked and can be damaged. Rinse the cleaner off (along with the dirt) with a damp (not wet) sponge. Cleaners are too harsh to be left on the leather. If the leather isn't clean yet, repeat this step. Don't forget to clean under all the buckles. Sometimes this takes castile soap and a toothbrush to remove the black areas that have built up, especially underneath buckles.

When you are finished, the leather should be clean and slightly damp. The stitching should stand out clean, and there will be no jockeys or dirty places. You can use a toothpick to clean stitching and holes for the buckles.

Conditioning

Now you must decide if the leather needs to be conditioned or oiled. Leather should be soft and supple with no cracks, and it should not squeak when you ride. How often your leather needs oiling or conditioning depends on the climate you live in and the use and care the leather has had. You should not oil your tack every time you clean it, because over-oiling can make the leather too greasy and flabby, and it may weaken the stitching. Only oil it if the leather seems dry or stiff.

If oil is needed, you can apply it by painting it on the *underside* of the leather in a thin coat, using a 1- or 2-inch paintbrush. It is better to oil the underside of the leather since it soaks up oil more easily than the outside, or smooth side, of the leather. Also, oiling the outside of your saddle will make oil stains on your riding pants. Next, bend the leather back and forth, and roll it and work it *gently* between your hands. This helps the leather soak up the oil or conditioner, and you can tell when it becomes supple. Use enough oil to make the leather easy to bend, but don't overdo it. You can let it soak in for a while and then wipe off any excess oil with a rag.

Be careful not to get oil on suede knee rolls or on cloth (like the saddle pad)—it will stain.

Protecting the Leather

This should always be done *after* cleaning and any oiling or conditioning. Glycerine saddle soap seals the pores of the leather, nourishing and protecting it. If you use oil or conditioner afterward, it cannot get deep into the pores and the leather will look dull.

Use a damp sponge to apply the saddle soap. If you use bar saddle soap, dip the bar in water, not the sponge. The sponge should be sticky and soapy, not wet or lathery. Rub the soap in on both sides of the leather. There should not be any lather, but if the holes in the bridle or stirrup leathers get filled with soap, you can blow through them or use a toothpick to clean them out. If you have used just enough soap, you should be able to see a fingerprint on the leather after you have rubbed the soap in, and the leather will feel smooth and supple. Any excess soap should be wiped off with a rag.

Here are a few other cleaning hints:

- **Bits, stirrup irons, and spurs** should be cleaned by soaking them in warm water and scrubbing them with a pot scrubber or steel wool. These all-metal items may also be put into the dishwasher to be cleaned. For a special shine, polish them with metal polish (except for the mouthpiece of the bit), and buff them with a clean, dry rag or paper towel.

- **Washable saddle pads, girths, and girth covers** should be laundered once a week. Don't use bleach, and be sure to rinse them thoroughly. Bleach or soap left in a pad can mix with the pony's sweat and irritate his skin.

For more information about tack care and cleaning, see the *USPC Horse Management Handbook*.

Tack Safety Check: Condition and Repair

Tack must be in good, safe condition or it may break while you are riding and cause an accident. Worn, cracked, or dirty tack can also cause sores on the pony or the rider. Check the condition of the tack before you buy or borrow it, when you clean it, and every time you use it. If you find a problem like cracked leather or stitches coming loose, don't use that tack. Show it to your parents or your instructor and arrange to get it fixed.

The following sections discuss the parts you should check.

Saddle Tree

The saddle tree is the framework inside your saddle. If it is cracked or broken, the saddle can hurt your pony's back or fall apart. Saddle trees can be broken by using a narrow saddle on a wide-backed pony (especially with a heavy rider), by a pony rolling on his saddle, or by a rider pulling on the cantle and twisting the tree while mounting. To check the tree, push against the pommel and cantle and look for telltale wrinkles across one or both sides of the seat. Pull sideways on the head or front of the saddle—any movement means the tree is broken. Some broken trees can be repaired by a *saddler* (a person who makes and repairs tack), but it is quite an expensive job.

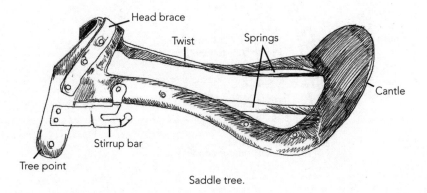

Saddle tree.

Leather

All leather must be strong and supple (easy to bend), free from cracks, and not dried out. Bend the leather back and forth and check for cracks. Cracks with brown powder in them are called *dry rot*. Stiff leather can sometimes be restored with cleaning and oiling, but dry-rotted or cracked leather cannot be used safely and cannot be restored. It is best to discard it. Any leather that bends around a piece of metal (like bit and rein fastenings or stirrup leathers) is likely to wear out and crack faster.

Saddle seat should not move or wrinkle when pressed end to end.

There should be no movement in the gullet when you try to squeeze and pull side to side.

Checking for a broken tree.

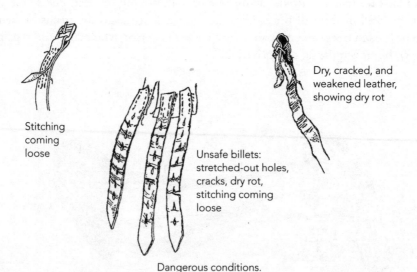

Stitching coming loose

Unsafe billets: stretched-out holes, cracks, dry rot, stitching coming loose

Dry, cracked, and weakened leather, showing dry rot

Dangerous conditions.

Stitching

Check the stitching on all your tack—saddle, bridle, girth, and all other items. Any stitching that is broken, missing, or coming loose should be fixed before you use that item again.

Billets

The billets must be sound and stitched firmly to the webbing. Billets that are thin, stretched, worn out, or cracked could break—the saddle would fall off. The holes in the billets should not be cracked or stretched out. The stitching that holds the billets must not be broken, worn, or missing any stitches. Billets can be easily replaced.

Stirrup Leathers

The stirrup leathers must be sound or you could lose a stirrup suddenly. The leather must be strong, without cracks, and not have too many extra holes too close together, which weakens the leather. The area where the stirrup iron rests must also be checked for cracks. The stitching that holds the buckle must be strong. If stitches are missing, or if the thread is wearing thin, the leather is not safe to use and must be restitched. This is a simple but important repair.

Stirrup Bars

The stirrup bars should always be in the open position to be safe for riding. They are supposed to let your stirrup leather slide away in case your foot gets caught in the stirrup during a fall. They should not be loose, bent, or slanted downward. If they are rusty, they may need oiling.

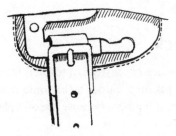
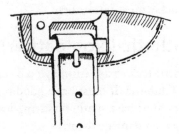

SAFE Stirrup bar open   DANGER! Stirrup bar closed

Safety stirrup bars.

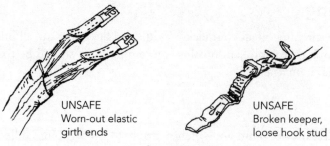

UNSAFE
Worn-out elastic
girth ends

UNSAFE
Broken keeper,
loose hook stud

Unsafe conditions.

Girth

The girth must be smooth, clean, and strong, with no cracks in the leather or rough places that could hurt the pony's skin. Check the stitching that holds the buckles on. If you have elastic ends on your girth, the elastic will eventually wear out and need replacing. On a string girth, be sure there are no broken or worn-out strings.

Keepers and Runners

Keepers and runners are little pieces of leather near the buckle that hold the end of a strap in place. They keep straps from flapping loose and getting caught on things and keep buckles from unbuckling by accident. If a keeper or runner gets so loose that it won't hold its strap, it should be fixed. The most important keepers are the ones at the bit fastenings on reins and cheekpieces. If one of these keepers breaks, your rein or bridle could come undone. The little hook that goes through the hole in the fastening is called a *hook stud*. It must not be loose or bent because it keeps the bit fastening from coming off. Some bridles and reins fasten with buckles instead. These must not have loose stitching, and the buckle must not be bent.

Synthetic (Nonleather) Tack

Synthetic tack (made from nylon or other materials instead of leather) is fine for Pony Club use. It must be in good repair, just like leather tack. Some synthetic saddles must have synthetic stirrup leathers and girths, because the oil in leather fittings can damage them.

Halters used in Pony Club should be made of full leather, synthetic with breakaway leather crownpieces, synthetic with a breakaway safety tab or loop,

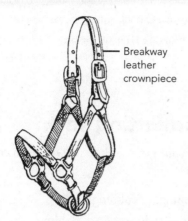

Breakway
leather
crownpiece

Nylon halter with leather safety crownpiece.

or a rope halter with a breakaway safety tab or loop. Breakaway features are necessary because nylon or synthetic halters are so strong that they might not break in an emergency if your pony should get his halter caught on something. This could hurt your pony badly. Synthetic bridles should also have leather or breakaway reins for safety.

Unsafe Tack Checklist

The following unsafe tack problems can cause tack to break, hurt you or your pony, or cause an accident. Any one of these means, "Do not use this tack!"

- Broken or cracked saddle tree
- Cracked or stretched-out holes in leather straps, such as bridle parts, billets, and stirrup leathers
- Loose, broken, or missing stitching, especially in stirrup leathers, billets, or around buckles or bit fastenings
- Leather showing cracks or dry rot
- Stirrup bars rusted or fixed in closed position
- Bits with rust or rough spots
- Girths with worn-out elastic
- Broken or missing runners or keepers
- Bent or broken buckles or loose hook studs
- Stirrup pads worn smooth

- Rotten or worn-out rubber bands on Peacock safety stirrups
- "Stressed" or bent metal, such as Peacock stirrups or bits
- Reins too long, especially on ponies

Adjusting and Fitting Tack

It is very important that your tack fits your pony and that all parts are correctly adjusted. Improperly adjusted tack can:

- Hurt your pony by pinching, slipping, or rubbing him
- Make your pony act up or cause you to lose control of him
- Make your saddle unsafe for you
- Make you uncomfortable when you ride

Every pony should have his own tack that is properly fitted to him. If you buy or borrow other tack, it must be carefully adjusted before you can ride with it. *You should check the adjustment of the tack every time you ride.*

To adjust tack, you will need the following:

- A leather punch
- A sharp knife to cut off long ends
- A nail or pencil to mark where extra holes should be punched

Saddle Fitting

A saddle must fit your pony's back without pinching, rocking, or pressing on his spine at any point. When the saddle sits on his back without a saddle pad, you should be able to see an open space all the way down the center of the gullet over the pony's spine. When you are sitting in the saddle, you must be able to fit at least two or three fingers between the head of the saddle and your pony's withers. The front of the saddle must be wide enough to fit his "saddle muscles" comfortably, without pinching or pressing on the top of his shoulder blades. To check this, slide your hand down each side under the front of the saddle to check for pinching while a rider is mounted. The panels must fit the pony's back muscles evenly, without rocking, rubbing, or making pressure points. When you remove the saddle after a ride, check the sweaty saddle mark. If you see smaller dry patches in the sweat mark, these show where the saddle makes pressure points and is hurting the skin and the tissues underneath.

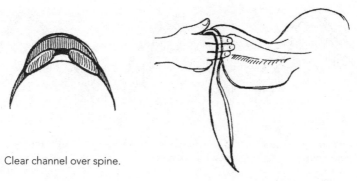

Clear channel over spine.

Three fingers fit between front of saddle and pony's withers.

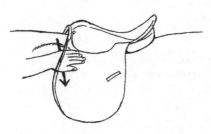

Slide hand under front of saddle, behind pony's shoulder blade (no pinching).

Sweat mark showing pressure point (dry spot).

Checking saddle fit.

Saddle Too Wide

If a saddle sits down too low on a pony's withers and spine, it is too wide for his back. (This can happen if a pony is thin or has a bony back.) If it is not too bad, it can be fixed by having the panels restuffed. A temporary solution is a *back protector pad*, which fills in the hollows on each side of the pony's spine, raising the saddle and protecting his back. This pad is always used on top of a regular saddle pad. Just stuffing padding under the front of the saddle will not do—this will lead to sore withers.

Saddle Too Narrow

A saddle that is too narrow will press down into the pony's back muscles and pinch the top of his shoulders. This makes him sore and can make him move stiffly, buck, or even rear. This cannot be fixed by padding; the only solution is to use a wider saddle.

Saddle tree fits shape of back correctly.

Tree is too wide, presses down on withers.

Tree is too narrow, digs into back muscles, pinches shoulder blades.

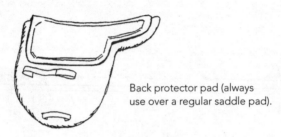

Back protector pad (always use over a regular saddle pad).

Saddle fitting.

Balance of Saddle

The seat of a saddle should be balanced so that the *dip*, or *seat* (the lowest point of the saddle), is in the center, not at the back. If the saddle is too high in front or if the back panels are too flat, it will throw the rider backward out of balance. This can give your pony a sore back. The best way to fix an unbalanced saddle is to have a saddler restuff the panels to fit your pony's back. A *lift-back, lollipop,* or *riser pad* can be used temporarily to balance the saddle, but you must be sure that this doesn't make the tree points dig into the pony's saddle muscles in front. Many saddles ride too high in front because they are really too narrow for the pony.

Girth Fitting

It is very important for the girth to fit right because it holds your saddle on. A girth that is too long cannot be tightened enough to be safe; it can make the saddle slip. A girth that is too short is hard to do up and may be tightened too much, making the pony uncomfortable. A *girth extender* is useful to extend a girth that is too short or if a girth must be used on ponies of various sizes.

A girth should have two spare holes above the buckles on each side when it is tightened, and at least one spare hole below the buckles.

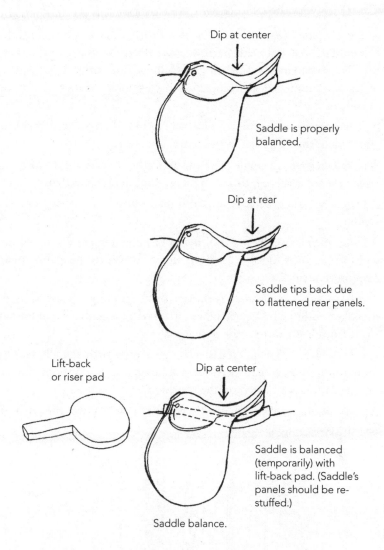

Dip at center

Saddle is properly balanced.

Dip at rear

Saddle tips back due to flattened rear panels.

Lift-back or riser pad

Dip at center

Saddle is balanced (temporarily) with lift-back pad. (Saddle's panels should be re-stuffed.)

Saddle balance.

Some ponies get sores behind their elbows from the girth. This is usually caused by a rough or dirty girth, but the type of girth and the way it fits can make a difference.

Types of Girths

There are many types of girths, which can be made from leather, synthetic materials, cotton or synthetic webbing, fleece lining, neoprene, or nylon strings. Some horses or ponies need a particular kind of girth in order to be comfortable and avoid sores and rubs. Types of girths include the following:

- A *shaped, contoured, overlay,* or *chafeless girth* is a shaped girth of soft leather or synthetic material made narrow at the elbows so as not to rub the sensitive elbow skin and cause girth galls. Some come with a 1- to 2-inch strip of leather running down the center or a smooth leather overlay on the outside of the girth.
- A *Balding girth* is a flat piece of leather cut into three strips that are crossed and folded, then stitched in the center.
- A *three-fold girth* is a single piece of soft leather folded to form three layers. Inside the folds there is usually a piece of fabric, such as flannel.
- A *lampwick girth* is a flat girth that is made with heavy cotton or synthetic webbing.
- A *string girth* is usually made of nylon or polyester strands joined to form a girth that grips tightly yet allows the air to get to the skin, which may help prevent sores.
- A *dressage* or *Lonsdale girth* is shorter than a usual girth and is used on a dressage saddle with longer billets. It may be straight or contoured and made from leather or synthetic material.
- An *elastic end girth* makes it easier to tighten the girth and allows the pony more room to breathe. The elastic can be on one end or both ends. If it is on one end, it is attached on the near side.
- A *girth cover* is a soft, washable fleece cover that fits over the girth to protect the pony's skin.

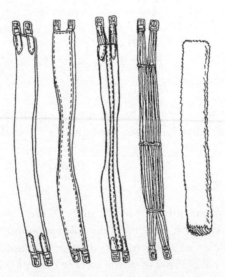

Left to right: folded leather girth, shaped girth, elastic end shaped girth, string girth, and fleece girth cover.

Types of girths.

Stirrup Leathers

Stirrup leathers should be long enough and have several spare holes so you can adjust them to a normal riding position. You may need to punch extra holes in them to make them adjustable to your best riding length. It's important to get the holes evenly spaced so you won't ride crooked. Don't punch lots of extra half-holes in your leathers—this weakens the leather. Changing your leathers from one side of the saddle to the other will help keep them even as they stretch out.

Here's how to measure stirrup leather hole spacing:

1. Put a nail through one hole in both leathers.
2. Insert a pencil or nail through the holes in the top leather to scratch a mark in the bottom leather.
3. Punch the holes with a leather punch.

Stirrup Irons

Stirrup irons are usually made of stainless steel. They should be 1 inch wider (½ inch on each side) than the rider's foot. If they are too big, the foot can slip right through. If they are too small, the foot can get stuck. Safety stirrups can be used, especially for small children. These may free the foot from the stirrup in case of a fall. If Peacock safety stirrup irons are used, the rubber band should be on the outside of the iron. Fillis stirrup irons must be used with stirrup pads. If you are riding with rubber boots or soles you should not use rubber stirrups pads as it will not let your foot slip out easily in an emergency.

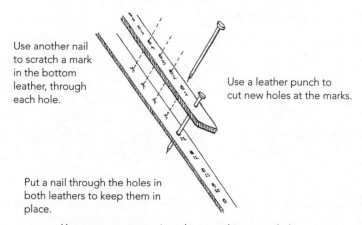

Use another nail to scratch a mark in the bottom leather, through each hole.

Use a leather punch to cut new holes at the marks.

Put a nail through the holes in both leathers to keep them in place.

How to measure spacing when punching extra holes.

Fitting Bits and Bridles

Bits and bridles must be carefully fitted because your control depends on them. If the bit fits badly, it can hurt your pony's mouth and make him toss his head, fuss with her mouth, pull, or even rear. The only way he can tell you it hurts is to act up.

Most snaffle and pelham bits should stick out ¼ inch on each side of your horse's mouth. The size of a bit is determined by measuring the width of the mouthpiece from the inside of the cheeks or rings.

All bits must be smooth and comfortable, with no rough or rusty spots or rotting rubber. They should not pinch or rub the pony's lips. Avoid nickel bits—they bend and develop thin spots and sharp edges as they get old.

Snaffles

A snaffle bit must rest high in the pony's mouth so he cannot get his tongue over it. A properly fitted snaffle should make one or two gentle wrinkles at the corners of the pony's lips, like a smile.

Pelhams, Kimberwickes, and Curb Chains

Pelhams and Kimberwickes should rest against the corners of the pony's mouth without making more than one small wrinkle. The curb chain must be flat against the pony's chin. It must not be too loose, or the bit will turn too far and you will have no control. It can also pinch the pony's lip. If it is too tight, it will make the bit "grab" and hurt the pony's mouth. The curb chain should be adjusted so that the bit turns 45 degrees to tighten the curb chain against the chin groove. It is usually right if you can fit two fingers (held sideways) between the curb chain and the chin groove.

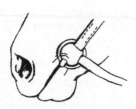

A snaffle bit should be adjusted so it makes two small wrinkles in the lips. It must not hang too low in the pony's mouth.

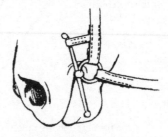

A full-cheek snaffle bit should have bit keepers on the upper cheeks.

Fit of snaffle bit.

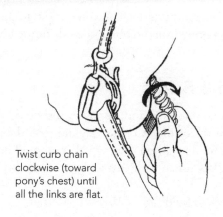

Twist curb chain
clockwise (toward
pony's chest) until
all the links are flat.

Making the curb chain lie flat.

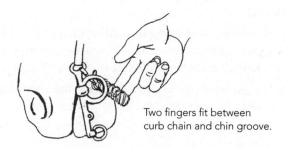

Two fingers fit between
curb chain and chin groove.

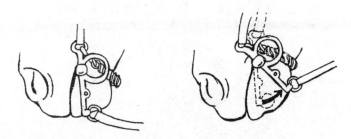

When curb chain is properly adjusted, bit
will rotate 45 degrees to tighten curb chain.

Lip strap is in place (through
center ring of curb chain).

Adjusting the curb chain.

A lip strap runs through the center link on the curb chain and buckles to the tiny rings on the bit shank. This keeps a pony from grabbing the side of the bit with her lip.

Fitting Other Parts of the Bridle

Other parts of the bridle should be snug, not loose and sloppy. You should be able to slip a finger under every part of the bridle. All straps should have their keepers and runners fastened. When a bridle is fitted properly, there should be two spare holes above each buckle to allow for adjustments and in case the bridle breaks.

Here's how each of the parts of the bridle should fit:

- **Browband.** Must be long enough so that the bridle doesn't rub and pinch the base of the ears
- **Throatlatch.** Should be loose enough to allow the pony to flex his neck without binding at the throat. You should be able to fit a fist or four fingers between the throatlatch and the pony's throat when pulled back.
- **Crownpiece.** Should have two extra holes above the cheekpiece buckles when the bit is correctly adjusted

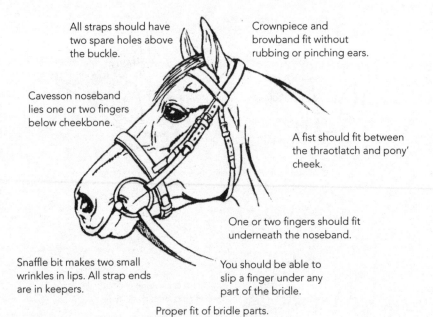

All straps should have two spare holes above the buckle.

Crownpiece and browband fit without rubbing or pinching ears.

Cavesson noseband lies one or two fingers below cheekbone.

A fist should fit between the thraotlatch and pony' cheek.

One or two fingers should fit underneath the noseband.

Snaffle bit makes two small wrinkles in lips. All strap ends are in keepers.

You should be able to slip a finger under any part of the bridle.

Proper fit of bridle parts.

A Pony Club member checks her pony's bridle for proper fit before riding.

- **Cavesson (headstall).** Adjusts the height of the noseband. It goes inside the crownpiece and cheekpieces.
- **Cavesson (noseband).** Should rest one or two adult-sized fingers below the pony's cheekbones. It goes inside the cheekpieces, next to the pony's face. It should be snug but never uncomfortably tight. You should be able to fit one or two fingers under the noseband.

How Other Items Should Fit

Halters

For a properly fitted halter, the noseband should lie halfway between the projecting cheekbone and the corner of the mouth. A halter should fit snugly but comfortably, without rubbing, pinching, or hanging too loose for safety and control. There should be space for no more than the width of three adult fingers between the noseband and the nose bone, and no more than a fist should fit between the throatlatch and the pony's cheek.

Saddle Pads

A saddle pad should fit well into the gullet and the pommel area so as not to put pressure on the pony's withers. It fastens to the billets above the buckle guard with billet tabs or a Velcro strip. A *girth loop* helps keep the pad from slipping back or wrinkling. A *baby pad* is a washable cotton pad that is used alone or underneath a show pad next to the pony's skin. It is easy to wash and it keeps the show pad clean.

Breastplate (Hunt Style)

A *breastplate* keeps the saddle from slipping back. The *yoke* fits around the shoulders, and the *center strap* goes between the front legs and fastens around the girth. The two top straps attach to the Dee rings at the front of the saddle. There should be room to fit one hand at the top of the yoke, and the center strap should be slightly loose so it will not cause a sore between the pony's front legs. The best breastplates have adjustable buckles on each side of the yoke.

Breast Collar (Event or Polo Type)

A *breast collar* keeps the saddle from sliding back. It should fit across the chest without binding at the base of the neck. It is buckled around the girth on both

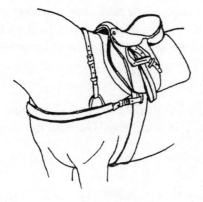

Event- or polo-style breast collar.

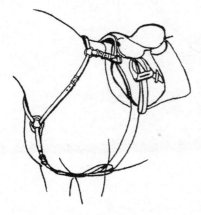

Hunt-style breastplate.

sides. The upper strap should be snug enough to keep the breast collar from slipping down.

Standing Martingale

A *standing martingale* has a *martingale strap* that attaches to the cavesson noseband (never to a dropped noseband!) and runs between the front legs to the girth. The *neck-strap* buckles on the left. It should be secured by a *rubber ring* at the chest, so that the martingale cannot hang down in a big loop, which is unsafe.

The martingale should be adjusted so that it can be pushed up to almost touch the pony's throat when his head is in a normal position. (Note: In Pony Club competitions, standing martingales are usually allowed only for D Level riders.)

Running Martingale

A *running martingale* has a martingale strap that fastens around the girth and splits at the chest, with each strap ending in a *rein ring*. The reins run through

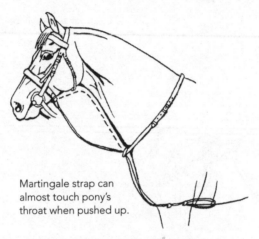

Martingale strap can
almost touch pony's
throat when pushed up.

Standing martingale, correctly adjusted.

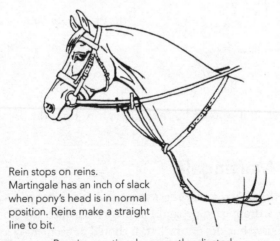

Rein stops on reins.
Martingale has an inch of slack
when pony's head is in normal
position. Reins make a straight
line to bit.

Running martingale, correctly adjusted.

these rings. For safety, the reins must have *rein stops*, which prevent the martingale rings from getting caught on the bit fastenings. A running martingale should be adjusted so that it has about an inch of slack when the pony's head is in a normal position and the reins make a straight line from the bit to the rider's elbows. A good way to check the length is to see of the rings will reach the withers or the throat. The *neck-strap* buckles on the left and should be secured with a *rubber ring* at the chest. (Note: Running martingales are training aids that should be used only by riders who know how to use them correctly. They are not for beginners!)

Neck-Strap

A *neck-strap* is a simple strap that goes around the pony's neck. It is designed to provide the rider with something to hang on to other than the reins. A stirrup leather can be used.

Dropped Noseband

A *dropped noseband* is used to keep a pony from opening his mouth to evade the bit. The noseband rests on the end of the nose bone just above the soft part of the nose. The chin-strap is buckled below the bit, in the curb groove. The noseband should be snug but not too tight. You should be able to slip a finger under it, and the pony should be able to chew easily.

Flash Noseband

A *flash noseband* is a *cavesson noseband* with a *flash strap* attached; it is used to keep a pony's mouth closed and to hold the bit in position. The cavesson noseband is adjusted fairly high and snugly. The chin-strap buckles below the bit, in the curb groove. Both should be snug but not tight—you should be able to slip a finger underneath.

Figure-Eight Noseband

A *figure-eight noseband* is also used to keep a pony's mouth closed, but it rests higher on his face and lets his nostrils expand better for fast work. The *upper strap* goes under the jaw behind the cheekbones, inside the bridle. The *lower strap* buckles below the bit, in the curb groove. A small *pad* rests high on the nose bone, where the straps cross. Both straps should be snug but not tight—you should be able to slip a finger underneath.

Dropped noseband: rests on end of nose bone with chin-strap below bit in chin groove.

Flash noseband: cavesson noseband adjusted high (just below cheekbone) and snugly; chin-strap below bit in chin groove.

Figure 8 noseband: upper jaw strap adjusted snugly above bit, just in front of cheekbone. Chin-strap below bit in chin groove.

Nosebands.

Selecting the Right Tack

There are many different kinds of tack. It is important to choose the right kind of tack for you, for your pony, and for the kind of riding you do in Pony Club. Buying the wrong kind of tack can be an expensive mistake, and it can make it much harder to ride well.

Tack may be bought new or used. Often, good used tack that has been well taken care of is a better buy than very cheap new tack. If you buy used tack, it should be checked carefully for soundness and condition. Many Pony Clubs have used tack sales from time to time where you may be able to find good used tack and outgrown riding clothes at reasonable prices.

Here are some things to remember when buying tack.

Saddle

An *all-purpose balanced seat saddle* makes it easier to learn a good balanced seat for riding and jumping. Either leather or synthetic saddles are acceptable.

There are special-purpose saddles that are designed to help the rider sit in a certain way for special events. These saddles make it difficult to ride with a good all-purpose balanced seat. Some examples are:

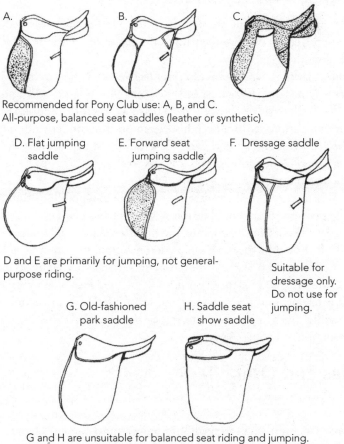

A.
B.
C.

Recommended for Pony Club use: A, B, and C.
All-purpose, balanced seat saddles (leather or synthetic).

D. Flat jumping
saddle

E. Forward seat
jumping saddle

F. Dressage saddle

D and E are primarily for jumping, not general-purpose riding.

Suitable for dressage only. Do not use for jumping.

G. Old-fashioned
park saddle

H. Saddle seat
show saddle

G and H are unsuitable for balanced seat riding and jumping.

Types of saddles.

- Western saddles
- Australian stock saddles
- Saddle seat show saddles (also called Lane Fox saddles)
- Racing saddles
- Polo saddles and old-fashioned "park" saddles
- Forward seat, or flat jumping saddles (acceptable for jumping, but not usually used for general-purpose riding)
- Dressage saddles (for dressage and flat work, but not designed for general-purpose riding, and never used for jumping)

Fitting Saddle to Rider

A saddle must be the right size for the rider. Saddles are measured from the pommel to the cantle or from the stud to the center of the cantle, depending on the type of saddle.

A saddle that is too small makes a rider feel stuck in an upright position, and his knees may be jammed against the knee rolls. A too-large saddle puts a small rider too far back to ride safely in a good balanced position, and the stirrup bars are too far forward to let him keep his legs in position underneath his body.

To check for rider fit, sit in the middle and deepest part of the saddle (preferably on a pony). Adjust the stirrup leathers so that the stirrups hang evenly to touch the bottom of your ankle bones when your leg is out of the stirrup and relaxed. When you sit in the center of the saddle in a good position with your feet in the stirrups, there should be room for one hand behind you at the cantle, and your legs should fall easily into the hollow of the saddle flap, behind the knee rolls. It should be easy to sit in a good position, to post, and to balance in a half-seat. The stirrup leathers should hang vertically (straight up and down) when you are in a good balanced position. It's a good idea to ask your instructor to check your position in a new saddle to see if it helps you ride well.

The saddle must fit the pony, too. (See the section "Adjusting and Fitting Tack" beginning on page 278.)

Bridles and Other Tack

Tack comes in several sizes:

- **Pony:** Fits most small to medium ponies (up to about 13 hands)
- **Cob:** Fits large ponies, smaller ponies with large heads, and small horses or those with fine heads, like Arabians
- **Horse:** Fits most full-sized horses

Saddle fits rider. Rider can sit in balanced position with one hand's width of cantle behind him, knees behind knee rolls.

Saddle too small. Rider is stuck in upright position between cantle and knee roll. No extra space behind seat or in front of knee.

Saddle too large. Dip in seat is too far back and stirrup bars are too far forward, causing rider to sit in "chair seat" with legs ahead of seat.

Fitting saddle to rider.

Peacock stirrup iron.

Caution: Bridles for ponies should not have horse-sized reins, long enough to make a very long *bight* (the loop of extra rein behind the rider's hands). A child's foot can get caught in this loop, which can be dangerous. It is not safe to shorten the loop by tying the end of the reins in a knot. If the reins are too long, they can be shortened by a saddler, or you can buy shorter pony-sized reins.

Learning More about Tack

Here are some things you might like to do to learn more about tack:

- **Go through a tack catalog and look up different kinds of tack and equipment.** Compare the differences among various brands and models. How much do they cost? Which ones would you like best? Make a wish list of the tack you would like to have. You might like to cut out pictures of the things you would buy if you were outfitting a stable and paste them in a scrapbook.

- **Visit a tack shop with your Pony Club.** (Your instructor can call ahead to see if it's okay to bring a group and to arrange a time.) Ask what kind of tack they recommend for Pony Club riders. Do they have bargains in used tack? Ask for tips on checking to see if a saddle fits the pony and the rider and on breaking in new tack. How can you tell if tack has good leather, just okay leather, or poor leather? What should it cost?

- **Visit a saddler or invite him to come and talk to your Pony Club.** Maybe he can show you a saddle tree and how a saddle is put together. Ask if he can teach you some simple tack repairs you can do yourself. How can you tell if a saddle needs repairs? Ask for tips on taking care of tack.

- **Have a tack-cleaning party with your friends.** Everyone brings his own tack and tack-cleaning equipment. You all clean and check the tack for safety. (Maybe your parents or Pony Club District Commissioner can help do minor repairs, too.) Music, friends, and maybe pizza can help make it fun.

- **Play tack parts tag.** To learn parts of tack, write the name of each item on tape or sticky notes. Each person draws a tag and tries to stick it on the correct part of the saddle or bridle.

- **Play bridle assembly race.** Each team (two or three people) gets a snaffle bridle (taken apart), with all the pieces on a blanket. The first team to put their bridle together correctly wins. (If you're really experienced, try it blindfolded!)

- **Play the whatizzit game.** Three or four people each bring an odd piece of tack. It can be something old or unusual that *they* know all about but that others would not know. Each person holds up his piece of tack and tells what it is and what it is used for. *Only one* tells the truth—the others make up a story. The rest of the club tries to guess who is telling the truth about their tack and what each object really is. (Set a time limit or a number of guesses.) If the audience can guess who is telling the truth, or what the tack really is, they win. If not, the person with the tack wins. After the guessing is over, each person tells what his tack really is and what it is used for.

- **Play the tack trunk game.** This can be played anywhere—in the car or on a trail ride. The first person says, "I'm going to a Pony Club rally, and in my tack trunk I've got an *ankle boot*" (a piece of tack beginning with *A*). The next person says, "I'm going to a Pony Club rally, and in my tack trunk I've got an *ankle boot* and a *bit*" (a piece of tack beginning with *B*). The next one has to say the whole thing, including *ankle boot, bit,* and a piece of tack beginning with *C*. How far can you go before somebody goofs?

Note to Parents
_____

Checking Tack

There is nothing more important than making sure your child rides with safe equipment, correctly adjusted and in good working order. Children should be taught to check their own tack every time they mount, but this is too important not to be double-checked by a responsible adult, especially where small children and inexperienced riders are concerned. This is also important for the comfort and welfare of the pony.

Be sure to examine your child's tack and equipment regularly for condition and wear. Helping with a thorough tack cleaning once a week is a good way to make sure that small problems don't develop into big hazards, and it emphasizes to the child the importance of taking good care of expensive equipment.

If you, or your child, notice a problem or a needed repair, get it mended right away. This is not something that children can do for themselves, and if you put it off, it can add up to a real riding hazard.

13

Dress and Turnout

Turnout means the way you and your pony are dressed and prepared to ride. Good turnout means being safe, neat, clean, and workmanlike, not fancy. *Workmanlike* describes being ready to work—to do the job. This means having the right clothes, tack, and equipment; having everything in good condition and fitting properly; and having your pony clean, properly prepared, and in good condition. You do not have to have expensive clothes or equipment to do this, but you do need to know what the proper turnout means.

Turnout can be everyday, informal, or formal. *Everyday turnout* is the way you dress, groom, and prepare yourself and your pony for ordinary riding at home. *Informal turnout* is for horse shows, informal hunting, and Pony Club rallies. *Formal turnout* attire can be worn at many of these activities as well but is different from informal turnout because of the color of coat worn and the additional appropriate appointments. The differences between informal attire and formal attire will be explained later in this chapter and can be found in the current *USPC Horse Management Handbook* as well.

What to Wear for Riding and Working Around Ponies

Everyday Attire

Your everyday riding clothes should be safe and easy to work in. They should fit comfortably and should be washable.

Boots or Shoes

The first thing you need is a safe pair of boots or shoes in which to ride and work around ponies. Riding shoes or boots with a heel like hunt boots made from leather, synthetic, or rubber; jodhpur boots; or paddock shoes are best. Paddock boots with smooth or suede half-chaps or leggings (leather or synthetic) may be worn as well. Riding boots must have enough heel to keep them from slipping through a stirrup (no sneakers or loafers!). Deep-tread hiking boots or waffle soles are unsafe for riding, as they can catch on a stirrup.

Dressed in turnout for an informal Mounted Games practice, this rider has a correctly fitted helmet and safe footwear.

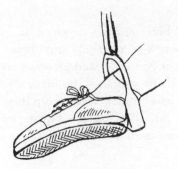

DANGER! Sneakers or shoes without heels can slip right through a stirrup.

DANGER! Stirrup can get caught in the gap between the heel and the deep tread of this kind of boot

Unsafe footwear.

For working around ponies on the ground, any substantial shoe that is securely fastened, covers the ankle, is entirely closed (no sandals or open toes!) and has a thick sole is okay. *Never* work around ponies in cloth or canvas shoes, sandals, or open-toed shoes, or in bare feet!

Helmet

You must wear an ASTM/SEI safety riding helmet whenever you are mounted, at home or anywhere else. It must be of the approved type that meets the ASTM (American Society for Testing and Materials) standards. The helmet must have a seal from the SEI (Safety Equipment Institute), which proves that it has been tested. No other type of helmet will do, as this is the safest type of helmet currently available. Your helmet must be worn with the harness and chin strap in place and properly fastened whenever you are riding, and at Pony Club pre-riding inspections. It's a good idea to wear your helmet when you are working around your pony, even if you are not riding, as it can save you a bang on the head if he should bump into you.

Your helmet must fit properly so it will protect you if you fall and be comfortable when riding. It should sit down on your head so the brim shades your eyes (not on the back of your head). It should fit as snugly as you can comfortably wear it, but it should not give you a headache. With the harness and chin strap on, your helmet should stay securely on your head without rocking, even when you bend over and shake your head; if you wiggle it gently, you should feel your scalp and the skin of your forehead move with it. The chin strap should be snug enough that it does not clear your chin. Be sure the buckles on each side don't slide down but stay up by your ear.

Safe footwear and an ASTM/SEI-certified helmet must always be worn when riding or working around ponies. Here are several types of suitable helmets, boots, and shoes.

If your helmet is slightly loose, use the spacers (pieces of foam with Velcro or sticky backs) that come with the hat to adjust the fit according to the manufacturer's directions.

Never get on a pony, even for a minute, without your helmet on, and never let anyone ride your pony unless she is wearing a helmet. Wearing a helmet isn't just a silly rule—*it can save your life!*

Pants

For comfortable riding, you need long pants that fit snugly in the lower legs and that don't ride up and wrinkle under your knees. Breeches or jodhpurs are best for riding because they are made to be comfortable when you are in a riding position. Jeans (especially stretch jeans) or slacks are okay if they fit right and don't give you sore knees from wrinkles. You can use pant clips with elastic straps that fit under your boots and hold the pants down.

Shirt

A shirt with long or short sleeves to cover and protect at least the tops of the arms and long enough to tuck in and cover the tummy is appropriate to wear for everyday riding. Shirts with sleeves and a collar (like a polo shirt, dress shirt or blouse, "ratcatcher" shirt, or turtleneck) look best for lessons, clinics, and Pony Club rallies. Shirts should always be tucked in.

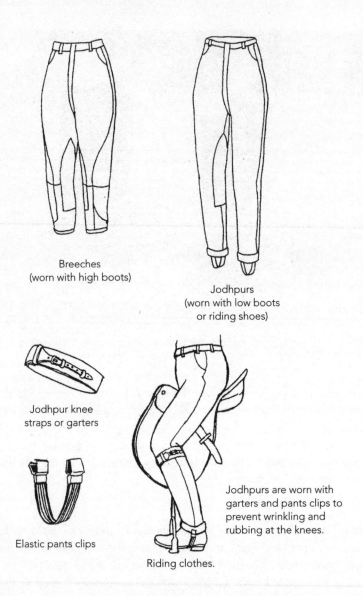

Breeches
(worn with high boots)

Jodhpurs
(worn with low boots
or riding shoes)

Jodhpur knee
straps or garters

Elastic pants clips

Jodhpurs are worn with
garters and pants clips to
prevent wrinkling and
rubbing at the knees.

Riding clothes.

Gloves

Gloves can save you from getting blisters on your fingers. Stretch cotton gloves are good for summer. Some have rubber or plastic grippers that hold the reins when they are wet. For winter, be sure your gloves are not too bulky to hold the reins easily.

Accessories

Don't wear dangle earrings, rings, or other jewelry that could catch on the reins or the pony's mane. Don't wear combs, barrettes, or pins in your hair that could

Everyday attire. This attire is proper for lessons, riding clinics, and working rallies. It should be neat and workmanlike.

hurt your head if you took a spill. Don't wear loose scarves or belts that could catch on things. Never chew gum or eat candy while you are riding. If something should happen to make you gasp, you could choke!

When you are riding outside in the sun, use sunscreen to prevent sunburn. In cold weather, wear layers of clothes to keep warm, but be sure your clothes let you move freely.

D Level Pony Club members may participate in regional Pony Club rallies wearing appropriate everyday attire, except when they are attempting to qualify for a USPC Championship Rally. In that case, either correct informal or formal attire is to be worn. For more information about this, check the current *USPC Horse Management Handbook*.

Informal Attire

This is what you might wear for a horse show, informal hunting, or a rally. You should be neat and tidy, with clothes clean, shirt tucked in, and boots should be clean and polished. Informal attire is expected at most Pony Club rallies and tests.

- **Helmet.** Must be a properly fitted ASTM/SEI-certified hunt cap type or event type.
- **Boots.** Black or brown riding boots, jodhpur boots or equivalent, as described in the previous section. Paddock boots with smooth or suede (suede is allowed for D Level riders only) half-chaps or leggings (leather or synthetic) may be worn. Boots and half-chaps should be clean.
- **Pants.** Breeches (worn with high boots) or jodhpurs (worn with jodhpur boots or paddock shoes), preferably beige, grey, or other conservative color. Garters (leather knee straps) and/or elastic foot straps should be worn with jodhpurs. A belt must be worn if pants have belt loops.
- **Shirt.** Ratcatcher, turtleneck, or plain collar, in white or any other color. Shirt must have sleeves, as a white shirt with sleeves (not a T-shirt) may be worn when the coat requirement is waived due to hot weather.

Informal attire. This attire is correct for Pony Club shows or rallies where informal attire is specified. (Jodhpurs and jodhpur boots or paddock boots are also correct, as are paddock boots with half-chaps.)

- **Tie.** Not required with turtleneck. Stock tie with plain gold stock pin (fastened horizontally through knot), or choker (pin optional) with neckband shirt. Plain or regimental stripe necktie optional with plain collar-style shirt.

- **Coat.** Hunt coat of any color other than solid black. In cold weather, a plain form-fitting sweater over a turtleneck is acceptable for riding lessons and clinics instead of a riding coat.

- **Gloves (optional).** Brown, black, or white, in cotton, synthetic, or leather.

- **Jewelry.** Pony Club pin should be worn on front of helmet or jacket lapel. Watches and medical identification bracelets are allowed. Small post-type earrings may be worn. No other jewelry except plain stock pin or tie tack.

- **Hair.** Neat and tidy. Long hair should be braided, done up in a bun, or put up under the helmet, as long as the hair does not affect the helmet's function or its fit and security on the rider's head. Medium-length hair may be put into a hair net. Hair should never be in the rider's eyes or cover her number.

A medical armband with the required medical information form completely filled out must be worn on the left arm at all Pony Club functions.

Formal Attire

Formal attire is worn for formal competitions, hunts, and formal Pony Club inspections at rallies.

- **Helmet.** Same as informal. Black ASTM/SEI hunt cap or event helmet with black cover.
- **Boots.** Black field or dress boots (jodhpur boots for young children). Paddock boots with smooth or suede (suede is allowed for D Level riders only) half-chaps or leggings (leather or synthetic) may be worn. Boots and half-chaps should be clean.
- **Pants.** White, buff, canary, or tan breeches (jodhpurs for young children, with leather garter straps and elastic foot straps). A belt is required if pants have belt loops.
- **Shirt.** White riding shirt with neckband collar. The shirt must have sleeves and a collar, as a white shirt with sleeves and collar may be worn when coat requirement is waived due to hot weather. (Check the current *USPC Horse Management Handbook* for complete details regarding attire requirements for the removal of jackets in competition.)

Formal attire. This is correct attire for formal competitions, hunts, and rallies where formal attire is specified. (Jodhpurs and jodhpur boots or paddock shoes are also correct, especially for younger children.)

- **Tie.** White stock tie with plain gold stock pin fastened horizontally through the knot. Standard stock ties are preferred, but "ready-tied" stock ties are allowed.
- **Coat.** Solid black, solid navy blue, or dark grey (charcoal) hunt coat (no pinstripes or patterns woven into the fabric).
- **Gloves (optional).** Same as informal.
- **Jewelry.** Same as informal.
- **Hair.** Same as informal.

A medical armband with the required medical information form completely filled out must be worn on the left arm at all Pony Club functions.

Formal and informal dress should not be mixed. For instance, don't wear a turtleneck sweater (informal) with a formal black coat. Clothes should fit well, be in good repair (no rips or missing buttons), and be clean and pressed. Boots should be clean and polished. (Refer to the current *USPC Horse Management Handbook* for complete information regarding appropriate riding attire.)

Turnout for Pony Club Inspections

Inspections are held before Pony Club mounted events to be sure that all riders are safely dressed for riding, ponies are clean and comfortable, and tack is safe, clean, and correctly adjusted. The inspection held before a first ride at a rally is called a *Turnout Inspection*. An inspection held before a lesson or before later rides at a rally is usually called a *Safety Check*.

Tack

Your tack should always be safe, clean, and fit well when you ride, but it should be especially clean, neat, and well adjusted for a Pony Club inspection. (See chapter 12, "Tack," for more about tack care, fitting, condition, and safety.) Tack is checked for safety, neatness, cleanliness, adjustment, and condition. Old or worn equipment is not penalized as long as it is in safe condition and shows proper care. The examiner or judge will check and inspect your tack and turnout according to the requirements for your rating level. (You can find those requirements in the current edition of the *USPC Horse Management Handbook*.)

It is better to take good care of your tack from day to day than to try to do a super cleaning of dirty, neglected tack right before a rally or competition. Good regular cleaning and conditioning will show up in the condition of the leather. Your leather should be clean and supple, with the stitches showing clearly, no jockeys (sticky dots of dirt), and the metal parts clean and bright. The saddle pad (and girth cover, if you use one) should be freshly laundered, and rubber stirrup pads should be scrubbed clean.

The condition of your tack is most important, as you will not be allowed to ride in a Pony Club event with tack that is broken or in need of repair. All tack must be in safe condition—all stitching must be sound and leather parts must be free of cracks and dry rot. The billets must not be worn out, and the stirrup leathers must be sound and cannot have cracks or loose stitching. The bit fastenings of the reins and bridle must be strong, supple, and tight, and there should not be any loose keepers, cracked leather, or missing stitching on the bridle or reins.

Adjustment of tack will be checked by the instructor, examiner, or judge to be sure your tack is safe and comfortable for you and your pony. The girth must have two buckles at each end and must be fitted so that after it is tightened there are at least two spare holes at the top and one at the bottom of the billets. You must have buckle guards in place. Your stirrup bars must be down (in the open position) for riding. If you wear rubber-soled boots, rubber stirrup pads are discouraged (but not penalized) because they make it harder to take your foot out of the stirrup. (Some stirrups like Fillis or "knife edge" irons are made to be used only with stirrup pads.) Your stirrup irons must be 1 inch wider than your boots for safety, but they should not be much wider than 1 inch or the rider's foot could slip through and become caught in the stirrup. The bit and bridle and any other equipment must be correctly adjusted (see chapter 12, "Tack," for how to adjust tack).

When you come to the place for your inspection, all your tack should be adjusted and ready to ride. Your girth should be tightened and your stirrups should be run up.

Your Pony

Your pony should always be clean and comfortable when you ride, whether at home or in formal competition. For ordinary riding, he should at least be brushed clean (especially under the saddle and girth), and have his feet picked out. For Informal Turnout and Formal Turnout Inspections, he will be checked for grooming and cleanliness, care and condition of his feet, and condition and fitness to do his job. If you have taken good care of your pony by grooming him thoroughly every day and taking regular care of his feet, he will show good care and will be in much better condition than if you just tried to do a big cleanup the day before the rally. Good care shows! (See chapter 8, "Your Pony's Feet and Shoeing," for how to groom and pick out feet.)

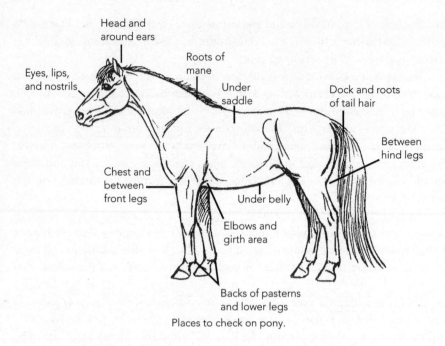

Head and
around ears

Roots of
mane

Eyes, lips,
and nostrils

Under
saddle

Dock and roots
of tail hair

Between
hind legs

Chest and
between
front legs

Under belly

Elbows and
girth area

Backs of pasterns
and lower legs

Places to check on pony.

Grooming and Turnout

Your pony should be curried and brushed clean so that his coat is free from dirt, dust, and scurf. Some places to check are:

- Under the saddle and girth
- Under the belly and between the hind legs
- The backs of the pasterns and the lower legs
- The head and around the ears
- The roots of the mane and tail hair
- The elbows and between the front legs

You should clean the skin around your pony's eyes and eyelids, his nostrils and lips, and under his tail. (Use alcohol-free wet wipes or baby wipes; clean his eyes first and under his tail last.)

Any botfly eggs should be removed. (They can be scraped off with a Styrofoam block after being lubricated with a dab of shampoo, or you can use a bot knife to scrape them off.)

Mane and Tail

The mane and tail should be brushed out and free of bedding and dirt. The roots of the hair should be clean. Light-colored tails should be washed to remove stains.

Braiding the mane or tail is not permitted for Pony Club events, except for dressage competitions at the upper levels. (See the *USPC Rules for Rallies*.)

Feet and Shoeing

Feet should be picked out. They must show evidence of regular trimming or shoeing. If you clean the feet and apply hoof dressing to the hoof, sole, and frog the night before Turnout Inspection, the feet can be toweled off in the morning, and they will be shiny and easier to pick out clean. It is not required to apply hoof dressing to your pony's feet for a Turnout Inspection, but if you do, wipe off the excess dressing so that none of it gets on your pony, on you, or on the person doing the inspection.

Turn-Back Inspections

A Turn-Back Inspection is held at a working rally or competition after riding. The pony's grooming and care after riding, care of tack, equipment, and personal gear, and the neatness of the stable area are all inspected. Ponies are not tacked up, and riders do not dress in formal attire for Turn-Back Inspections. Requirements for Turn-Back Inspections are found in the *USPC Horse Management Handbook* and *USPC Rules for Rallies*.

Note to Parents

Turnout and Pony Club Inspections

Turnout Inspection is intended to be sure that all Pony Club riders are safely dressed for riding; ponies are clean and comfortable; and tack is safe, clean, and correctly adjusted. It also teaches children the value of neatness, regular and conscientious care of the pony and tack, and pride in a job well done. Turnout should be approached with common sense and intelligent attention to details, not nit-picking. Planning ahead with your child for assembling necessary clothes and equipment, regular care and cleaning, and preparation of the pony can help your child learn to be prepared, organized, and well turned out. Children should receive the help they need appropriate for their age and level, but Pony Club members are expected to take as much responsibility as possible for preparing themselves and their ponies.

Index